Breast Wishes

Remember, we all stumble, every one of us. That's why it's a comfort to go hand in hand... Emily Kimbrough

We are excited to share our recipes of hope with you. These are recipes that have been shared with us from family, good friends and women that we have been fortunate to meet on this journey as Breast Friends.

Women Working for a Cure

Written and published by
Breast Friends Cookbooks Inc.
Box 436, Foam Lake, SK Canada S0A 1A0
Phone: 306-272-4547
Website   www.breastfriends.ca
Email   breastfriends@sasktel.net
Printed by Gateway Publishing Co. Ltd.
385 Debaets Street, Winnipeg R2J 4J8
Ph: 222-4294 1-800-665-4878 Fax: 224-4410
Cover design -Photography by Brian Gould
Graphic Design — T-C4 Graphics Ltd. Winnipeg, MB
Dedication Collage — Paula Tolver, Regina, SK
Book photography by Backyard Studios, Foam Lake
All accessories and props supplied by
Golden Ocean Giftware, Foam Lake, SK.
Copyright @2008 by Breast Friends Publishing

Canadian Cataloguing in Publication Data

Main entry under title:
Breast Wishes

Includes index.
ISBN 978-0-9735239-2-8

         1. Cookery   1. Breast Friends

TX714.C44 2006   641.5   C04-900651-9

First Printing — 2008

THE BREAST FRIENDS

Left to right- Linda Helgason, Charlene Rokochy, Cecile Halyk, Nat Dunlop, Jacquie Klebeck, Anne Reynolds, Jeannie Johnson, Patti Hack, Val Helgason and Darlene Cooper

We have decided to do it again! Good things come in threes, and we consider these books and this journey a good thing. For those of you who have followed our story and supported the cause by purchasing our books, thank you and welcome back. We know you will find "Breast Wishes" a great addition to your kitchen, and will complete the Breast Friends Cookbook set. We are the same ten women that started this journey. We have a few more grey hairs, many more wrinkles, and hopefully more wisdom; certainly more wisdom about cancer and breast cancer. We have 9 more grandchildren - bringing the total to 60. We have less career time — 4 more have retired. During the past four years we have learned so much and we have listened to virtually thousands of women's stories about their fight with cancer. We have had the pleasure of spending time with women affected by this disease from all across Canada. Our first book was written to help deal with grief — sisters, friends and a mom lost to breast cancer. Our second book was written again in the midst of grief — this time, a husband lost to melanoma, and special family and friends lost to other cancers.

For awhile we got frustrated and said, "Why are we still raising awareness? Women not only know about this hideous disease but they are scared stiff of it. The disease continues — there doesn't appear to be advancements — are we spending too much money on awareness?" But then, you read the recent stats — the wonderful stats that say the death rate is down 25% - that mammography, although it isn't the answer, or the cure, is helping to save lives. Pink ribbons and breast cancer campaigns are reminding women to do what they need to do. Do you know the most shocking new statistic is that still only 34% of Canadian woman over the age of 50 are going for annual mammograms? Even with that low number, early detection is saving thousands of lives. Imagine how much those stats would change if every woman would get tested.

We decided that awareness still has a place. Breast cancer scares us — but we have to continue getting those horrible, boob-squeezing tests and finding those lumps early until we learn what else we can do to protect ourselves. Therefore, Breast Friends continue to contribute toward awareness. We also support research into lifestyles and environment. A portion of the profits generated by the books go to large cancer research foundations, but we also donate to smaller research projects and studies. We listen to the patients and front line workers about where they perceive needs, and try to help in those areas. Donations go to the Breast Assessment Centres for diagnostics and treatment, to action groups and hope centres that support and educate newly diagnosed women and their families. We supply funds to shuttle services that take women to treatment centres from the hospices and have purchased chemotherapy infusion pumps enabling women to receive treatment closer to home. We have purchased education kits that circulate to schools and health districts teaching young girls how to do breast self exams and have supplied new beds for a Cancer Lodge in need. Contributions have been made toward a mobile mammogram machine that will service women in far northern communities and we have donated $30,000. toward digital mammography in our province.

We are very proud that, at the time of printing, the sales of the cookbooks have generated over $609,363 dollars in donations—we can't believe it either!!

Breast Wishes was written to celebrate the thousands living in spite of this frightening disease — Survivors, Warriors, Women of Strength. This is a book of hope; our focus will be on life. It will be on the positive steps, small but positive happenings in cancer treatment. The women we have met on our journey are amazing. They have taught us so much. The women: walking the cancer walks, running the runs, counseling other women and those just hanging on and learning how to live with the overwhelming change, the young moms coping with the fatigue at the same time as raising little ones and trying so hard to be strong, the grandmas sharing the news and seeing the look of panic in their family's eyes. With courage and strength, day by day they laugh, live and love despite the changes and despite the adversity. They are the 'Women of Strength' this book is dedicated to and who inspire us all on our life journey. Theirs are the stories that we have shared throughout the book. We celebrate them and their families.

Breast Wishes from Breast Friends!

BREAST WISHES

This book is dedicated to Cancer Warriors — to women (and men) and their families who are battling breast cancer. We have met hundreds of wonderful women on this journey, many who have shared their stories and experiences with us.

Our dedication page is a collage of pictures of breast cancer survivors.

At the end of each chapter, you will find some stories, some memories, some information and some favorite ponderings that we would like to share with you.

Our hope is that Breast Wishes will bring you comfort and enjoyment.

Breast Wishes from the Breast Friends

"The ten women that have compiled these recipes collectively have 33 children, 24 children-in-law, 60 grandchildren, and 356 years of marital experience."

Women of Strength
and man

Men get breast
cancer too.

Male incidence of
breast cancer
accounts for 2%
of all cases

Women of Strength

Breast Wishes

is dedicated to Women of Strength - to Breast Cancer Survivors. Thank you to all who submitted pictures for these pages. You are an inspiration.

"Call it a clan, call it a network, call it a tribe, call it a family. Whatever you call it, whoever you are, you need one." ~Jane Howard

Table of Contents

Appetizers..1

Beverages.. 35

Brunches.. 49

Breads and Muffins 69

Soups..111

Salads.. 139

Entrees 169

Vegetables and Side Dishes.............................235

Desserts 273

Cakes and Pastries... 307

Cookies and Treats 341

Recipe Index 381

Appetizers

A strong woman works out every day to keep her body in shape, but a woman of strength looks deep inside to keep her soul in shape.

APPLE DIP
(An apple a day -
dipped is the best way!)

6 apples, cored and sliced, (Granny Smith are best)
2 -355 ml cans 7 Up or Sprite

1 -250 gram package cream cheese, softened
1 cup Skor Bits
½ cup brown sugar
¼ cup white sugar
1 teaspoon vanilla

Dip sliced apples into 7 Up or Sprite, so they don't turn brown.
Mix rest of ingredients, but reserve a few Skor bits to sprinkle on the top.
Put dip in a bowl and arrange apple slices around it.

We all get heavier as we get older because there's
a lot more information in our heads. So I am not getting
fat, I'm just really intelligent and my head couldn't hold
anymore so it started filling up the rest of me.
That's my story and I'm sticking to it!!!!

ARTICHOKE AND LEEK DIP

1 cup mayonnaise
1 package leek soup mix
1 cup sour cream
1 -398 ml can artichoke hearts, drained
1 ½ cups Mozzarella cheese, grated

Mix all ingredients and place in shallow round or square baking dish. Bake at 350° F. for 20-25 minutes or until well heated. Serve with crackers or crusty bread.

MONKEY BREAD

1 package Pillsbury dinner rolls
¾ cup margarine, melted
1 teaspoon garlic salt
1 teaspoon Italian spice

Cut each roll into 4 pieces. Mix the last 3 ingredients. Dip roll pieces in margarine mixture and place in a small cake pan or bundt pan. Pour remaining margarine over rolls and bake at 350° F. for about 30 minutes or until browned. Serve warm.

It's not hard to meet expenses - they're everywhere!

BAKED ATLANTIC SCALLOPS

2 pounds scallops
2 teaspoons salt, divided
1 ½ cups celery, diced
1 cup mushrooms, chopped
1 cup green pepper, chopped
6 tablespoons butter
¼ cup flour
2 cups milk
1 cup buttered soft bread crumbs
¼ cup Cheddar cheese, grated

Separate scallops and sprinkle with 1 teaspoon salt. Cook celery, mushrooms and green peppers in 2 tablespoons of butter until tender. Melt remaining butter over low heat. Blend in flour and 1 teaspoon salt. Gradually add milk; cook and stir until thickened. Combine scallops, and vegetables with sauce; place in a greased shallow baking dish. Top with bread crumbs and sprinkle with grated cheese. Bake in oven set at 350° F. for 20-30 minutes.

*Few of us get dizzy
from doing too many good turns.*

BREAD FONDUE

1 loaf sourdough bread
1 cup sour cream
1 -250 gram package cream cheese, softened
4 ounces red chilies, chopped
4 green onions, finely chopped
1 small can flakes of ham

Cut lid off bread and hollow until ¾ shell remains. Mix all other ingredients well and pour into bread shell. Replace lid, wrap in heavy foil and bake 1 hour at 350°F.

FETA CHEESE DIP
(If you love Feta cheese, you'll love this dip!)

1 -250 gram package cream cheese, softened
1 cup Feta cheese, crumbled
½ cup mayonnaise
½ teaspoon dill weed
¼ teaspoon dried basil
¼ teaspoon garlic powder
¼ teaspoon oregano
¼ teaspoon thyme
Mix all ingredients with mixer, until well blended. Cover and chill. Serve with vegetables or crackers.

CALIFORNIA ROLLS

1 cup Jasmine rice, uncooked
1 English cucumber, seeded
3 carrots (optional: celery, red pepper, and bean sprouts)
250 grams crab strips (optional: smoked salmon, lobster, shrimp)

8-10 seaweed wraps
wasabi paste (Japanese horseradish)
soya sauce
pickled ginger

Note: A bamboo mat is used for rolling.

Cook rice as directed on package. While rice is cooking, cut cucumber and carrots into Julienne strips. (Other vegetables used must be cut into Julienne strips.) Lay seaweed wrap on bamboo mat. Place warm rice approximately ¼ inch thick and 1/3 inch from edges. (Moisten hands when working with rice.) Add strips of vegetables and crab placing on the rice, but no closer than 1 inch from the edge of the seaweed wrap. Using the bamboo mat, roll up wrap and cut into 1 inch sections. Place on serving plate and refrigerate, covered, until cool and ready to serve. Serve with condiments: soya sauce, pickled ginger and wasabi paste.

CHEESY BITS

1 pre-baked round flat bread or pizza crust
1 cup Italian salad dressing
2 cups Mozzarella cheese, grated

Place bread on a pizza pan and poke holes into it with a fork. Pour salad dressing over entire bread and let sit for about an hour. Sprinkle with cheese and place in oven at 350° F. until cheese is melted and heated thoroughly. Cut into pieces and serve warm.

TORTILLA CRISPS
(These are great served with almost any dip)

¾ cup margarine, softened
½ cup Parmesan cheese
1 tablespoon parsley
¼ cup sesame seeds
¼ teaspoon oregano
¼ teaspoon onion powder
¼ teaspoon garlic salt
12 tortillas

Mix the top 7 ingredients. Spread the mixture over tortillas and cut each tortilla into 8 wedges. Place wedges on cookie sheet and bake at 350° F. for 12-15 minutes or until crispy.

CORNMEAL TORTILLAS

(Make a double batch, these freeze well, great for tacos, wraps, quesadillas or use with Tortilla Beef Tidbits.)

2 cups flour
1 cup yellow cornmeal
1 teaspoon salt
1 egg
3 cups water

Combine flour, cornmeal and salt. In a small bowl, beat egg and combine with water. Stir into flour mixture. Use about 1/3 cup of batter for each tortilla. Pour into greased skillet or griddle, tilt to cover bottom with a thin layer of batter. Cook until dry on top, then flip. Makes about 10 tortillas.

"If children have the ability to ignore all odds and percentages, then maybe we can all learn from them. When you think about it, what other choice is there but to hope? We have two options, medically and emotionally: give up, or fight like hell." .....Lance Armstrong

CRAB PHYLLO TARTS

3 -2 ounce packages frozen miniature phyllo tart shells
½ cup Swiss cheese, shredded
2 eggs
1/3 cup mayonnaise
¼ cup light cream
1 green onion, finely chopped
¼ teaspoon salt
¼ teaspoon ground mustard
1/8 teaspoon pepper
1 -314 gram can crabmeat - drained, flaked and cartilage removed

Place tart shells on an ungreased baking sheet. Sprinkle cheese into each shell. In a mixing bowl, combine the remaining ingredients. Spoon a teaspoonful of crab mixture into each tart shell. Bake at 375° F. for 18-20 minutes or until pastry is browned. Serve warm.

"Marriage is like a 5,000 piece jigsaw puzzle - all sky."
Cathy Ladman

DEVILLED EGGS

6 eggs, hard boiled
1/8 teaspoon pepper
½ teaspoon salt
1 ½ teaspoons sugar
2 tablespoons onion, finely chopped
¼ teaspoon dry mustard
2 tablespoons mayonnaise
6 - 8 tablespoons cream
1/8 teaspoon vinegar
1/8 teaspoon parsley flakes
sprinkle of paprika

Cut cooled eggs in half, lengthwise. Lift out yolks and put in small bowl. Mash well with fork. In a cup or small bowl, mix the rest of the ingredients, except parsley flakes and paprika. Add to the mashed yolks. Mix well to form a smooth consistency. Spoon into whites, heaping slightly. Sprinkle with parsley flakes and paprika. Serve on a bed of lettuce.

"Flattery is like chewing gum.
Enjoy it but don't swallow it." .....*Hank Ketcham*

FOUR CHEESE CRAB DIP

1 -250 gram package cream cheese, softened
1 ½ cups 4 cheese Italiano, shredded
1/3 cup Miracle Whip
1 -106 gram crab meat, drained
2 green onions, chopped
½ cup flaked almonds, toasted
Preheat oven at 350° F. Combine all ingredients except almonds, and spread into an ungreased pie plate or shallow baking dish of similar size. Bake 15 minutes; stirring once during baking. Garnish with toasted almonds and serve warm with crackers or vegetables.

CHEDDAR ROASTED RED PEPPER DIP

1 -250 gram package cream cheese, softened
1 ½ cups medium Cheddar cheese, shredded
1/3 cup Miracle Whip
1/3 cup bacon, cooked and crumbled
3 green onions, chopped
1/3 cup roasted red pepper (you can buy this pureed in a jar or chop them finely if full peppers)
½ cup walnuts or pecans, chopped and toasted
Preheat oven to 350° F. Combine all ingredients except nuts, and spread into an ungreased pie plate or shallow baking dish of similar size. Bake 15 minutes; stirring once during baking. Garnish with toasted nuts and serve warm with crackers or vegetables.

FRESH MEXICAN SALSA
(Colourful and easy to make)

1 large red pepper, finely chopped
1 large green pepper, finely chopped
½ onion, finely chopped
3 Roma tomatoes, finely chopped
3 garlic cloves, minced
1-3 jalapeño peppers with seeds (to taste)
½ teaspoon salt
1 tablespoon lemon juice
few sprigs of cilantro (optional)

Place red and green peppers, onions, and tomatoes in bowl.
Blend together; garlic, jalapeño peppers, salt, lemon juice and
cilantro. Add to bowl of veggies. Serve with crackers or scoops.

❧

*"Forget what you have done for your friends
And remember what they have done for you.
Disregard what the world owes you and
Concentrate on what you owe the world."*
The Talmud

GUACAMOLE

4 ripe avocados, peeled, pitted and cut
¼ cup lemon juice
½ cup Miracle Whip
¼ cup onion, chopped
1 teaspoon chili powder
½ teaspoon garlic powder
¼ teaspoon cayenne pepper
2 medium tomatoes, seeded and diced

Mix first 9 ingredients in blender or food processor. Stir in tomatoes just before serving. This dip goes well with Tortilla Crisps.

TACO DIP

4 cups salsa (your choice of strength)
1 -284 ml can Cheddar cheese soup

Mix ingredients and warm in microwave until hot. Serve with your favourite flavour of tacos.

"Fatherhood is pretending the present you love most is soap on-a-rope." .....Bill Cosby

HAM AND CHEESE PUFF

1 cup water

½ cup margarine or butter

salt

pepper

1 cup flour

4 eggs

1 cup ham, diced

¾ cup Swiss cheese, grated

½ cup Parmesan cheese

½ teaspoon dry mustard

Preheat oven to 425° F. Grease cookie sheet. Bring water and margarine to boil. Remove from heat and add flour, salt and pepper. Stir quickly until it forms into a soft ball. Add eggs, one at a time beating vigorously. Add ham and cheeses and dry mustard. Form into a ring on cookie sheet or drop as individual rounds. Bake 40-50 minutes. Serve warm with honey mustard.

"Having children is like living in a frat house- nobody sleeps, everything is broken and there is a lot of throwing up."
...... Ray Romano

13

HOMEMADE SALAMI

10 pounds ground beef, lean
8 tablespoons tender quick
2 tablespoons garlic powder
2 tablespoons onion powder
8 tablespoons ketchup
1 -165 gram bottle or bag mustard seed
2 tablespoons brown sugar
2 teaspoons cayenne pepper

Mix all ingredients and let sit for 24 hours in refrigerator. Mix
again. Make rolls and wrap in tin foil. Place on cookie sheet
and bake at 325° F for 2 hours. Open foil while hot and let
sit. Keep turning as it cools. When completely cool, wrap and
freeze.

*"The person who risks nothing, does nothing,
has nothing, is nothing, and becomes nothing.
He may avoid suffering and sorrow, but simply cannot
learn and feel and change and grow and love and live."
.....Leo F. Buscaglia*

HOT MUSHROOM DIP

3 slices bacon
8 ounces fresh mushrooms, sliced
½ medium onion, chopped
1 clove garlic, minced
2 tablespoons flour
¼ teaspoon salt
1/8 teaspoon ground black pepper
1 -250 gram package cream cheese, cut into cubes
2 teaspoons Worcestershire sauce
2 teaspoons soya sauce
½ cup sour cream

Place bacon slices in a large skillet over medium-high heat. Fry until crisp. Remove bacon, crumble and set aside. Drain off all but 2 tablespoons of the bacon drippings. Add mushrooms, onion and garlic to the bacon drippings, and cook over medium heat, stirring, until tender and most of the liquid has evaporated. Sprinkle flour, salt, and pepper over the top, and stir to blend. Mix in cream cheese, Worcestershire sauce, and soya sauce. Reduce heat to low, and stir until cream cheese is melted. Remove from heat. Stir in sour cream and bacon. Serve warm with bread sticks and assorted crackers.

**If things get any worse,
I will have to ask you to stop helping me.**

LEMON PEPPER CHICKEN WINGS

5 pounds chicken wings
1/3 cup lemon juice
3 tablespoons honey
¾ teaspoon thyme
1 ¼ teaspoons lemon peel, grated
2 ½ teaspoons peppercorns, coarsely ground
salt to taste

Cut wings apart at joints. Discard tips. Place wings on shallow foil-lined baking pan. Bake at 400° F. until brown, about 1 hour and 10 minutes, turning pieces occasionally. In bowl stir together; lemon juice, honey, thyme, lemon peel and peppercorns. Drain fat off wings. Leave wings on the foil-lined pan and pour lemon juice mixture over wings and stir well. Return to oven and bake until sauce thickens, 12-15 minutes, turning often. Place in chafing dish and sprinkle with salt.

May your troubles be less,
your blessings more,
and nothing but happiness
come through your door.

Shown on previous page:

- ❖ Shrimp Wheels.....page 25

- ❖ Tortilla Beef Tidbits.....page 28

- ❖ Fresh Mexican Salsa.....page 11

- ❖ Savory Party Bread.....page 24

- ❖ Yummy Potato Skins.....page 32

Promotional material approved for publication by Saskatchewan Roughrider Football Club Inc.

MARITIME SHRIMP DIP

1 -10 ounce can tomato soup, undiluted
1 envelope unflavoured gelatin
1 -250 gram package cream cheese
1 -106 gram can crabmeat, drained and rinsed
1 -106 gram can shrimp, drained and rinsed
¾ cup celery, finely chopped
½ cup onions, finely chopped
1 cup mayonnaise
1 tablespoon lemon juice

Heat soup and dissolve gelatin in it; add cheese and beat with electric beater until entirely incorporated. Add remaining ingredients. Mix well and put in oiled 8 cup mold. Refrigerate for 4 hours. Serve on lettuce with crackers.

*"The grand essentials of happiness are:
something to do,
something to love,
and something to hope for."*
..... *Allan K. Chalmers*

17

MEXICAN CHERRY CHEESE DIP

1 -250 gram package cream cheese
¼ cup sugar or Splenda
1 teaspoon vanilla
1 -540 ml can cherry pie filling

Mix cheese, sugar and vanilla. Line the bottom and sides of bowl with the mixture. Pour pie filling in center of bowl. Serve with Cinnamon 'n Sugar Tortillas.

CINNAMON 'N SUGAR TORTILLAS

8 tortillas
½ cup white sugar or Splenda
1 teaspoon cinnamon
½ cup margarine, melted

Cut tortillas into 2 inch pieces in any shape you want. Spread or spray each piece with melted margarine and sprinkle with sugar and cinnamon mixture.
Place on a lightly greased cookie sheet and bake at 350° F. for 5-8 minutes or until crispy.

PARMESAN BISCUIT STICKS

2 ¼ cups flour
1 tablespoon sugar
1 tablespoon parsley
3 tablespoons Parmesan cheese
4 teaspoons baking powder
1 teaspoon basil
1 cup milk
1/3 cup butter

Mix well together; flour, sugar, parsley, cheese, baking powder, basil and milk. On floured surface; roll out dough to ½ inch thickness. With sharp knife cut into desired lengths and widths. Preheat oven to 400° F. and melt butter in 9 x 13 inch pan. Roll dough in melted butter and line in pan. Bake for 20-30 minutes. Good dipped in pizza sauce.

"The difference between great people and everyone else is that great people create their lives actively, while everyone else is created by their lives, passively waiting to see where life takes them next. The difference between the two is the difference between living fully and just existing."... Michael E. Gerber

PIZZA SPREAD

1 -250 gram package cream cheese
¼ teaspoon garlic salt
½ cup pizza sauce
½ cup red pepper, chopped
½ cup green pepper, chopped
1 cup Cheddar cheese, shredded
1 cup Mozzarella cheese, shredded

Mix cream cheese and garlic salt and spread in 9 x 13 pan.
Spread pizza sauce on cheese and layer the rest of ingredients.
Bake at 350° F. for 20 minutes. Serve warm with taco chips
for dipping.

Time passes, Life happens,
Distance separates, Children grow up,
Jobs come and go, Love waxes and wanes,
Men don't do what they are supposed to do,
Hearts break, Parents die,
Colleagues forget favours,
Careers end, BUT
Sisters and girl friends are there, no matter how much
time and how many miles are between you.

PUMPKIN DIP

1 -250 gram package cream cheese, softened
2 cups icing sugar
1 cup canned pumpkin
½ cup sour cream
1 teaspoon ground cinnamon
1 teaspoon pumpkin pie spice
½ teaspoon ground ginger

In a large mixing bowl, beat cream cheese and icing sugar until smooth. Beat in pumpkin, sour cream, and spices. Serve with sweet crisps or ginger snaps. Refrigerate leftovers.

CREAM CHEESE AND PEPPER JELLY
(Keep these ingredients on hand and when company says they are dropping over in 5 minutes — this is the one!)
1 -250 gram package cream cheese, softened
½ cup mild pepper jelly (raspberry chipotle, jalapeño, cranberry, red pepper or any other you can find) Spread jelly over the block of cream cheese. Serve with assorted crackers, Fritos "Scoops" chips work great. If you want to get a little fancier arrange the cream cheese and jelly on each cracker ahead of time.

You never know what you can do till you try.

21

SALMON BALL

1 -250 gram package cream cheese, softened
1 tablespoon fresh lemon juice
1 tablespoon onion, finely chopped or grated
1 teaspoon prepared horseradish
1/8 teaspoon dill weed
salt, pepper and garlic powder, to taste
1 -213 gram can salmon
3-4 tablespoons fresh parsley, chopped
¼ cup walnuts or pecans, chopped

In a mixing bowl with a hand-held electric mixer at medium
speed, beat cream cheese, lemon juice, onion, horseradish, dill,
salt, pepper, and garlic powder until well blended. Drain and
flake salmon, removing skin and bone. Beat salmon into cheese
mixture at low speed until well blended. Chill until firm enough
to handle. Shape into a ball with wet hands. Coat with parsley
and walnut mixture. Cover and chill thoroughly; serve with
crackers.

I saw a woman wearing a sweat shirt with "Guess" on it.
So I said "Implants?" She hit me.

SASSY SAUCY MEATBALLS

1 pound lean ground beef
1/3 cup water chestnuts, finely chopped
2 tablespoons onion, grated
½ teaspoon salt
1 tablespoon prepared horseradish
2/3 cup orange marmalade
1/8 teaspoon garlic powder
1 ½ tablespoons flour
2 tablespoons soya sauce
1 tablespoon lemon juice
1 cup ketchup
½ teaspoon ground ginger
2 tablespoons brown sugar, packed
3 tablespoons water

Combine ground beef, water chestnuts, onion, salt and horseradish. Form in ¾ to 1 inch balls and place in baking dish. Combine remaining ingredients. Pour over meatballs. Bake 30-40 minutes at 350° F. Makes about 2 dozen meatballs, depending on size. These meatballs freeze well.

We are often our own worst enemy.

23

SAVORY PARTY BREAD

1 round sourdough loaf, unsliced
1 pound Monterey Jack cheese, sliced
½ cup margarine, melted
½ cup green onion, chopped
2-3 teaspoons poppy seeds

Cut the bread lengthwise and crosswise without cutting through bottom crust. Insert cheese between cuts. Combine margarine, onions and poppy seeds. Drizzle margarine mixture over the bread. Wrap in foil and place on a baking sheet. Bake at 350° F. for 15 minutes. Uncover, bake for 10 minutes longer or until cheese is melted.

"Stop sweating the small stuff. Don't worry about who doesn't like you, who has more, or who is doing what!
Instead, let's cherish the relationships we have with those who love us. Let's think about what you have been blessed with, and what we are doing each day to promote ourselves mentally, physically, emotionally."
..... Erma Bombeck

SHRIMP WHEELS

1 -106 gram can shrimp, drained, mashed
¼ cup mayonnaise
2 tablespoons olives, chopped
2 tablespoons chili sauce
1 tablespoon celery, chopped
1 -8 ounce package crescent rolls

Combine shrimp, mayonnaise, olives, chili sauce and celery. Unroll dough and separate crescents into 4 rectangles (not triangles). Spread ¼ cup shrimp mixture on each rectangle. Roll each rectangle and cut each roll into 10 slices. Place, cut side down on greased baking sheet. Bake at 375° F. for 10-12 minutes. Serve hot. Makes 40 wheels.

"It's like magic. When you live by yourself,
all of your annoying habits are gone."
..... Merril Markoe

SPINACH CHEESE BAKE

(As a side dish or an appetizer - delicious and nutritious!)

1/3 cup canola oil

2 cups fine bread crumbs

3 tablespoons Parmesan cheese

1 -300 gram package of frozen spinach, thawed, liquid
squeezed out, or 4 cups fresh spinach, washed, chopped

2 green onions, thinly sliced

2 cups creamed cottage cheese

¼ cup Feta cheese, crumbled

3 tablespoons flour

2 eggs, beaten

1 tablespoon fresh dill, chopped or ¾ teaspoon dried dill

¼ teaspoon salt

¼ teaspoon pepper

Preheat oven to 350° F. Mix together; oil, bread crumbs and
Parmesan cheese. Pack ¾ of mixture into a 9 x 13 inch
greased pan. In another bowl, mix; spinach, onion, cheeses,
flour, eggs, dill, salt and pepper. Pour spinach mixture into
prepared pan, sprinkle remaining crumbs on top. Bake 45
minutes, or until the center looks and feels set. Cut into squares.
Serve warm.

STUFFED MUSHROOMS

12 large fresh mushrooms, stems removed
1 -6 ounce package chicken flavored dry stuffing mix
2 cups butter
2 cloves garlic, peeled and minced
1 -250 gram package cream cheese, softened
2 cups imitation crabmeat, flaked
salt and pepper to taste
garlic powder to taste
crushed red pepper to taste

Arrange mushrooms on medium baking sheet, bottoms up. Chop and reserve mushroom stems. Prepare stuffing according to package directions. In a medium saucepan over medium heat melt butter. Mix in garlic and cook until tender, about 5 minutes. In a medium bowl mix together mushroom stems, stuffing mix, cream cheese and crabmeat. Liberally stuff mushrooms with mixture. Drizzle with the butter and garlic. Season with salt, pepper, garlic powder and red pepper. Bake uncovered in preheated oven at 350° F. for 12-15 minutes or until stuffing is lightly browned.

Hors d'oeuvres; a sandwich cut into twenty pieces.

TORTILLA BEEF TIDBITS
(A hit as a healthy appetizer or lunch alternative, use Cornmeal Tortillas, your own tortillas, or use bought shells.)

1 cup cream cheese, softened
2 tablespoons mayonnaise
1 ½ teaspoons Dijon mustard
1 teaspoon regular mustard
¼ cup dill pickles, finely chopped and blotted dry
½ pound roast beef, shaved (cooked ham may be substituted)
4 tortillas

Combine cream cheese, mayonnaise and mustards in a small bowl, until smooth. Add pickles, mix well. Divide and spread cream cheese mixture on each tortilla. Place a layer of beef on top. Roll up each tortilla very tightly. Wrap in plastic wrap. Chill for at least one hour. To serve, slice chilled rolls into 1 inch pieces. Skewer with tooth picks. Makes about 30 tidbits.

"People of mediocre ability sometimes achieve outstanding success, because they don't know when to quit. Most men succeed because they are determined to."
..... George E. Allen

TRAVERSE BAY DIP

1 -250 gram package cream cheese
1 cup sour cream
1 -14 ounce can re-fried beans
10 drops Tabasco sauce
1 tablespoon dried chopped chives
or 3 tablespoons fresh
chili powder, to taste
1 ½ cups Monterey Jack cheese, grated
1 ½ cups Cheddar cheese, grated

Combine cream cheese, sour cream, re-fried beans, Tabasco, and chives. Spread in 9 x 13 inch pan. Sprinkle chili powder over top. Cover with grated cheeses. Sprinkle more chili powder over top. Bake at 350° F. for 20 minutes. Serve hot with taco chips.

Don't argue with an idiot, people watching may
not be able to tell the difference.

TZAZIKI DIP
(Also a great spread on pita pockets!)

1 English cucumber, grated
1 cup plain yogurt
¼ cup mayonnaise
2 teaspoons extra virgin olive oil
½ teaspoon garlic powder
1 teaspoon salt
½ teaspoon pepper

Mix and refrigerate, covered. Serve with pita chips or vegetables.

SPINACH BACON DIP

1 -250 gram package cream cheese
1 cup mayonnaise
1 cup Cheddar cheese, grated
1 cup bacon, fried and crumbled
1 -300 gram package frozen spinach, thawed and squeezed dry
¼ cup purple onion, minced
1 teaspoon dill weed

Beat cream cheese and mayonnaise until smooth. Stir in rest of ingredients. Bake at 250 ° F. for 20 minutes or microwave for a few minutes until warm. Serve with crackers or bread pieces.

WELSH CAKES
(Serve these cold with a soft cheese, such as;
Brie, Camembert or a flavored cream cheese.)

2 cups flour
½ cup white sugar
2 teaspoons baking powder
½ teaspoon salt
¼ teaspoon nutmeg
¼ teaspoon cinnamon
½ cup butter
½ cup currants
¼ cup mixed peel, finely chopped
1 egg, beaten
1/3 cup milk

In large bowl put flour, sugar, baking powder, salt, nutmeg and cinnamon. Cut in butter until crumbly. Stir in currants and peel. Add eggs and milk. Stir to form ball of dough. Roll ¼ inch thick on floured surface. Cut into 2 or 3 inch rounds. Fry in non-stick frying pan over medium heat browning both sides. Pan should be lower temperature than for cooking pancakes. Makes about 3 dozen.
Hint: A pancake griddle set at 340° F. works really well.

YUMMY POTATO SKINS

4 large baking potatoes, baked
3 tablespoons canola oil
1 tablespoon Parmesan cheese, grated
½ teaspoon salt
¼ teaspoon garlic powder
¼ teaspoon paprika
1/8 teaspoon pepper
½ cup bacon bits or cooked bacon, fried and crumbled
½ cup Cheddar cheese, shredded
½ cup sour cream
4 green onions, sliced

Cut potatoes in half lengthwise and scoop out pulp, leaving a ¼ inch shell (save pulp for another use). Place potatoes skins on a greased baking sheet. Combine oil, Parmesan cheese, salt, garlic powder, paprika and pepper; brush over both sides of skins. Bake at 475° F. for 7 minutes and then turn. Bake until crisp, about 7 minutes more. Sprinkle bacon and Cheddar cheese inside skins. Bake 2 minutes longer or until the cheese is melted. Top with sour cream and onions. Serve immediately.

"Hope never abandons you, you abandon it." .....George Weinberg

"My mom has cancer and from the moment she was diagnosed, it has taken our collective breath away. She is fighting a brilliant battle and is recovering from grueling treatment. The cancer cells have moved around and have taken root in her lungs. All of the medical jargon and explanations aside, two weekends ago, my husband and I and our children arrived at my parents' house for a visit. The sky was blue, the back yard inviting, the barbeque smoking. I took my Mom shopping while the guys hung out. It was so painfully normal that it broke my heart. I couldn't understand why I was so upset, but after a day or so of reflection, I realized the weekend was a snapshot of our former lives as a family. You know, the one you know you are lucky to have, but don't grasp the miracle of until it is taken away by that hideous diagnosis of cancer. The greatest fear is losing your old life. While we have lost that life, we are determined to forge a new one with just as many laughs and memories."

"Fear has taken on a new meaning in our lives. It is no longer something that we sit and dread – we take it on.

F???ind
E???radicate
A???ssessment
R???emission

You find the MONSTER, you eradicate, you make an assessment of your treatments, and then you go to remission. When you have done this the first time, you start over as many times as necessary. I welcome F.E.A.R. everyday when I wake up, because I wake up."

Cancer gave me the gift of time off. I had been too busy raising two daughters as a single parent for 14 years, followed by nursing my second husband through cancer. Now I had time to take stock and to do the emotional and spiritual work I knew was essential for my health. However, I had to take issues in smaller doses than previously. And I had to be kind to myself, taking time out and telling myself it was OK to take longer than I had anticipated. This wasn't going to be a quick fix – no TV sitcom half-hour solutions. This was real.

My sister is presently going through treatment. She was diagnosed in May, had two surgeries, chemo and now is having daily radiation . . . My sister has been very private in her struggle and hasn't "allowed" any of us (3 siblings) personal visits or attendance at any of her medical treatments. We are on the phone daily, but we ALL need to hold her and we need to cry together. But. . . we respect that it is "her own race" and that she has given herself permission to handle it in the way that suits her best.

I have to live knowing that I can't do it all. I am choosing friends and activities that nurture me. Yes, I'm back, but I have to make wiser choices about how I pace myself. Do I succeed at this all the time? No, I'm finding it very easy to get overly busy. I have to monitor myself continually.

Beverages

A strong woman isn't afraid of anything,
but a woman of strength shows
courage in the midst of her fear.

FLOATS, SHAKES, SODAS AND MALTS

(These are all tastes of our youth, but tall glasses of these beverages served to grandchildren today, are a big hit too!)

<u>Float</u> - a float is a cold beverage that has ice cream floating in it. Often it is made from pop but can actually be any kind of a drink.

<u>Shake</u> - is a sweet, cold beverage, which is made from milk, ice cream or iced milk, and sweet flavorings such as fruit syrup or chocolate sauce.

<u>Soda</u> - is a treat made by mixing ice cream with either a soft drink or flavoured syrup and carbonated water, often with some special technique to encourage the partial slushing of the ice cream itself.

<u>Malt</u> - is a milkshake made with malt powder, which is made from dried milk and malted cereals. Today we can substitute malted candies which are made from malted milk and will give the malt flavour.

Shakes, Sodas and Malts continued on next page....

ROOT BEER FLOAT
(Any pop will work for a delicious float, substitute orange juice for the little ones.)

1 cup vanilla ice cream
1 -12 ounce can or bottle root beer
½ cup whipped cream
4 maraschino cherries
Place 1 scoop of ice cream into each of two tall glasses. Pour root beer carefully over the ice cream. Add another scoop and repeat. If possible, repeat again. Decorate with whipped cream and cherries and serve immediately. Serves 2.

YUMMY STRAWBERRY MILKSHAKE
(Any flavour you love is the one to use....vanilla and vanilla ice cream, or chocolate syrup and chocolate ice cream...even blended whole bananas and vanilla ice cream)

4 cups strawberries, hulled
2 cups milk
4 cups strawberry ice cream
2 teaspoons white sugar
In a blender combine strawberries, milk, ice cream and sugar. Blend until smooth. Makes two large shakes.

Let old friends know you haven't forgotten them, and tell new friends you never will.

OLD FASHIONED SODA

1/3 cup vanilla ice cream

3 tablespoons chocolate syrup or fruit syrup

¼ cup milk

¾ cup club soda (or until the glass is full)

Place syrup and milk in the bottom of a tall glass and stir to make a smooth paste. Add vanilla ice cream, pour in club soda until glass is almost full. Stir until well blended. Garnish with whipped cream and cherry. Serves 1.

CHOCOLATE MALT

½ cup Whoppers (malted milk ball candies)

½ cup milk

2 scoops ice cream

Combine and mix all the ingredients in a blender. Serves 1.

Work, as if you don't need the money.
Love, as though nobody has hurt you.
Dance, as if nobody is watching.
Sing, as if nobody is listening.
Live, as if this was paradise on earth.

WAKE UP SHAKE
(Makes 2 large servings)

1 banana
1 cup frozen berries (strawberries or raspberries)
1 cup vanilla yogurt
½ cup orange juice
¼ cup Splenda or sugar
1 cup ice cubes

Place all ingredients in blender. Cover and blend on high speed until smooth. Enjoy immediately!

BANANA YOGURT SHAKE

1 ½ cups milk
2 bananas, peeled
1 cup non-fat yogurt
¼ cup honey
1 teaspoon vanilla
½ teaspoon cinnamon
1/8 teaspoon nutmeg
¼ cup ice cubes

Combine milk, bananas, yogurt, honey, vanilla, cinnamon and nutmeg in a blender. Process until thick and creamy, about 2 minutes. Add ice and blend until smooth. Serve immediately.

NO TIME FOR BREAKFAST SMOOTHIE
(Tastes great and a great start to the day!)

½ cup low-fat milk
½ cup fat-free plain yogurt
½ frozen banana, peeled and chopped
2 tablespoons powdered protein supplement
1 ½ tablespoons flax seed
1 teaspoon honey
½ cup frozen strawberries

In a blender, blend the milk, yogurt, banana, protein supplement, flax seed, honey, and strawberries until smooth.

SUN TEA
(Fun to make and tastes extraordinary on a warm summer day!)

4 litres or 1 gallon cold water
5 orange pekoe tea bags
½ cup sugar
1 can frozen lemonade

Mix the water with the tea bags in it and pour into a large glass container with a lid. Place in the sun for 4 - 6 hours. Add sugar and lemonade. Chill thoroughly. Enjoy!

*"It is better to look ahead and prepare
than to look back and regret."*
.... *Jackie Joyner-Kersee*

MOCK CHAMPAGNE

1 -2 litre bottle ginger ale, chilled

1 -46 fluid ounce can pineapple juice, chilled

1 -64 fluid ounce bottle white grape juice, chilled

In a large punch bowl, combine ginger ale, pineapple juice and white grape juice. This is nice decorated with an ice ring.

To make ice ring you will need another bottle of ginger ale: Fill a ring-shaped cake pan to ½ with ginger ale. Freeze until partially frozen. At this stage you can place edible flowers, or pieces of fruit around the ring. Fill pan with ginger ale and freeze until solid. Place in punch bowl just before serving.

HARVEST COFFEE CIDER

¼ cup ground coffee, any variety

¼ teaspoon ground cinnamon

¼ cup brown sugar, firmly packed

1 cup apple juice or apple cider

3 cups cold water

Place coffee in filter in brew basket of coffee maker, sprinkle with cinnamon. Place sugar and apple juice or cider in empty pot of coffee maker. Add water to coffee maker; brew. When brewing is complete, stir until well blended. Makes 4 servings.

For every action, there is an equal and
opposite government program.

TROPICAL FRUIT PUNCH
(This punch has been our traditional
Christmas punch for over 30 years.)

4 cups sugar
2 cups water
2 cups strong tea, cooled
7 cups orange juice
3 cups lemon juice
5 cups pineapple juice
2 bottles ginger ale
orange slices
maraschino cherries

Boil sugar and water for 10 minutes. Remove from heat. Add and stir in tea. Chill thoroughly. At serving time, combine tea mixture, orange, lemon and pineapple juices. Add ice cubes. Add ginger ale and stir. Garnish with orange slices and maraschino cherries. Great with vodka or gin.

Success........
Age 4 success is....not piddling in your pants.
Age 12 success is....having friends.
Age 17 success is.....having a drivers license.
Age 35 success is....having money.
Age 50 success is.... having money.
Age 70 success is....having a drivers license.
Age 75 success is......having friends.
Age 80 success is ....not piddling in your pants.

CRANBERRY PUNCH

1 can frozen concentrate cranberry juice
1-2 liter bottle ginger ale
1 can frozen concentrate raspberry juice

Mix all of the above in a punch bowl. Add ice cubes and serve. Note: Freeze whole berries in some of the cranberry juice in circles and use in place of ice cubes. It adds variety to the punch.

MORNING MOCHA
(This is a great replacement for your morning coffee.)

1 teaspoon instant coffee
1 teaspoon sugar or Splenda
2 tablespoons light hot chocolate or 1 ½ tablespoons regular
1 ½ cups boiling water
¼ cup milk

Place all dry ingredients in a large mug. Pour in boiling water and then add milk. Enjoy.

May you always have love to share,
Health to spare,
And friends that care.

Shown on previous page:

❖ Sun Tea.....page 39

❖ Yummy Strawberry Milkshake.....page 36

❖ Old Fashioned Soda.....page 37

❖ Chocolate Malt.....page 37

❖ Root Beer Float.....page 36

HOT SPICY PUNCH
(Easily doubled for a large group)

4 cups water
1 ½ tablespoons gingerroot, peeled and chopped
4 tea bags
2 cinnamon sticks, broken
3 whole cloves
4 cups boiling water
½ cup sugar
½ cup lemon juice
½ cup orange juice
2 cups pineapple juice
2 cups cranberry cocktail
4 cups apple juice
1 orange, sliced thick
extra whole cloves for garnish

Heat 4 cups water in large pot. Add gingerroot, bring to a boil, turn down heat, cover and simmer 15 minutes. Let stand until cool. Strain, returning liquid to pot, discarding ginger. Put tea bags, cinnamon sticks, and 3 cloves into a bowl. Add 4 cups boiling water and stir. Cover bowl and let steep for 10 minutes. Strain into ginger water. Add all remaining ingredients, except orange slices and cloves. Heat well and pour into punch bowl. Stick a clove in the rind of each orange and float on top of punch. Serve.

Old age is like everything else, to make a success of it, you've got to start young.

43

PUERTO RICAN COQUITO
(A great change from our Christmas eggnog. Add some chocolate, to taste, and call it "Choquito")

2 egg yolks, beaten

1 -12 ounce can evaporated milk

1 -14 ounce can cream of coconut

1 -14 ounce can sweetened condensed milk

2/3 cup white rum

½ cup water

¼ teaspoon ground cloves

½ teaspoon ground cinnamon

1 teaspoon vanilla

In the top of a double boiler, over lightly simmering water, or in a heavy saucepan, combine egg yolks and evaporated milk. Stir constantly until mixture reaches a temperature of 160° F. The mixture should be thick enough to coat the back of a spoon. Transfer mixture to a blender, and add cream of coconut, sweetened condensed milk, rum, water, cloves, cinnamon, and vanilla. Blend for about 30 seconds. Pour into glass bottles, and chill overnight. Store in refrigerator.

"Remember not only to say the right thing in the right place, but far more difficult still, to leave unsaid the wrong thing at the tempting moment."
........*Benjamin Franklin*

COCOMOKA COLD

7 cups coffee, freshly made
2 cups whipping cream (whip an additional ½ cup for garnish)
8 cups chocolate ice cream
¼ cup rum or 1 teaspoon almond extract
¼ teaspoon salt
nutmeg or sweet chocolate, grated

Prepare coffee and chill. Whip cream until stiff. Pour chilled coffee into a large chilled bowl, stir in the whipped cream. Add 4 cups of the ice cream and beat until it is partially melted. Add rum (or almond extract) and salt. Fold in the remainder of the ice cream. Pour into tall glasses. Garnish with the extra whipped cream. Sprinkle with grated nutmeg or grated sweet chocolate.

"I have heard there are troubles of more than one kind.
Some come from ahead and some come from behind.
But I've bought a big bat. I'm all ready you see.
Now my troubles are going to have troubles with me!"
......Dr. Seuss

SLUSHIE PUNCH
(Slush your way through a hot day!)

2 cups sugar

6 cups water

2 -3 ounce packages strawberry flavored gelatin

1 -46 fluid ounce can pineapple juice

2/3 cup lemon juice

4 cups orange juice

2 -2 litre bottles lemon-lime flavored carbonated beverage

In a large saucepan, combine sugar, water, and strawberry flavored gelatin. Boil for 3 minutes. Stir in pineapple juice, lemon juice, and orange juice. Divide mixture in half, and freeze in 2 separate containers. The mixture takes 6-8 hours to freeze enough to get the slushy consistency. When ready to serve, place the frozen contents of one container in a punch bowl, and stir in 1 bottle of the lemon-lime soda until slushy. Save the other frozen container for another hot day!

I don't have hot flashes, I have short, private vacations in the tropics.

SANGRIA BLANCA
(Enjoy on your deck with a friend or that special someone)

1 orange, sliced
1 lemon, sliced
orange liqueur/brandy
2 tablespoons sugar
1 cup Ocean Spray White Cranberry Cocktail
1 cup white wine
1 small bag mixed frozen fruit (strawberries, peaches, pineapple)

Place orange and lemon slices in a large jug. Add sugar, orange liqueur/brandy to cover fruit. Stir to release juices and dissolve sugar. Add white cranberry cocktail and wine. Add frozen fruit to glasses and pour sangria over fruit. Makes 4 servings.

I've learned that making a living is not the same thing as making a life.

I've learned that sometimes life gives you a second chance.

I've learned that if you pursue happiness, it will elude you. But if you focus on your family, your friends, the needs of others, your work and doing the very best you can, happiness will find you.

I've learned that whenever I decide something with an open heart, I usually make the right decision.

A friend of mine saw me at the garden store with a cart full of perennial plants. He noted that buying perennials instead of annuals must be a sign that I'm planning to be around longer than an annual plant. You bet! I want to be able to look at every one of those plants I place in my garden and think back to when I used to be a stage 4 cancer patient.

I knew I was tough, I just didn't know how much so. The lessons I've learned aren't lessons I would have chosen to learn, but it's what life has handed me and I'll make the best of it and muddle through. I've learned that by leaning on family and friends, I can somehow get from morning to night, even in the worst of times. I've learned that isolating is not OK, and I've learned that to say thanks, I have friends who just want to help however they can.

After that day, your life is never the same. "That day" is the day the doctor tells you, "You have cancer." Every one of us knows someone who's had to face that news. It's scary, it's sad. But it's still life, and it's a life worth living. "My Cancer" is a daily account of my life and my fight with cancer. There is still sunshine through the clouds.

48

Brunches

A strong woman won't let anyone get the best of her, but a woman of strength gives the best of herself to everyone.

APPLE AND CINNAMON BAKED FRENCH TOAST
(Just like having apple pie for breakfast!)

1 loaf French bread
6 eggs
3 cups milk
½ cup white sugar
1 tablespoon vanilla
6 apples, peeled, cored, and sliced
½ cup brown sugar
2 tablespoons cinnamon

Slice bread 1 inch thick. Place close together in a 9 x 13 inch greased glass pan. In a bowl, beat eggs, milk, white sugar, and vanilla. Pour half the mixture over the bread. Place apples over bread. Pour remainder of egg mixture over apples. Cover and refrigerate overnight. Sprinkle with brown sugar and cinnamon in the morning. Bake uncovered at 350° F. for about 1 hour or until browned. Serve with maple syrup and/or whipped cream.

Worry gives a small thing a big shadow.
..... Swedish Proverb

APPLE FLAX PANCAKES
(A family favourite, and they get their omegas too!!)

1 ¼ cups flour
1/3 cup flax seed, coarsely ground
3 tablespoons sugar
1 tablespoon baking powder
½ teaspoon salt
¼ teaspoon cinnamon
dash of nutmeg
2 eggs, separated, whites beaten stiffly
1 ¼ cups milk
3 tablespoons butter, melted
1 cup apple, pared and shredded

In a large bowl, combine flour, flax, sugar, baking powder, salt, cinnamon and nutmeg. In a medium bowl, lightly beat together egg yolks, milk and butter. Add liquid ingredients to the dry, and stir until just combined. Add apple to batter, stir until just combined. Fold in egg whites. Using a 1/3 cup measure, pour batter onto a medium hot, greased, griddle or frying pan. Cook pancakes until bubbles appear on the surface, flip and cook on the other side.
Yield: 12 pancakes

"Darkness cannot drive out darkness, only light can do that."
..... Rev. Martin Luther King, Jr.

BAKED BREAKFAST FRITTATAS
(Delicious and wholesome.)

1 cup broccoli, chopped, partly cooked (if frozen, partly thawed)
1 cup seasoned croutons
½ sweet red pepper, diced
8 eggs
½ cup milk
1/8 teaspoon salt
1/8 teaspoon pepper
½ cup Swiss or Cheddar cheese, shredded

Sprinkle broccoli, croutons and red pepper evenly over bottom of greased 8 inch square cake pan. In bowl, whisk together; eggs, milk, salt and pepper. Pour over vegetables, sprinkle evenly with cheese. Bake in 350° F. oven for 30 minutes. Cut into squares. Serve warm.

Lady Aster: "If you were my husband
I'd put poison in your tea."
Churchill: "Madam, if you were my wife, I'd drink it"
..........Roger Bates

BREAKFAST COUSCOUS

¼ cup water
1 cup milk
½ cup uncooked couscous
¼ cup dried cranberries
¼ cup raisins
¼ cup walnuts, chopped and toasted
2 tablespoons brown sugar
½ teaspoon cinnamon
¼ teaspoon salt

Bring water to a boil in a small saucepan. Stir in milk and warm through. Stir in remaining ingredients. Remove from heat. Cover. Let stand for 10 minutes. Mixture will thicken as it cools.

"Living consciously involves being genuine; it involves listening and responding to others honestly and openly; it involves being in the moment."
.... Sidney Poitier

BREAKFAST LASAGNA

Crepes:
1 ½ cups milk
1 cup flour
2 eggs
1 tablespoon canola oil
½ teaspoon almond extract
2 tablespoons sugar
whipped cream, for garnish

Filling:
1 box instant vanilla pudding
1 cup orange juice
½ cup sour cream
2 cups fresh strawberries, sliced
2 bananas, sliced
1 cup fresh blueberries

Crepes: whisk together; milk, flour, eggs, oil, almond extract, and sugar in a bowl until you have a smooth batter. Lightly grease a small skillet and place over medium heat. Spoon in 2 tablespoons of batter and gently tilt the skillet to spread the batter to the edges of the pan. Cook until brown, 1-2 minutes. Flip the crepe and cook the other side until brown. Remove to a plate. Repeat with remaining batter until it is all used.

Filling: whisk together; pudding mix, orange juice, and sour cream in a bowl. Gently fold strawberries, bananas and blueberries into the sour cream mixture. Lightly grease the bottom of a baking dish. Cover the bottom of the dish with 1/3 of the crepes. Spoon ½ of the fruit mixture over the crepes. Repeat with remaining fruit and crepes, finishing with the crepes as the top layer. Garnish with whipped cream. Allow to sit 30 minutes before serving.

CARAMEL CREAM BANANA STUFFED CREPES
(Peaches are delicious in this recipe as well.)

Crepes:

1 cup flour	¼ cup icing sugar
2 eggs	1 cup milk
3 tablespoons butter, melted	1 teaspoon vanilla
¼ teaspoon salt	

Filling:

¼ cup butter	¼ cup brown sugar, packed
¼ teaspoon ground cinnamon	¼ cup heavy cream
6 bananas, halved lengthwise	

Garnish:

1 ½ cups whipping cream, whipped   1 pinch ground cinnamon

Sift flour and icing sugar into a mixing bowl. Add eggs, milk, butter, vanilla, and salt; beat until smooth. Heat a lightly greased 6 inch skillet. Add about 3 tablespoons batter. Tilt skillet so that batter spreads to almost cover the bottom of skillet. Cook until top is set and golden; turn and brown the other side. Repeat process with remaining batter, grease skillet as needed. Slip cooked crepes onto waxed paper. Melt butter in a large skillet. Stir in brown sugar, and cinnamon. Stir in cream and cook until slightly thickened. Add bananas to skillet; cook for 2-3 minutes, spooning sauce over them. Remove from heat.

Roll a crepe around each banana half and place on serving platter. Spoon sauce over crepes. Top with whipped cream and a pinch of cinnamon.

CLASSIC CHEESE SOUFFLÉ

(A soufflé is not nearly as daunting as we think. There are a few steps, but once in a while, it is well worth it!)

¼ cup butter or margarine

¼ cup flour

1 teaspoon salt

1/8 teaspoon cayenne pepper

1 ½ cups milk

2 cups Cheddar cheese, shredded

6 eggs, separated

Melt butter in a medium saucepan over medium heat, stir in flour, salt and cayenne pepper until smooth. Slowly add milk and stir until thickened. Add cheese and keep stirring just until the cheese melts. Remove pan from heat and preheat oven to 325° F. In a small bowl beat egg yolks with a fork and add a little of the hot mixture while beating to warm the egg yolks. This will prevent lumping when they are added to the hot mixture. Slowly pour warm egg yolks into hot sauce stirring quickly to avoid lumping. In a large bowl beat egg whites until stiff peaks form. Lightly grease bottom only of a 2 quart soufflé dish or straight sided casserole dish. With rubber spatula, gently fold cheese sauce into beaten egg whites. Pour mixture gently into casserole dish. If you want your soufflé to have a top hat appearance - cut a circle with a knife in the mixture about one inch deep and one inch in from the side. Bake in centre of oven for one hour and serve immediately.

FAVORITE EGG CASSEROLE

1 dozen eggs
1 cup plain yogurt
1 teaspoon seasoned salt
1/3 cup butter or margarine
2 cups shredded hash brown potatoes, thawed
¼ cup onion, chopped
1 cup sharp Cheddar cheese, grated

Beat eggs, yogurt, and salt together. Melt butter and lightly sauté onion. Add potatoes. Stir to mix. Pour in egg mixture and lightly stir to blend ingredients. Pour into casserole dish. Sprinkle grated cheese over casserole. Bake at 350° F. for about 25 minutes or until knife comes out clean when inserted. Serves 8.

"Whatever course you decide upon, there is always someone to tell you that you are wrong. There are always difficulties arising which tempt you to believe that your critics are right. To map out a course of action and follow it to an end requires courage."
............*Ralph Waldo Emerson*

FAVORITE NEIGHBOURS' WAFFLES

¾ cup flour

¼ cup cornstarch

½ teaspoon salt

½ teaspoon baking powder

¼ teaspoon baking soda

¾ cup buttermilk

¼ cup milk

6 tablespoons canola oil

1 egg yolk

1 egg white

1 tablespoon sugar

½ teaspoon vanilla

Preheat oven to 200° F. Preheat your waffle iron. In a medium bowl, stir together; flour, cornstarch, salt, baking powder and baking soda. Combine; milk, buttermilk and oil in another bowl. Whisk in egg yolk with a fork, and set aside. In a small bowl, beat egg white with an electric mixer until almost soft peaks. Gradually sprinkle in sugar, while continuing to whip until thick and glossy, add vanilla. Pour milk mixture into dry ingredients, and whisk just until blended. Fold in egg white using a spatula. Pour batter onto hot waffle iron in the recommended amount for your iron. Usually waffle irons take a generous ½ cup. Close the iron, and cook until golden brown. Keep finished waffles in the warm oven directly on the rack. Do not stack, or they will become soggy. Freeze leftovers and heat in toaster.

"Children are a great comfort in your old age and they help you reach it faster too." ..... Lionel Kaufman

FLAX PORRIDGE
(A new delicious twist on a hearty old time favorite)

3 cups water
2 teaspoons salt
1 ½ cups quick cooking oats
1/3 cup dried apple, craisins or raisins
¼ cup maple syrup
½ teaspoon ground cinnamon
¼ cup sliced almonds
2 tablespoons whole flax seed
2 tablespoons ground flax seed

In a medium saucepan, bring water and salt to a rolling boil. Add oats, apple or raisins, maple syrup and cinnamon. Stir. Cook 3 to 5 minutes over medium low heat, stirring occasionally. Stir in almonds and flax. Cover remove from heat and let sit 2 minutes. Serve with milk. Drizzle with extra maple syrup if desired.

"There's nothing better than a good friend, except a good friend with chocolate".......Linda Grayson

"Here is a test to see if your mission on earth is complete – if you are alive then it isn't...Richard Bach

58

HAM AND SWISS QUICHE
(Mozzarella or Cheddar will work too.)

1 -9 inch pie shell
1 ½ cups ham, finely chopped
2 cups Swiss cheese, shredded
3 eggs, beaten
1 cup cream
2 tablespoons onion, chopped
1 teaspoon dry mustard
½ teaspoon salt
1 tablespoon Parmesan cheese

Place ham in the bottom of pie shell, and top with Swiss cheese. In a bowl, combine eggs, cream, onion, mustard, and salt. Pour over ham and cheese. Sprinkle with Parmesan cheese. Bake at 350° F. for 30 minutes.

"You should never marry anybody unless you have seen each other miserable with the flu." ....Dr. Phil McGraw

Don't cry because it is over - smile because it happened!

KICK START BREAKFAST
(The kids won't even know this is a healthy breakfast!)

1 cup powdered milk
1 tablespoon peanut butter
1 tablespoon liquid Nesquick Syrup
water
cereal, high fibre

Mix milk, peanut butter, chocolate sauce, and just enough water to make a thick liquid. Add enough cereal so that all the cereal is coated with mixture. Divide into 3 portions. Enjoy!

EGGS ON BAGELS WITH HOLLANDAISE SAUCE

2 bagels, cut in half
4 eggs, scrambled
Hollandaise sauce, your favorite recipe (homemade or commercial)
Prepare Hollandaise sauce. Place bagels on cookie sheet. Divide eggs into 4 and place on bagels. Cover eggs with sauce and serve immediately.

"Be nice to your children, for they will choose your rest home."
..... Phyllis Diller

Shown on previous page:

❖ Orange Almond Brunch Biscuits.....page 62

❖ Breakfast Lasagna.....page 53

❖ Mock Champagne.....page 40

❖ Apple Dip.....page 1

❖ Orange Cottage Crepes.....page 63

❖ Caramel Cream Banana Stuffed Crepes....page 54

❖ Ricotta Pineapple Muffins.....page 107

❖ Cherry Muffins.....page 99

MAKE AHEAD BREAKFAST CASSEROLE

12 slices bacon
5 hash brown potato patties
½ cup onions, chopped
2 cans sliced mushrooms
3 cups Cheddar cheese, cubed
3 cups ham, cubed
6 eggs
½ cup milk

Lightly grease a 9 x 13 inch baking pan. Fry hash brown patties until crisp and put in baking pan. Fry bacon until crisp and crumbly put on top of hash browns. Layer onions, mushrooms, cheese and ham evenly in pan. In bowl beat eggs and milk together. Pour over all ingredients in baking dish. Cover with foil and keep in fridge overnight. Bake at 350° F. for 45 minutes covered. Remove foil and bake 25 minutes longer. Let stand 5 to 10 minutes before serving.

"Happiness does not depend on outward things, but on the way we see them." ......*Leo Tolstoy*

ORANGE ALMOND BRUNCH BISCUITS
(Low fat, tasty and wholesome)

1 ¾ cups flour

½ cup whole wheat flour

4 teaspoons baking powder

2 tablespoons sugar

½ teaspoon salt

½ cup applesauce

1 egg

½ cup milk

2 tablespoons orange juice

2 tablespoons butter, melted

¼ cup sugar

¼ cup orange rind, grated

½ cup sliced almonds

Glaze:

1 cup icing sugar

2 tablespoons orange juice

1 tablespoon orange rind

Combine flour, baking powder, 2 tablespoons sugar, salt and applesauce. In another bowl, beat egg, milk and orange juice. add to dry ingredients. Knead and roll to approximately a 10 x 12 inch rectangle. Brush with melted butter and sprinkle with ¼ cup sugar, 1 tablespoon of the orange rind, and ¼ cup almonds (reserve the rest.) Roll from the widest side. Cut into 1 inch slices. Place in greased 9 x 12 inch pan and bake for 20 minutes at 425° F. Mix glaze ingredients. Drizzle over biscuits and sprinkle remaining ¼ cup almonds and orange rind on top.

"If you are old enough to know better,
you're old enough to do it..... George Burns

ORANGE COTTAGE CREPES
(Worth the time! Make a double batch; they freeze well)

4 eggs
1 cup milk
2 teaspoons butter, melted
1 cup flour
1 tablespoon sugar
½ teaspoon salt

Sauce:
½ cup orange juice
½ cup sugar
½ cup butter or margarine

Filling:
1 cup creamed cottage cheese
2 tablespoons light cream
1 tablespoon orange rind, grated
2 tablespoons sugar

Beat eggs, milk, butter, flour, sugar and salt for about 3 minutes. Cover and let stand for one hour. Pour ¼ cup batter onto lightly greased griddle. Fry crepes. Mix filling ingredients together. Divide filling into the number of crepes. Spread on and roll up tightly. Place in a lightly greased 9 x 12 inch pan. Mix sauce ingredients and pour over crepes. Bake in a 350° F. oven for approximately 30 minutes.

"The face I see is furrowed now.
In fact it's rather rutty,
Revlon and Clinique won't do,
I need a can of putty."
..... Jane Thomas Noland

63

OVERNIGHT BREAKFAST
(Great served with tomato wedges.)

6 eggs, hard boiled
1 -10 ounce can mushroom soup
½ cup mayonnaise
½ cup milk
1 teaspoon chives
6 slices bacon, cooked and crumbled

Slice eggs in quarters. Put all ingredients except bacon in a 1 quart greased casserole. Cover with plastic wrap and chill overnight. Bake uncovered at 350° F. for 20-25 minutes. Top with the bacon. Bake 5 minutes longer. Serves 4.

"The life I touch for good or ill will touch another life, and that in turn another, until who knows where the trembling stops or in what far place my touch will be felt."
.......Frederick Beuchner

"You know you're getting old when your wife gives up sex for Lent, and you don't realize it till the Fourth of July."
..... Milton Berle

PEACH PUFF PANCAKE
(Great with any fresh fruit!)

2 eggs, beaten
¾ cup buttermilk
2 tablespoons canola oil
2 tablespoons brown sugar
1 cup flour
½ teaspoon salt
1 teaspoon baking powder
1 teaspoon baking soda
2 peaches, peeled and sliced
1 tablespoon brown sugar

Mix eggs, buttermilk, oil, and 2 tablespoons brown sugar. Stir in flour, salt, baking powder, and baking soda. Fold in peaches. Pour into large greased pie plate. Sprinkle with brown sugar. Bake at 350° F. for 25-30 minutes. Serve with syrup and whipped cream. Serves 6.

Note: If you use apples sprinkle the top with sugar and cinnamon.

"I love gardening ... it is nice raising something
that doesn't talk back to you."
.....Ed Fisher

65

PINK RIBBON BREAKFAST CASSEROLE

1 pound sausage meat
½ cup onion, diced
¼ cup green pepper, diced
2 cups Mozzarella and Cheddar cheese blend, grated
1 -8 ounce can refrigerated crescent dinner rolls
6 eggs, beaten
1 cup milk
¼ teaspoon salt
1/8 teaspoon pepper

Preheat oven to 375° F. Crumble and cook sausage, onion and green pepper in medium skillet until browned. Drain. Line bottom of greased 9 x 13 inch baking dish with crescent roll dough, firmly pressing perforations to seal. Pop into oven and pre-bake for 5 minutes. Sprinkle with skillet mixture and cheese. Combine remaining ingredients in medium bowl until blended; pour over sausage. Bake 30 - 35 minutes or until set. Let stand 5 minutes before cutting into squares; serve hot. Refrigerate leftovers.

"Trouble is part of your life... If you don't share it, you don't give the person who loves you a chance to love you enough." ..... *Dinah Shore*

UNIQUE EGG CASSEROLE

12 eggs, hard boiled, peeled and sliced
½ pound bacon, fried crisp and crumbled
¼ cup butter
¼ cup flour
1 cup light cream
1 cup milk
2 cloves garlic, minced
¼ teaspoon thyme, marjoram, basil and parsley
2 cups Cheddar cheese, shredded
¾ cup bread crumbs

In saucepan over medium heat melt butter, stir in flour, gradually add cream and milk and heat until sauce is thick. Add cheese and seasonings. Grease a 9 x 13 inch casserole dish and pour half the sauce in it. Add eggs and bacon and top with remaining sauce. Sprinkle bread crumbs on top. Bake at 350° F. for 30 minutes.

"Most folks are about as happy as they make up
their minds to be."........Abraham Lincoln

"I had a four year old daughter and a healthy five month old baby boy and I thought life couldn't be better, until one day in May when my life fell apart. I was diagnosed with cancer. What kind of mother could I be? What kind of wife could I be? How could I face the world as this horrible new me? A family crisis had definitely hit. This is something you hear about all the time, but never expect to happen to you. Suddenly my family and I were experiencing all this change and I felt as though it was all my fault. But here I am still alive, and after two months of chemo, I am rid of the cancer that had plagued my body. I've learned that through the power of prayer, miracles do happen. We must remember that when we hear the word cancer, it's not necessarily the end of the world, but the beginning of a more appreciative life. No longer will my family sweat the small stuff, life really is too short. Along with the gift of a second chance at life, I received the gift of generosity from so many people."

When I was first diagnosed, I was fearful that I wouldn't see the day when my babies grew into beautiful people. That was the limited vision I faced at the beginning of my journey with breast cancer. It wasn't until words from another survivor ("Stop feeling sorry for yourself") was shared with me, that I was able to refocus and begin to live each day to its fullest. The old "cruel to be kind" psychology set me back on track to the principles of positive thinking. A second onset of the disease, twenty-one months later after the birth of my twins, proved yet another challenge. With a different prescription of treatment and an attitude of determination, I was successful once more. My vision now, as I celebrate five years "cancer free", is one of hope, progress and growth.

Breads and Muffins

A strong woman makes mistakes and avoids the same in the future, but a women of strength realizes life's mistakes can also be blessings and capitalizes on them.

BRAN AND OAT SCONES
(Lovely served warm with fruit for breakfast.)

1 cup 100% bran cereal

1 cup quick cooking oats

½ cup raisins or currants

1 ¼ cups plain yogurt

1 cup flour

¼ cup sugar

1 tablespoon baking powder

1 teaspoon baking soda

½ teaspoon salt

½ teaspoon cinnamon

¼ teaspoon nutmeg

1/3 cup margarine

Combine cereal, oats, raisins and yogurt. Let stand to soften. Combine flour, sugar, baking powder, baking soda, salt, cinnamon and nutmeg in a large bowl. Cut in margarine until crumbly. Add cereal mixture and stir just until moistened. Turn onto a floured surface and knead 10 times or until smooth. Flatten to a 9 inch circle or two 6 inch circles. Sprinkle with sugar and cinnamon. Place on a greased cookie sheet. Bake at 425° F. for 20 minutes. Cut into wedges.

"You've reached old age when the gleam in your eye is just the sun on your bifocals." .....Henny Youngman

LEMON-FILLED GINGER SCONES
(The lemon and ginger combination creates a unique and delicious flavour.)

2 cups flour
¼ cup sugar
1 tablespoon baking powder
1/3 cup butter
2/3 cup buttermilk
1 tablespoon ginger root, grated
1/3 cup lemon curd
sprinkle sugar

Mix flour, sugar, and baking powder. Cut in butter. Stir in buttermilk and ginger root. Form into ball. Divide in half. Line a pie plate or pan with greased foil. Place half of dough on foil and pat into a 7 inch circle, creating a pie crust effect. Cover with lemon curd then cover with other circle. Fold up edges and seal really well. Sprinkle with sugar and bake at 400° F. for 20-25 minutes.

"Until you become a parent, you can't begin to discover your capacity for strength, love and fatigue." ..... *Peter Gallagher*

ORANGE RAISIN SCONES WITH ORANGE BUTTER

1 ¾ cups flour

2 ½ teaspoons baking powder

3 tablespoons sugar

2 teaspoons orange zest, grated

1/3 cup butter, cut into pieces

½ cup raisins

1 large egg, lightly beaten

4-6 tablespoons half and half cream

1 large egg, lightly beaten

½ cup butter, softened

2 tablespoons orange marmalade

Preheat oven to 400° F. Combine flour, baking powder, sugar and orange zest in a medium bowl; cut in butter with a fork until crumbly. Stir in raisin, 1 egg, and enough cream just until ingredients are moistened. Turn dough out onto a lightly floured surface; knead lightly 10 times. Roll into a 9 inch circle and cut into 12 wedges. Places wedges 1 inch apart on a lightly greased baking sheet and brush with beaten egg. Bake at 400° F. for 10-12 minutes or until golden brown. Remove from baking sheet immediately and serve with orange butter (mix butter and marmalade).

Energizer Bunny arrested, charged with battery!

71

POTATO BEST BISCUITS
(Use up those mashed potatoes! Great with soup, stew, or as a snack with cheese.)

1 ½ cups flour
¼ cup cornmeal
4 teaspoons baking powder
½ teaspoon salt
1 ½ cups cold mashed potatoes
¼ cup canola oil
1/3 cup milk

In large bowl mix together; flour, cornmeal, baking powder and salt. Add mashed potatoes and oil. Blend until thoroughly mixed and texture is crumbly. Add milk to make soft dough. Turn the dough out onto a floured surface and knead for six turns. Roll the dough to about ¾ inch (2 cm) thick. Cut with a floured 2 inch (5 cm) round cutter, a small glass works well. Place biscuits on a baking sheet, lightly sprayed with a nonstick cooking spray. Bake in a 400° F. oven for 12-15 minutes, or until nicely golden.

"The beaten path is the safest, but the traffic is terrible."
Jeff Taylor

SCOTTISH OAT CRISPS
(They go nicely with Cheddar cheese and homemade soup!)

2 cups oatmeal
1 cup flour
1 teaspoon sugar
1 teaspoon baking powder
½ teaspoon salt
6 tablespoons margarine
water

Cut first six ingredients together with a pastry wire. Add water a little at a time to make a stiff dough. Roll out on a greased pizza pan. Bake at 350° F. for 10-15 minutes until slightly brown. Cut into wedges.

When you have to walk that lonesome valley and you have to walk it by yourself, the women in your life will be on the valley's rim, cheering you on, praying for you, pulling for you, intervening on your behalf, and waiting with open arms at valley's end. Sometimes, they will even break the rules and walk beside you ... or come in and carry you out.

SPINACH FETA BISCUITS
(Serve with your favourite soup.)

2 eggs
¼ cup canola oil
¼ cup brown sugar
1 cup water
2 teaspoons baking powder
¼ teaspoon salt
2 teaspoons oregano
1 package frozen spinach, thawed, drained, squeezed
2 cups flour
1 cup Feta cheese, crumbled

Beat eggs, oil, and sugar. Add water and then rest of ingredients, stirring cheese in last. Drop into greased muffin tins. Bake at 350° F. for 12 minutes. Yields 12 biscuits.

Whoever one is, and wherever one is, one is always in the wrong if one is rude." ….. Maurice Baring

BANNOCK
(Grandpa can hardly wait when this is served up for the grandkids after school snack!)

3 cups flour
1 tablespoon baking powder
½ teaspoon salt
1 ¼ cups water
canola oil for frying (about ¼ cup)

Measure flour, baking powder and salt into medium bowl. Add water. Mix and knead until dough forms into a ball. Place on floured surface and flatten with rolling pin to a ½ inch thick circle. Cut into pie-shaped wedges. Make a slash in the center of each wedge so it cooks through. Heat canola oil in frying pan on medium-high. Fry on both sides until a golden brown. Place on paper towels to absorb oil. Serve warm with butter, jam, corn syrup or just plain. This recipe is easily doubled and is great on those camping trips!

"Hot heads and cold hearts never solved anything."
.....Billy Graham

GREAT BROWN BREAD

1 cup warm water
2 teaspoons sugar
2 tablespoons yeast
Mix sugar in water and add yeast. Set aside for 10 minutes.

4 cups warm water
½ cup sugar
2 teaspoons salt
¾ cup canola oil
¾ cup molasses
Mix ingredients in large bowl and add yeast mixture.

Mix:
5 cups white flour
4 cups whole wheat flour
1 cup oatmeal
1 cup bran

Gradually add the flour mixture stirring until mixed. Knead until firm. Add flour if mixture is too sticky. Let rise for 1 ½ hours. Knead again and let rise again until doubled. Divide the dough into five portions and place in well greased bread pans. Let rise until double and bake at 350° F. for about 35 minutes.

What are the three words guaranteed to
humiliate men everywhere?   "Hold my purse."

CHAPATTIS BREAD
(This bread is used for dipping. Serve with dishes that have a lot of sauce.)

3 ½ cups whole wheat flour
sea salt (to taste)
2 teaspoons canola oil
1 cup water

In large bowl, stir together flour and salt. Stir in oil gradually. Add water and knead on floured surface for 3 minutes. Divide into 8 equal portions. On floured surface roll thin into circles. Heat heavy based frying pan. When thoroughly hot, fry in batches for 1-2 minutes, turning frequently until speckled brown. Remove and keep warm. Serves 4.

"I hate the word housewife;
I don't like the word home-maker either.
I want to be called Domestic Goddess."
.....Roseanne Barr

CINNAMON BUNS

(These very popular buns were made by a chef at a local restaurant.)

¼ cup warm water

1 teaspoon sugar

2 teaspoons yeast

3 eggs, well beaten

½ cup sugar

¾ cup canola oil

¾ teaspoon salt

1 tablespoon baking powder

2 cups water (hotter than lukewarm)

4-5 cups flour

¾ cup butter, melted (approximately)

1 cup brown sugar

2 tablespoons cinnamon

1 tablespoon flour

Glaze:

1 tablespoon butter

1 ½ cups brown sugar

½ cup cream

1 teaspoon vanilla

Continued on next page......

CINNAMON BUNS continued....

Dissolve sugar in water. Stir in yeast and let sit for 10 minutes. Beat together; eggs, sugar, oil, salt, baking powder, and water. Add the yeast. Add enough flour to make a *soft* dough (watch your flour after fourth cup). Place in greased bowl, cover, and let rise for 45 minutes. Punch down and let rise again until doubled in size. Divide dough in half; roll into rectangle about 8 x 12 inches. Mix together brown sugar, cinnamon and flour. Spread dough with melted butter, sprinkle brown sugar mixture and roll up. Work on the roll to stretch it to about 24 inches in length and cut in 2 inch thick slices. Place in greased 9 x 13 inch cake pans. Cover and let rise. Turn each bun over after 15 minutes and let rise for 1 hour. Bake at 350° F. for 30-40 minutes. Remove from oven and tip upside down on tinfoil.

Glaze:
Melt butter in small saucepan. Remove from heat; stir in brown sugar, cream and vanilla. Spread on the bottom side of the warm cinnamon buns. Yummy!

"Shopping is a woman thing. It's a contact sport like football. Women enjoy the scrimmage, the noisy crowds, the danger of being trampled to death, and the ecstasy of the purchase."
..... Erma Bombeck

EASTER BABKA
(A traditional Ukrainian Easter bread.)

2 tablespoons yeast   1 tablespoon grated lemon rind

1 teaspoon sugar   2 tablespoons orange juice

½ cup lukewarm water   ½ teaspoon vanilla

½ cup butter, melted   3 ½ cups flour

1 cup milk, scalded   ½ cup light raisins

5 eggs yolks plus 1 egg, well-beaten

½ cup sugar

½ teaspoon salt

sprinkle of cornmeal or dry bread crumbs

In small bowl dissolve sugar in lukewarm water, add yeast and let
stand for 10 minutes. Combine butter and milk in large bowl;
cool. Add eggs, sugar, salt, lemon rind, orange juice, vanilla
and yeast. Beat in 2 cups of the flour until elastic. Add raisins
and enough of remaining flour to make very soft dough. Put a
damp towel over bowl and let rise until double in bulk. (Maybe
punched down for a second rising.) When dough has risen, take
3 one pound coffee tins and butter well. Sprinkle with cornmeal,
shaking the can so the cornmeal sticks to the sides and bottom of
tin. Make a large bun from the dough and drop it in the tin.
Let rise until the tin is full. Bake at 325° F. for 45-60
minutes or until brown and hollow sounding when tapped.
Makes 3 loaves. Serve with Lemon Spread on next page.

DELICIOUS LEMON SPREAD
(This is a scrumptious spread to be served
with traditional Easter Bread.)

2 cups cottage cheese (dry curd)
4 eggs, hard-boiled
½ cup cream, boiled then cooled
½ cup butter
½ cup white sugar
1 teaspoon lemon rind
1 tablespoon lemon juice

Place all ingredients in a blender and puree.

CORN BREAD

2 eggs
½ cup sugar
1 ¼ cups buttermilk
1 cup cornmeal
1 cup flour
1 teaspoon baking powder
¼ teaspoon salt

Beat eggs. Beat in remaining ingredients. Pour batter into a hot
greased 8 x 8 inch pan. Bake at 350° F. for 20 minutes.
Cut into squares and serve with a salad or soup.

ENGLISH MUFFINS
(Make your own Egg McMuffins!)

2 cups warm water
1/3 cup sugar
2 tablespoons yeast
1 tablespoon salt
6 ½ cups flour
2 eggs, beaten
1/3 cup canola oil

Combine water, sugar and yeast; stir until dissolved. Add salt and 2 cups flour, beat for 2 minutes. Add eggs and oil, beat for 1 minute. Work in remaining flour and let rise for 20 minutes. Roll dough to ½ inch thick and cut with 3 inch cutter. (A salmon can will work.) Cover and let rise for 45 minutes. Preheat ungreased electric fry pan to 375° F. Cook for 7-8 minutes on each side - be careful not to burn. They will sound hollow when done. Serve with a slice of ham, cheese and a fried egg.

You block your dream when you allow your fear to grow bigger than your faith." ..... *Mary Marin Morrissey*

FANTASTIC FOCACIA BREAD
(A quick way to impress your guests.
This truly is a fantastic bread.)

1 tube refrigerated pizza crust
2 garlic cloves, crushed
2 cups Mozzarella cheese, shredded
2/3 cup Parmesan cheese, grated
2 teaspoons oregano (or less, to taste)
2 Roma tomatoes, sliced

Spread dough on pizza stone or pan. Spread crushed garlic on dough. Sprinkle half of the Mozzarella cheese, half of the Parmesan cheese and half of the oregano on the dough. Place sliced tomatoes on the cheese in a single layer. Repeat cheeses and oregano. Bake at 350° F. for 30-35 minutes. Cut into wedges.

"Having a two year old is like having a blender
you don't have a top for."
Jerry Seinfeld

MOLASSES CORNMEAL

1 egg
1 cup buttermilk
2 tablespoons canola oil
2 tablespoons molasses
1 cup flour
¼ cup sugar
½ teaspoon salt
1 teaspoon baking powder
½ teaspoon baking soda
1 cup cornmeal

Beat egg until thick. Blend in buttermilk, oil, and molasses. Set aside. Sift together; flour, sugar, salt, baking powder, and baking soda. Mix in cornmeal. Make a well in the centre of the dry ingredients. Add liquid ingredients and mix until smooth. Do not over-beat. Pour batter into a greased 8 x 8 inch pan or large pie plate. Bake at 350° F. for about 20 minutes. Cut into 2 inch squares or wedges. Serve warm.

It is all right to try and fail,
but don't fail to try.

NAAN BREAD

(A leavened Indian flatbread. Accompanies any meal or serve straight from the oven with a little butter as a healthy snack.)

2 large eggs
¼ cup plain yogurt
¾ cup milk
¼ cup canola oil

4 cups flour
1 tablespoon sugar
1 tablespoon baking powder
½ teaspoon baking soda
1 ½ teaspoons salt

In large bowl beat eggs until frothy. Add yogurt, milk and canola oil. Mix. In separate bowl mix together flour, sugar, baking powder, baking soda and salt. Stir into egg mixture. Turn out onto floured surface and knead until dough is smooth. Cut into 30 golf ball size pieces. Cover with damp tea towel. Let stand 1 hour. On floured surface, roll or pat each ball into 6 inch long ovals. Arrange on greased baking sheets. Bake at 450° F. for 5-6 minutes until puffed and browned. Makes 30.

"I'm growing old by myself -
My wife hasn't had a birthday in years."......Milton Berle

ORANGE CRESCENTS

3 ounces cream cheese, softened
3 tablespoons sugar
¼ teaspoon almond extract
1 teaspoon orange zest, grated
1 -8 ounce package refrigerated crescent rolls

Blend cream cheese, sugar, almond extract and orange zest. Separate dough into triangles. Divide cheese mixture among dough triangles, spread, leaving a ¼ inch border. Roll each triangle, starting at the long edge. Place on a lightly greased cookie sheet, shaping into crescents. Bake at 350° F for 15 minutes or until lightly browned.

Topping:
½ cup icing sugar
1 tablespoon orange juice
1 teaspoon orange zest, grated
1 teaspoon margarine, melted
1/8 teaspoon almond extract
Combine all ingredients while rolls are baking. Spread over hot crescent rolls and serve immediately.

*"That shows how long we've been married -
Now you kiss me to calm me down."...... Bette Davis*

THE BEST PIZZA CRUST

1 package instant yeast
1 tablespoon salt
1 tablespoon sugar
3 ½ cups white flour
1 ½ cups warm water
2 tablespoons canola oil
1 tablespoon olive oil

Mix yeast, salt, sugar and flour in medium bowl. In larger bowl mix water and canola oil. Slowly add flour mixture to liquids, mix well and knead until mixture forms a soft consistent ball. Divide in two and place on a lightly floured surface, roll out into circles to fit 2 lightly greased pizza pans. Press into pans. Slit fitted dough in a few places with a sharp knife to prevent bubbles from forming. Brush with olive oil. Add your favorite toppings. Bake for 25-30 minutes in a 350° F. oven.
This recipe doubles well. Make pizza crusts ahead of time, partially bake (about 10 minutes), cool and wrap in plastic and then foil. Freeze. Thaw, deck with your favorite toppings, and bake for another 20-25 minutes.

**Despite the cost of living,
have you noticed how popular it remains?**

CHOCOLATE ZUCCHINI BREAD

2 eggs
1/3 cup canola oil
1 cup sugar
1 ½ cups zucchini, grated
1/3 cup water
1 teaspoon vanilla
1 2/3 cups flour
1 teaspoon baking soda
½ teaspoon baking powder
½ teaspoon salt
1 teaspoon pumpkin pie spice
1/3 cup walnuts, chopped
3 tablespoons cocoa
1/3 cup chocolate chips

Beat eggs, add oil and sugar. Add zucchini, water, and vanilla; stir. Blend in flour, baking soda, baking powder, salt, and spice. Stir in nuts. Divide batter in half, and add cocoa and chocolate chips to one half. Pour plain batter into bottom of a greased 9 x 5 inch loaf pan. Pour chocolate batter on top and swirl with a knife for marble effect. Bake at 350° F. for about 1 hour or until toothpick inserted into the centre comes out clean. Cool 10 minutes and remove from pan.

The number of people watching you is directly proportional to the stupidity of your action.

CRANBERRY ORANGE LOAF

2 cups flour
1 cup fresh or frozen cranberries, coarsely chopped
¾ cup sugar
½ cup walnuts
2 ½ teaspoons baking powder
¼ teaspoon salt
1 egg, slightly beaten
1 teaspoon orange rind, grated
2/3 cup orange juice
½ cup mayonnaise

Preheat oven to 350° F. Grease a loaf pan. In a large bowl, combine flour, cranberries, sugar, walnuts, baking powder, and salt. In a small bowl beat; egg, orange rind, orange juice, and mayonnaise until smooth. Stir into flour mixture, just until moistened. Bake for 60-70 minutes. Cool on rack for 10 minutes.

"Most people can do extraordinary things if they have the confidence or take the risks. Yet most people don't. They sit in front of the telly and treat life as if it goes on forever."
..... Phillip Andrew Adams

DOUBLE LEMON ZUCCHINI POPPY LOAF
(Zucchini never tasted so good!)

4 eggs
1 ¼ cups sugar
½ cup canola oil
1 teaspoon lemon extract
1 ¼ cups milk
3 cups zucchini, shredded
1 whole lemon
¼ cup canola oil
4 ½ cups flour
1 tablespoon baking powder
1 ¼ teaspoons baking soda
1 -102 gram package lemon instant pudding
½ cup poppy seeds

Beat eggs, sugar, oil, and lemon extract until fluffy, add milk, mix well. Finely grate the lemon peel and add zest to egg mixture. Chop remaining lemon, add ¼ cup oil and blend well in a blender. Add lemon mixture and zucchini to egg mixture. In another bowl, mix flour, baking powder, baking soda, pudding and poppy seed, add to above mixture. Mix lightly, do not beat. Pour into three lightly greased loaf pans. Bake at 350° F. for 1 hour.

Mistakes are the best teachers.

GLAZED LEMON NUT BREAD

4 tablespoons butter, softened
¾ cup sugar
2 eggs
2 teaspoons lemon zest
2 cups flour
1 teaspoon salt
1 ½ teaspoons baking powder
¾ cup milk
½ cup walnuts, chopped

Note: Zest is the finely grated yellow peel of the lemon.

Cream butter and sugar until light and fluffy; add eggs and lemon zest. Sift together dry ingredients and add alternately with milk to batter. Stir in nuts. Pour into greased loaf pan. Bake at 350° F. for 50-55 minutes. Let cool in pan for 10 minutes and top with glaze.

Glaze:
Combine 2 teaspoons lemon juice and 2 tablespoons sugar. Spoon over bread. Remove from pan and cool. Wrap and store overnight.

I have this theory that chocolate slows down
the aging process...It may not be true,
but do I dare take the chance?

LEMON POPPY SEED BREAD

2 cups white sugar
1 cup canola oil
3 eggs
1 ½ cups milk
1 ½ teaspoons vanilla extract
1 teaspoon lemon extract
2 tablespoons poppy seeds
3 cups flour
1 ½ teaspoons baking powder
1 ½ teaspoons salt

Icing:
2 tablespoons lemon juice
¾ cup icing sugar

Preheat oven to 350° F. Grease and flour 2 loaf pans.
Combine sugar, oil, eggs, milk, vanilla and lemon extract in a
large bowl. Mix well. Stir in poppy seeds. Sift together flour,
baking powder and salt. Add flour mixture to milk mixture
alternately, mixing well after each addition. Divide batter evenly
between prepared pans. Bake loaves for 45 minutes or until a
toothpick inserted in center comes out clean. Loosen edges from
sides of pans. Cool loaves in pans for 10 minutes, then turn out
onto wire rack.
Icing Directions: Blend lemon juice and icing sugar in a small
bowl. Drizzle over warm loaves.

SOUR CREAM BANANA BREAD
(Sour cream makes this very moist and flavourful!
Serve this for breakfast.)

½ cup butter

1 cup sugar

2 eggs

1 teaspoon vanilla

1 ½ cups flour

1 teaspoon baking soda

½ teaspoon salt

1 cup bananas, mashed

½ cup nuts, chopped

½ cup sour cream

Cream butter with the sugar. Beat in eggs and vanilla. Add dry ingredients; mix. Add bananas, nuts, and sour cream. Pour into a greased 8½ x 4½ inch loaf pan. Bake at 350° F. for 1 hour. Makes 1 loaf.

"Kids - they're not easy,
but there has to be some penalty for sex."
..... Bill Maher

SWEET POTATO BREAD
(Your friends will be asking you for this recipe!)

3 eggs
1 ½ cups sugar
1 ½ cups cooked sweet potatoes, mashed
1 cup canola oil
2 teaspoons vanilla
2 ¼ cups flour
1 ½ teaspoons baking powder
1 ½ teaspoons baking soda
1 ½ teaspoons cinnamon
1 teaspoon salt
¼ teaspoon ground cloves
¼ teaspoon ginger
¼ teaspoon nutmeg

In large mixing bowl, combine eggs, sugar, sweet potatoes, oil, and vanilla. Mix well. Mix together flour, baking powder, baking soda, cinnamon, salt, cloves, ginger and nutmeg. Add to sweet potato mixture. Beat only enough to blend. Pour into 2 greased and floured 8 ½ x 4 ½ inch loaf pans. Bake at 350° F. for 50-60 minutes. These freeze well.
Makes 2 loaves.

If you know all the answers,
you haven't asked all the questions.

6 WEEK YOGURT BRAN MUFFINS
(This is an easy way to make fresh hot muffins every morning!)

2 cups boiling water

2 cups bran

3 cups sugar

1 cup canola oil

4 eggs

4 cups vanilla yogurt or buttermilk

4 cups bran flakes

5 cups flour

3 tablespoons baking soda

1 tablespoon salt

3 cups raisins

Pour boiling water over bran in small bowl. In large bowl beat sugar, oil and eggs; add yogurt, bran and bran flakes. Sift flour, soda and salt; fold into large bowl until moist, add raisins. Fill cup liners 2/3 full. Bake at 350° F. for 25 minutes. Use as much batter as required; store remainder in fridge. Batter will keep 4 to 6 weeks.

"Getting old has its advantages, I can no longer read the bathroom scale."......Brad Shreiber

APPLESAUCE WALNUT LOW FAT MUFFINS
(Tasty and low fat!!)

3 eggs

1 cup sugar

¾ cup canola oil

2 ½ cups applesauce

3 cups flour

1 tablespoon cinnamon

2 teaspoons baking powder

½ teaspoon salt

½ cup raisins

½ cup walnuts, chopped

¼ cup brown sugar (for sprinkling on top)

Beat eggs slightly, add sugar, oil and applesauce, beat well. Add dry ingredients, blend until smooth. Stir in raisins and nuts. Fill muffin tins 2/3 full and sprinkle with brown sugar. Bake in 375° F. oven for 20 minutes. Makes 24 muffins.

*"Manners are a sensitive awareness of the feelings of others.
If you have that awareness, you have good manners,
no matter which fork you use."*
..... *Emily Post*

BANANA BRAN APPLESAUCE MUFFINS
(These low fat muffins are a very tasty option)

2 cups applesauce
4 eggs
1 ½ cups sugar or Splenda
6 bananas, mashed
1 cup milk
2 cups bran
4 ¼ cups flour
4 teaspoons vanilla
2 teaspoons baking soda
2 teaspoons baking powder
3 teaspoons cinnamon
1 teaspoon cloves
1 teaspoon salt
1 cup chocolate chips (or 1 cup raisins)

Beat applesauce, eggs, sugar, bananas and milk. Add rest of ingredients and mix well. Bake at 350° F. for 20 minutes. Makes 3 to 4 dozen muffins.

A hangover; the wrath of grapes!

BERRY LEMON MUFFINS
(With Saskatoons or Blueberries, guaranteed a favourite!)

2 cups flour
½ cup sugar
1 tablespoon baking powder
½ teaspoon salt
rind of one lemon, grated
1 egg
1 cup milk
½ cup butter, melted
1 cup Saskatoons or Blueberries, (fresh or frozen)
Topping:
¼ cup butter, melted
3 tablespoons lemon juice
½ cup white sugar

Mix flour, sugar, baking powder, salt and lemon rind in a large bowl. Beat egg in a medium bowl, add milk and butter. Add egg mixture to dry ingredients, stir until just blended. Stir in fruit. Fill greased muffin tins 2/3 full, bake at 350° F. for 25 minutes.
Combine topping ingredients, brush on warm muffins. Makes 16 muffins.

"In general, my children refused to eat anything that hadn't danced on T.V." ..... Erma Bombeck

98

CHERRY MUFFINS

6 tablespoons margarine, softened
1/3 cup brown sugar, packed
1/3 cup sugar
1 large egg
1 cup milk
2 tablespoons maraschino cherry syrup
1 teaspoon vanilla
2 cups flour
1 tablespoon baking powder
½ teaspoon salt
12 maraschino cherries, blotted dry
1/3 cup pecans, chopped

Cream margarine and both sugars together in large bowl. Beat in egg and add milk, cherry syrup and vanilla. Beat until mixed. Combine flour, baking powder and salt in a medium bowl and add to margarine mixture. Stir until moistened. Fill greased muffin cups ¾ full. Press 1 cherry into centre of batter in each muffin cup and sprinkle with pecans. Bake at 400° F. for about 18 minutes.

"Life would be infinitely happier if we could be born at the age of 80 and gradually approach 18." .....Mark Twain

CHOCOLATE SQUASH MUFFINS
(Low fat and no sugar, but still awesome!)

3 eggs

2 cups squash, peeled and grated

2 cups Splenda

1 cup applesauce

1 cup skim milk

4 tablespoons cocoa

1 teaspoon vanilla

2 teaspoons baking powder

2 teaspoons baking soda

1 teaspoon salt

3 cups flour

1 cup mini chocolate chips (optional)

Mix eggs, squash, Splenda, applesauce, and milk. Add remaining ingredients and stir by hand until blended. Spoon into greased muffin tins. Bake at 350° F. for about 20 minutes. Makes 24 muffins.

Hints: - You may use zucchini instead of squash.
- Over beating muffins will create holes and cause them to be tough.

DOUGHNUT MUFFINS
(These really do taste like cake doughnuts.)

1 ¾ cups flour
1 ½ teaspoons baking powder
½ teaspoon salt
½ teaspoon nutmeg
¼ teaspoon cinnamon
1/3 cup canola oil
¾ cup sugar
1 egg
¾ cup milk

Glaze:
½ cup butter, melted
¾ cup sugar
1 teaspoon cinnamon

In a bowl combine flour, baking powder, salt, nutmeg and cinnamon. Set aside. In another bowl combine thoroughly; oil, sugar, egg and milk. Add liquid ingredients to dry and stir only to combine. Spoon into well greased muffin tins. Bake at 350° F. for 20-25 minutes. Melt butter in small dish. In another small dish, mix together sugar and cinnamon. Shake muffins out immediately and while hot, dip in melted butter, then into the sugar and cinnamon mixture. Makes 16-24 muffins.

CORN MUFFINS

¼ cup shortening
¼ cup sugar
2 tablespoons cornstarch
2 tablespoons vinegar
1 teaspoon salt
1 ½ cups flour
1 cup cornmeal
1 cup water

Cream shortening and sugar. Add cornstarch, vinegar and salt. Beat in all remaining ingredients, mixing thoroughly. Spoon into greased muffin tins. Bake at 400° F. for 20 minutes or until a toothpick inserted in the middle comes out clean.

FLAX SEED MUFFINS

3 cups ground flax seed
1 ¼ cups flour
1 tablespoon baking powder

1 cup skim milk
½ cup molasses
2 tablespoons canola oil
2 eggs, beaten

Preheat oven to 350° F. Whisk together flax seed, flour and baking powder. In separate bowl, stir milk, molasses, canola oil, and eggs. Stir this mixture into dry ingredients. Pour into greased muffin tins. Bake for 20 minutes or until toothpick inserted in the middle comes out clean.

Shown on previous page:

❖ Naan Bread.....page 85

❖ Great Brown Bread.....page 76

❖ Lettuce Cream Soup.....page 131

❖ Fantastic Focacia Bread.....page 83

IRISH COFFEE MUFFINS
(Now this is the way to start your mornings!)

2 cups flour
1 tablespoon baking powder
½ teaspoon salt
½ cup sugar
1 egg, beaten
½ cup butter, melted
½ cup heavy cream
¼ cup coffee liqueur
¼ cup Irish whiskey

Preheat oven to 400° F. Sift together; flour, baking powder, salt and sugar. Stir in remaining ingredients until moistened. Fill paper lined or greased muffin tins. Bake for about 20 minutes or until a toothpick inserted in the middle comes out clean.

'Think about it: look at the studies of awareness and treatment
and tests that women have had with breast cancer.
It is because they're active and they talk about it."
..... Herbie Mann

103

ORANGE BRAN FLAX MUFFINS
(Fresh oranges give these muffins great flavour.)

1 ½ cups oat bran
1 cup flour
1 cup flax seed, ground
1 cup wheat bran
1 tablespoon baking powder
½ teaspoon salt
2 oranges, quartered and seeded
1 cup brown sugar
1 cup buttermilk
½ cup canola oil
2 eggs
1 teaspoon baking soda
1 ½ cups raisins

Preheat oven to 375° F. In a large bowl, combine; oat bran, flour, flax seed, wheat bran, baking powder and salt. Set aside. In a blender or food processor, combine; oranges, brown sugar, buttermilk, oil, eggs, and baking soda. Blend well. Pour orange mixture into dry ingredients. Mix until well blended. Stir in raisins. Bake for 18-20 minutes. For variety, you may add chocolate chips or nuts of your choice. Makes 2 dozen muffins.

Look out for number one,
And don't step on number two either.

ORANGE TEA MUFFINS

1 ½ cups flour
½ cup sugar
2 teaspoons baking powder
½ teaspoon salt
1 cup fresh or frozen raspberries (optional)
½ cup coconut (optional)
½ cup butter, melted
½ cup fresh orange juice
2 eggs
rind of 1 orange, grated

Combine and blend well; flour, sugar, baking powder, and salt. Add raspberries and coconut, if desired. Beat together; butter, orange juice, eggs, and orange rind. Stir the liquid into the dry mixture and blend just until moistened. Spoon into well-greased muffin tins. Bake at 375° F. for 20 minutes. Makes 24 muffins.

**If only the good die young,
what does that say about senior citizens?**

Delegate but don't forget!

RHUBARB ORANGE MUFFINS
(A great flavour combination.)

2 cups flour
¾ cup sugar
1 ½ teaspoons baking powder
½ teaspoon baking soda
½ teaspoon salt
¾ cup pecans, chopped
1 egg
¼ cup canola oil
2 teaspoons orange peel, grated
¾ cup orange juice
1 ½ cups rhubarb, finely chopped (fresh or frozen)

Combine flour, sugar, baking powder, baking soda, salt and nuts in a large bowl. In another bowl combine egg, oil, orange peel and orange juice. Add liquid to dry ingredients all at once, stir just until moistened. Stir in rhubarb. Fill lightly greased muffin tins ¾ full. Bake at 375° F. for 25-30 minutes. Yield: 12-18 muffins.

"The formula for a successful relationship is simple:
Treat all disasters as if they were trivialities,
but never treat a triviality as if it were a disaster."
.....Quentin Crisp

RICOTTA PINEAPPLE MUFFINS
(A very tasty and moist muffin)

1 egg
canola oil
1 ½ cups Ricotta cheese
1 cup crushed pineapple, well drained
2 cups flour
½ cup sugar
1 tablespoon baking powder
½ teaspoon baking soda
½ teaspoon salt

In a measuring cup place egg and add enough oil to make
½ cup. Add egg and oil mixture to the Ricotta cheese and mix
until smooth. Add crushed pineapple. In separate bowl
combine; flour, sugar, baking powder, baking soda and salt.
Add to the wet ingredients and blend gently. This dough is quite
stiff. Fill greased muffin tins 2/3 full. Bake at 400° F. for
25 minutes. Makes 24 large muffins.

"Love your neighbor as yourself,
but choose your neighborhood."
..... Louise Beal

SPICED CARROT BRAN MUFFINS

1 cup all bran cereal
1 cup buttermilk or sour milk
1 egg, beaten
¾ cup carrots, finely shredded (about 2 medium carrots)
3 tablespoons canola oil
1 cup flour
¼ cup brown sugar, packed
2 teaspoons baking powder
½ teaspoon baking soda
¾ teaspoon cinnamon or allspice
½ teaspoon salt

Preheat oven to 400° F. In a bowl combine bran cereal and buttermilk. Let stand for about 5 minutes. Add egg, carrots and oil. Mix well. In another bowl combine flour, brown sugar, baking powder, baking soda, cinnamon, and salt. Add bran mixture. Stir just until blended. Spoon batter into greased muffin tins. Bake for 15-20 minutes.

"Cheerfulness keeps us with a kind of daylight in the mind, and fills it with a steady and perpetual serenity."
..... Joseph Addison

SPICY LOW FAT SQUASH MUFFINS
(These muffins were a hit, healthy too, and a great way to use up all those garden squash or zucchini!)

3 eggs
3 cups squash, peeled, cored and grated
2 cups Splenda
2 cups applesauce
1 cup skim milk
3 ½ cups flour
1 teaspoon vanilla
2 teaspoons baking powder
2 teaspoons baking soda
1 teaspoon salt
1 teaspoon cinnamon
1 teaspoon nutmeg
1 teaspoon allspice
1 cup raisins

Mix eggs, squash, Splenda, applesauce, and milk. Add remaining ingredients and mix only until blended. Spoon into greased muffin tins. Bake at 350° F. for 20 minutes. Makes 24 muffins.

"I always say shopping is cheaper than a psychiatrist."
...Tammy Faye Baker

I just passed my three year mark with breast cancer. I stopped at the cancer agency to take some goodies for the nurses. The room was full - evidently they had seen 56 people that day and I felt so guilty walking thru the room, feeling good. I felt like I should stop and say "been there, done that and moved on" so they can see it can get better, but I know not everyone will. I put on a very brave face to everyone that it's over but I know, there are still days that I am afraid, I don't want to get back in those chairs and back under the knife. I have learned to live for today, and today I am going to watch my grandchild's concert at playschool. I will push all of this far out of my mind, and I will forget, and enjoy what I have. I have a quote posted on my fridge that says **"Worrying does not empty tomorrow of troubles, rather it empties today of its strengths."** I have learned how true that statement can be and how much energy I have wasted worrying.

Those words,"...get over it." I have heard them soooo many times at our Support Group meetings, when members are talking about comments by friends and family members. I'm quite sure you've never heard them from a survivor. Your family and friends are well meaning. They think they can jolt you out of your sadness; they're asking you to, somehow, by sheer willpower, become the old self. It doesn't work that way in Cancer Country. You will heal, you will regain a happy outlook, but not their way. Try to be patient with them; they want the best for you.

Soups

A strong woman walks surefootedly,

but a woman of strength knows

when to ask for help.

BEEF NOODLE SOUP
(Great on a cold winter day, served with fresh bread or buns!)

1 ½ pounds meaty beef soup bones

7 cups water

1 tablespoon salt

½ teaspoon pepper

4 cups canned tomatoes, mashed

½ cup onion, chopped

2 large carrots, chopped

½ cup celery, chopped

1 teaspoon parsley flakes

½ teaspoon sugar

1 cup frozen mixed vegetables

2 cups egg noodles or macaroni

Option: 1 cup pot barley to replace 1 cup noodles or macaroni

Put soup bone, water, salt and pepper into large stock pot. Bring to boil. Cover and simmer for at least 2 hours. Skim if needed. Remove bones from stock and cut meat off into bite size pieces. Return meat to stock. Add pot barley (option), tomatoes, carrots, onion, celery, parsley flakes and sugar. Bring to a boil and simmer for at least ½ hour. Add mixed vegetables, bring to boil, then add the noodles. Simmer for 15 minutes or until noodles are tender. This soup freezes well. Note: For a stronger beef flavour, add beef bouillon or Oxo cubes, following the directions on package. Your favorite vegetables may also replace or be added to the soup.

111

BORSCHT

2 cups beets, diced

2 cups potatoes, diced

1 teaspoon salt

1 tablespoon vinegar

2 cups cabbage, shredded

½ cup butter

1 tablespoon parsley, chopped

1 tablespoon dried dill weed / 1 ½ teaspoons dried dill weed

¾ cup onion, chopped

2 cups carrots, sliced

1 cup green beans, cut into 1 inch pieces

1 cup peas

1 -28 ounce can tomatoes, pureed

salt and pepper to taste

1 tablespoon sugar

sour cream (optional)

Put potatoes, beets, salt, and vinegar in a Dutch oven and cover with water; boil. Put cabbage, butter, parsley, 1 tablespoon dill, and onion in a large frying pan; cook until clear. Add carrots, beans, and peas to beet mixture in Dutch oven and enough water to cover vegetables; boil for 15 more minutes. Add cabbage mixture and tomatoes. Add salt and pepper and more water, if too thick. Boil for 30 minutes. Add 1 ½ teaspoons dill and sugar; boil for 10 more minutes. Remove from heat and rest for ½ hour. Serves 6. * A large tablespoon of sour cream added to every bowl while serving is the perfect finish for this soup.

CABBAGE AND KIELBASA SOUP

(A thick soup zipped up with kielbasa sausage and made into a whole meal with potatoes and carrots. This makes a wonderful cold-weather supper.)

2 teaspoons canola oil
1 cup onions, chopped
1 cup carrots, thinly sliced
1 cup potatoes, diced
¼ pound kielbasa sausage, sliced and quartered
1 -19 ounce can tomatoes, coarsely chopped
4 cups cabbage, shredded
2 ½ cups beef stock
¼ cup parsley, chopped
1 tablespoon sugar
½ teaspoon paprika
½ teaspoon pepper

In large heavy saucepan, heat oil over medium heat; cook onions, carrots, potatoes and kielbasa for 5 minutes or until onions are softened. Stir in tomatoes, cabbage, beef stock, parsley, sugar, paprika and pepper; cover and bring to boil. Reduce heat to medium-low; cover and simmer for 20 minutes or until vegetables are tender. Serves 4.

May your home be warm and
your friends be many.

CANADIAN HAM-BONE SOUP

1 ham bone (leftover from roast ham is best)
3 cups ham, cubed
1 onion, chopped
1 stalk celery, chopped
1 clove garlic, minced
3 potatoes, cubed
1 cup lentils or white beans
6 cups ham broth

To prepare broth, place ham bone in stock pot, add onion and celery. Cover with 8 cups water. Simmer for 4 hours. Add salt and pepper to taste. Remove ham bone. Add the rest of the ingredients and cook until lentils or white beans are tender.

TOMATO PASTA SOUP

2 cups chicken broth
2 cups tomato juice
1 cup water
1 cup pasta (macaroni)
½ teaspoon salt
1/8 teaspoon pepper

Mix all ingredients in large saucepan and bring to a boil. Stir for 7-10 minutes, stirring often until pasta is tender. Makes about 6 cups. Tastes like you fussed!

CAROLLERS' POTATO SOUP

(This is a nourishing, delicious potato soup that welcomed us home after Christmas caroling for many years.)

2 tablespoons butter
1 medium onion, diced
3 stalks inside celery stalks (with leaves), diced
12 cups water
4-5 carrots, grated
10-12 potatoes, cubed
4 tablespoons margarine
4 tablespoons flour
3 cups whole milk
1 cup light or whipping cream
8 slices bacon, cooked and crumbled
or ½ cup real bacon bits

Sauté butter, onions and celery. Add water and bring to boil. Add carrots. Let simmer for 15 minutes. Add potatoes, let simmer for 15 minutes. While simmering mix margarine and flour in a small saucepan to make a paste. Add milk to make a white sauce. Add to soup and let thicken. Add cream and bacon, simmer until all flavors blend, 15- 20 minutes.

"Getting my lifelong weight struggle under control has come from a process of treating myself as well as I treat others in every way."......Oprah Winfrey

CHEESE SOUP
(Simple title, gourmet taste.)

2 celery stalks, finely chopped
2 carrots, finely chopped
1 small onion, finely chopped
1 cup cauliflower, chopped
1 cup broccoli, finely chopped
1 small clove garlic, crushed and minced
½ cup butter
½ cup flour
3 cups chicken broth
salt to taste
½ teaspoon pepper
2 ½ cups milk
2 cups Cheddar cheese, grated
1 tablespoon Worcestershire sauce
¼ cup sliced almonds

In a large pot; cook celery, carrots, onion, cauliflower, broccoli, and garlic in butter over medium heat for 6 minutes, stirring constantly. Stir in flour. Cook, stirring constantly, for 3 minutes. Slowly add broth, salt and pepper. Simmer, covered, over very low heat for 20 minutes, stirring occasionally to prevent scorching. Add milk, cheese and Worcestershire sauce. Cook over low heat for 10 minutes. Garnish with almonds. Can be made ahead, refrigerated and reheated carefully. This actually enhances the flavour. Serves 6.

CHEESY BROCOLLI SOUP

1 ½ cups chicken broth
1 -10 ounce package broccoli, frozen, drained
1 carrot, sliced thin
1 large potato, diced
1 medium onion, chopped
1 pound Velveeta cheese, cubed
1 can cream of chicken soup
1 cup milk or cream
¼ pound bacon, cooked, crumbled
1 teaspoon parsley
salt to taste

In large saucepan, combine broth, broccoli, carrots, potatoes and onion. Boil until vegetables are tender. Stir in cheese, chicken soup, and milk. Add bacon and parsley and stir constantly until heated through.

If you can start the day without caffeine,
If you can resist complaining and boring people
with your troubles,
If you can eat the same food everyday and be thankful for it,
If you can take criticism and blame without resentment,
If you can ignore a friend's limited education
and never correct him,
If you can resist treating a rich friend better than a poor one,
If you can conquer tension without medical help,
If you can relax without liquor and sleep without drugs,
Then you are probably THE FAMILY DOG!

CHEESY HAM AND RICE SOUP

4 celery stalks, chopped
1 large onion, chopped
¼ cup margarine
4 carrots, sliced
2 cups light cream
1/3 cup flour
10 cups water
8 ounces Velveeta cheese, cubed
4 cups wild rice, cooked
3 cups cooked ham, cubed
3 cups brown rice, cooked
3 tablespoons chicken soup base, powdered
1 teaspoon salt
½ teaspoon pepper

In heavy soup pot, sauté onion and celery in margarine.
Add carrots and cook for 15 minutes until carrots are tender.
Gradually stir in cream. Mix flour and 1 cup water in shaker
and shake until smooth. Add flour mixture to vegetables and stir
until thickened. Bring to a gentle boil. Stir in cheese until
melted. Add the rice, ham, soup base, salt, pepper and the
rest of the water. (Add additional water if needed.) Bring back
to a boil. This makes a large pot and freezes well.

*"It is good to have an end to journey toward, but it is the
journey that matters, in the end." ... Ursula K. Le Guin*

CHICKEN CHOWDER SUPREME

1 tablespoon canola oil
1 onion, chopped
2-3 celery stalks, chopped
1 clove garlic, minced
4-6 potatoes, cubed
1 large carrot, chopped
2-3 cups chicken, cooked and chopped
6 cups chicken broth
2 cups cream
2 tablespoons dill
salt and pepper to taste
pinch of white sugar

Sauté onion, celery and garlic in canola oil in soup pot.
Add rest of ingredients except cream and seasonings. When
vegetables are tender, add cream and seasonings.

I find it helps to organize chores into three categories::
Things I won't do now, things I won't do later,
and things I will never do.

CHICKEN MUSHROOM SOUP

2 tablespoons butter
1 tablespoon canola oil
2 boneless chicken breasts, diced
½ cup carrots, diced
2 celery stalks, diced
2 cups fresh mushrooms, sliced
4 green onions, chopped
3 tablespoons flour
4 cups chicken broth
½ teaspoon thyme
salt and pepper to taste
1 cup whipping cream

In a large saucepan, heat butter and oil over medium heat. Add chicken, carrots and celery. Cook stirring until chicken is nearly cooked through. Add the mushrooms and onion and continue cooking, stirring until mushrooms are tender. Stir in flour until blended, add chicken broth and thyme. Bring to a simmer, stirring continually. Cover and reduce heat to low, cook for about 10-16 minutes until vegetables are tender. Season with salt and pepper, stir in cream and heat through. Serves 4 to 6.

"Time is the coin of your life. It is the only coin you have, and only you can determine how it will be spent. Be careful lest you let other people spend it for you."....Carl Sandberg

CHICKPEA CHOWDER

2 medium onions, chopped

4 cloves garlic, minced

1 tablespoon canola oil

3 cups potatoes, peeled and cubed

3 stalks celery, sliced

1 ½ cups carrots, sliced

½ small green jalapeno pepper, chopped (optional)

2 tablespoons lemon juice

2 tablespoons mild curry powder

½ teaspoon dried sage

½ teaspoon dried thyme

¼ teaspoon salt

¼ teaspoon pepper

4 bay leaves

4 cups chicken broth

1 -28 ounce can chickpeas, drained and rinsed

½ cup fresh parsley, chopped

In a large soup pot, stir fry onions and garlic in oil for about 3 minutes. Add potatoes, celery, carrots and peppers; stir fry for another few minutes. Add lemon juice and the herbs except parsley; stir fry briefly to coat the vegetables. Add broth and chickpeas. Bring to boil; simmer for about 20 minutes, or until vegetables are cooked. Stir in parsley and serve. Yields 6 large bowls.

CORN AND CHICKEN CHOWDER

(This is a great way to use left-over roast chicken.)

2 large onions, chopped
4 stalks of celery, diced
1 teaspoon margarine
4 potatoes, peeled and cubed
4 carrots, chopped
1 can chicken broth
2 cups water
2 cups whole milk
1 can corn, do not drain
1 can cream corn
2 cups cooked chicken, cubed
2 cups whipping cream
2 teaspoons dill weed
½ teaspoon thyme
salt and pepper to taste

Sauté onions, celery and margarine in soup pot. Add potatoes, carrots, chicken broth, water and milk. Cook until tender. Add corn, cream corn and chicken. Heat thoroughly. Add cream and spices.

""Every evening I turn my worries over to God.
He's going to be up all night anyway.".....Mary C. Crowley

CREAMED POTATO AND CABBAGE SOUP
(Great for using up leftover cooked potatoes.)

½ cup onions, chopped
½ cup celery, chopped
2 cups potatoes, cooked and mashed
5 cups water
3 tablespoons chicken bouillon
3 cups cabbage, chopped
1 teaspoon dill
½ cup bacon, fried crisp and crumbled
3 cups milk

Mix onions, celery, potatoes, water, bouillon, dill, and cabbage in a large Dutch oven. Simmer for at least one hour or until vegetables are done. Add milk and bring to a boil. Add bacon, simmer for 15 more minutes. If the soup is too thin, mix 1 tablespoon of cornstarch with ¼ cup of cold water and add to soup. Bring to a boil again and serve.

"You know you have been out of college a long time when;
...You keep more food in the fridge than beer
...6:00 a.m. is when you get up now, not when you go to sleep
...You go from 130 days of vacation to 14
...Dinner and a movie is the whole date instead of just the beginning of one.
...You actually eat breakfast foods at breakfast time.
...Grocery lists are longer than mac and cheese, diet Pepsi and Ho-Ho's
....Having sex in a twin size bed is absurd.

CREAMY POTATO AND HAM SOUP
(They'll all love it and ask for seconds!)

6 cups water

4 cups potatoes, diced

2 cups carrots, sliced

1 medium onion, chopped

2 celery stalks, chopped

2 teaspoon salt

½ teaspoon pepper

1/3 cup margarine

½ cup flour

2 cups milk

2 cups Cheddar cheese, shredded

1 cup corn

2 cups cooked ham, cubed

In a large pot, bring to boil; water, potatoes, carrots, onion, celery, salt and pepper. Reduce heat and simmer until vegetables are tender, about 10 minutes. In another saucepan, melt margarine, stir in flour to make a smooth paste, slowly pour and whisk in milk, cook and stir until thickened. Add cheese and stir until melted. Add cheese mixture to undrained vegetable pot. Add corn and ham, and continue to simmer and stir for a few minutes until heated. Top with grated cheese. Serves 10.

"My cancer scare changed my life. I'm grateful for every new, healthy day I have. It has helped me prioritize my life."
.........*Olivia Newton-John*

CURRIED TOMATO SOUP
(Lovely flavour to warm up with, on those cold winter days.)

1 carrot, grated
1 onion, grated
½ green pepper, finely chopped
1 cup celery, chopped
1/3 cup canola oil
5-6 cups chicken bouillon
4 cups tomatoes, pealed and chopped
½ teaspoon curry powder
1 teaspoon salt
¼ teaspoon pepper
¼ teaspoon lemon pepper
2 tablespoons flour
sour cream
Mozzarella cheese, grated

In a large pot sauté carrot, onion, pepper and celery in canola oil. Add 4 cups of bouillon, tomatoes, curry powder, salt, pepper, and lemon pepper. Bring to a boil, simmer 20 minutes. In a covered container shake remaining bouillon with flour. Add slowly into soup, stirring constantly. Top each serving with a healthy dollop of sour cream and a teaspoon or so of Mozzarella cheese. Makes about 2 quarts.

I've learned that, regardless of your relationship with your parents, you'll miss them when they're gone from your life.

GARDEN CREAMY TOMATO VEGETABLE SOUP
(This is best made with fresh garden produce.)

10 cups water
1 tablespoon salt
1 cup new potatoes, chopped
1 cup carrots, chopped
1 cup green or yellow beans, diced
1 cup peas
1 cup onion, chopped
3 tablespoons fresh dill, chopped
2 envelopes Lipton tomato vegetable soup mix

1 tablespoon flour
¾ cup milk

In large stockpot, bring water, salt, potatoes, carrots, beans, peas, onion, and dill to boil. Add soup mix and simmer 10-15 minutes. Prior to serving, in a separate bowl, add flour slowly to milk, stirring to prevent lumps. Add to soup mixture, heat through and serve.

Ever Wonder?
Why the sun lightens our hair, but darkens our skin?
Why is it that doctors call what they do "practice"?
Why is lemon juice made with artificial flavour and
dishwashing detergent made with real lemons?
Why is the man who invests all your money called a "broker"?
Why didn't Noah swat those two mosquitoes?
Why don't sheep shrink when it rains?

126

GRANDMA'S TOMATO MILK SOUP
(Creamy and delicious, the kid's favourite!)

4 cups canned tomatoes in juice, mashed
1 cup water
1/8 teaspoon pepper
1 teaspoon sugar
½ teaspoon salt
¼ teaspoon celery salt
½ teaspoon onion powder
¾ cup macaroni
¼ teaspoon baking soda
6 cups milk
3 heaping tablespoons Cheez Whiz

In a medium sized pot, combine tomatoes and water, bring to a boil, and add: pepper, sugar, salt, celery salt, onion powder, and macaroni. Cook for 10 minutes on medium low heat stirring often. Add baking soda, stir and take off heat. Let cool for about 3-5 minutes. Meanwhile in a larger pot combine milk and Cheez Whiz, mix well and bring to a boil, stirring often. Take off burner. When the ingredients of both pots have cooled a little, slowly pour tomato macaroni mixture into milk mixture, stir to blend. Serves 6 hearty appetites!

A good laugh is sunshine in a home!

GREEN SPLIT PEA SOUP

(There are many versions of this soup but this is a must try, especially on a cold winter day.)

½ pound bacon, chopped fine
1 medium onion, chopped
2-4 celery stalks, chopped
3 large carrots, shredded
2 bay leaves
2 cups split green peas, washed
2 litres water
3-4 tablespoons chicken soup base
salt and pepper, to taste

In a large stockpot, fry bacon, onions and celery. Add carrots, bay leaves, split green peas, water, chicken soup base, salt and pepper. Simmer for approximately 1 ½ hours. Remove bay leaves. This is a very thick and delicious soup. Serves 8-10. This recipe is easily doubled to serve a large group.

"When you are faced with a decision, make the decision as wisely as possible - then forget it The moment of absolute certainty never arrives."........The Talmud

HARVEST PUMPKIN SOUP

2 tablespoons pumpkin seeds
2 tablespoons butter
½ pound fresh mushrooms, cleaned and sliced
½ cup onion, chopped
2 tablespoons flour
1 ½ - 2 tablespoons curry powder
3 cups vegetable broth
1 -15 ounce can pumpkin
1 ½ cups evaporated milk
1 tablespoon honey
½ teaspoon salt
¼ teaspoon pepper
2 tablespoons chives, minced

Preheat oven to 375° F. Arrange pumpkin seeds in a single layer on a baking sheet. Toast in preheated oven for about 10 minutes, or until seeds begin to brown. Melt butter in a large skillet, sauté the mushrooms and onion in butter until tender. Stir in flour and curry powder until smooth. Cook, stirring, until mixture begins to bubble. Gradually whisk in broth, and cook until thickened. Stir in pumpkin and milk. Add honey, salt, and pepper. Bring just to a boil, then remove from heat. Garnish with roasted pumpkin seeds and chives.

Fancy Restaurant: One that serves cold soup on purpose.

LEMON CHICKEN RICE SOUP
(Remember the lemon rice soup in your favourite restaurant- this is it!)

8 cups chicken broth

1/3 cup rice

1/3 cup carrots, diced

1/3 cup celery, chopped

¼ cup onion, finely chopped

1 cup cooked chicken, cubed

2 tablespoons butter

2 tablespoons flour

3 eggs

3 tablespoons lemon juice

salt and pepper to taste

green onions or parsley, chopped

In large saucepan, combine chicken broth, rice, carrots, celery and onion. Bring to a boil. Reduce heat, cover and simmer for 20 minutes or until rice and vegetables are tender. Stir in chicken. Remove broth mixture from heat.
In small saucepan, melt butter. Stir in flour. Cook 1 minute, stirring constantly until smooth and bubbly. Gradually stir in 2 cups broth mixture; cook until slightly thickened, stirring constantly. Beat eggs in a small bowl. Gradually beat in lemon juice and 2 cups thickened broth mixture. Slowly add egg mixture to broth mixture in large saucepan, stirring constantly. Heat gently until mixture thickens a little, stirring frequently; do not boil. Salt and pepper to taste. Garnish, if you like, with parsley or onions.

"There is a fountain of youth: it is your mind, your talents, the creativity you bring to your life and the lives of people you love. When you learn to tap this source, you will truly have defeated age." ......Sophia Loren

LETTUCE CREAM SOUP
(Excellent for that surplus wilted lettuce in the fridge!)

2 heads romaine lettuce (8 cups of spinach works well too)
¼ cup butter
½ cup onions, sliced
2 ½ cups chicken stock
salt and pepper to taste

2 tablespoons butter
1 ½ tablespoons flour
1 ½ cups milk
salt to taste

Wash, dry, and break up lettuce. Melt butter in large saucepan over medium heat. Add onions and lettuce and sauté for 15 minutes, stirring occasionally. Add salt and pepper. Add stock and simmer 15 minutes. Cool enough to puree in blender. In saucepan, over medium heat, melt butter and whisk in flour until dissolved. Gradually pour in the milk, stirring constantly to prevent lumps. Add salt to taste. Cook for 5 minutes or until thickened. Add to puree. Adjust seasoning. Serves 4-6.

"If we all worked on the assumption that what is accepted as true was really true, there would be little hope of advance"...Orville Wright

131

MINESTRONE SOUP

3 large carrots, sliced
2 celery stalks, sliced
1 large onion, chopped
1 garlic clove, minced
3 cups cabbage, shredded
1 medium zucchini, cubed
2 potatoes, cubed
3 beef bouillon cubes
8 cups water
1 -14 ounce can tomatoes
1 teaspoon salt
½ teaspoon pepper
1 teaspoon dried basil
1 teaspoon oregano
1 -14 ounce can kidney beans, drained and washed
½ cup macaroni
½ cup Parmesan cheese, grated

In a large pot put first 8 ingredients in water, bring to a boil, reduce heat and simmer about 30 minutes. Add tomatoes, spices, beans, and macaroni; simmer about 10 minutes until macaroni is tender. Add more water if necessary. Serve with cheese.

Worries go down better with soup.   Jewish Proverb

QUICK AND EASY MUSHROOM SOUP

1 pound mushrooms, sliced

½ cup margarine

1 teaspoon lemon juice

1 small onion, diced

1/3 cup flour

4 cups chicken broth

1 teaspoon salt

¼ teaspoon pepper

1 cup cream

Slice mushrooms and cook in margarine and lemon juice until tender. Remove mushrooms and cook onion in remaining liquid. Stir in flour. Gradually stir in chicken broth. Add mushrooms, salt and pepper and cream at the end.

QUICK CREAM CORN SOUP

1 can cream corn

3 cups milk

½ teaspoon dried dill weed

3 tablespoons bacon, fried and crumbled

1 tablespoon of powdered chicken bouillon

2 tablespoons cornstarch

¼ cup cold water

Pour corn, milk, dill, bouillon and bacon into a 2 quart saucepan. Heat for about 15 minutes. Be careful not to burn!! Mix cornstarch and water. After corn mixture comes to a boil add the cornstarch and continue to heat until thickened.

ROASTED CARROT, ONION AND GARLIC SOUP

¼ cup canola oil
5 medium carrots, peeled and cut into 1 inch pieces
3 large onions, chopped
salt and pepper to taste
1 clove garlic
2 teaspoons chopped thyme
10 cups chicken or vegetable broth
2 tablespoons butter

Heat all but 1 teaspoon canola oil in large skillet. Add carrots and onions. Cook until onions are translucent (8-10 minutes). Season with salt and pepper. Remove and discard top ¼ inch of garlic. Place garlic on small sheet of foil. Pour reserved 1 teaspoon of canola oil over garlic, season with salt and pepper, twist foil around garlic. Transfer carrots and onions to a lightly oiled baking pan. Place garlic in corner of pan. Bake at 350° F. for 45 minutes stirring occasionally. Transfer carrots and onions to a soup pot. Squeeze individual cloves of garlic into the mixture (discard skins). Add thyme to stock and bring to boil. Reduce heat and simmer for 30 minutes. Let cool slightly. In a food processor or blender, process soup in small batches until smooth. Return soup to clean saucepan. Bring soup to simmer. Add the butter and adjust seasonings.

Worry is the darkroom in which negatives are developed.

SPICY CURRIED CARROT SOUP

5 medium carrots, chopped
3 cloves garlic, minced
5 cups chicken broth, canned or homemade
1 dried chili pepper, any type (optional)
4 teaspoons fresh ginger, minced
1 teaspoon curry powder
1 teaspoon ground cumin
½ teaspoon freshly ground black pepper
3 tablespoons cilantro, fresh and chopped

Prepare carrots and garlic. In a large saucepan, combine all ingredients except cilantro. Bring mixture to a boil, then reduce and simmer for 30 minutes or until carrots are tender. Cool slightly. Transfer mixture to food processor or blender in small batches. Puree until smooth. Stir in chopped cilantro.

"We participants, in the front lines of the "Cancer Wars", are just ordinary men and women drafted without our consent into this service. We need not be victims. We can turn this experience to ultimate good in service to others. The choice is ours.".......*Gerald W. White*

VEGETABLE CHOWDER

3 cups potatoes, chopped
2 ½ cups broccoli, chopped
¾ cup onion, chopped
1 cup carrots, grated
2 stalks celery, chopped
4 teaspoons chicken soup base, powdered
3 ½ cups water
¾ cup margarine
¾ cup flour
4 cups milk
1 teaspoon salt
¼ teaspoon pepper
1 cup Cheddar cheese, shredded

Combine potatoes, broccoli, onion, carrots, celery, chicken soup base and water in large soup pot and bring to a boil. Reduce heat and simmer for 20 minutes until vegetables are tender. Melt margarine in a saucepan and stir in flour. Cook over medium heat for 2 minutes, stirring constantly. Whisk in milk, salt and pepper. Bring to a boil and boil for 2 minutes stirring constantly. Add to vegetable mixture. Simmer for 10 minutes. Stir in cheese and heat until melted.

The advantage of a bad memory is that one enjoys several times the same good things for the first time.

VEGETABLE SOUP

3 cups water
2 chicken bouillon cubes
2 carrots, diced
2 celery stalks, diced
1 small onion, chopped
1 tablespoon parsley, chopped
salt and pepper to taste

Add one of the following:
2 tomatoes, diced or
1 -19 ounce can diced tomatoes or
2 tomatoes, diced and 1 cup tomato juice

Other vegetables such as sliced fresh mushrooms, chopped zucchini, chopped cabbage or cubed squash, may be added.

Bring water and bouillon cubes to boil in large pot. Add carrots, celery, onion and parsley (and whatever other vegetables you have on hand) and simmer until tender. Add one of the variation of tomatoes and simmer for about 10 minutes.

Always remember........When life hands you
lemons, ask for tequila and salt.

We have to share with you one of the cutest stories we've heard through breast friends functions. We were speaking at a fund-raising event and at the end of the evening a small neat little elderly lady approached us. She said "You are dears and I want to thank you for working so hard against this disease .....because it is primarily a women's' disease, I am not sure for years it got the attention that it deserved from the big boys in the corporations that deem where the money is spent. I have been married for 51 years....and you know" she said, "I never really liked sex very much.....I am not sure why - maybe my husband just isn't very good at it......but about ten years ago, he seemed to lose interest a bit. I was so enjoying his company without all that testosterone. Then what happens, they invent a pill - so that not only does he want it again but more and longer......yikes! Now tell me what they are doing spending research money on that kind of thing when we still don't have a cure for breast cancer......You can sure tell we still live in a man's world.

We all smile and think about that lady every time we see a Viagra commercial on TV. But you know she may have had a point. We have to make sure that women's issues do find a place in the corporate world. We have come a long way but we have a long way to go.

Salads

A strong woman wears the look of confidence on her face, but a woman of strength wears grace.

FRESH BEET SALAD

(Store those beets in your fridge in a hole-punched plastic bag, they keep all winter! Beets are the most under rated, available, nutritious and delicious vegetable.)

1 cup beets, peeled, cooked (undercooked a little), grated
1 cup carrots, grated
½ cup apple, grated
¼ cup green onion, finely chopped
¼ cup celery, finely chopped
1 teaspoon garlic, minced
1 teaspoon horseradish, minced
1 teaspoon sugar
3 tablespoons canola oil
2 tablespoons lemon juice
½ teaspoon sea salt

Mix ingredients gently together, chill and serve. Keeps well for a few days in the fridge, so you can prepare ahead!

Blessed is the person who is too busy to worry in the daytime, and too sleepy to worry at night.

BALSAMIC GRAPE AND WALNUT SALAD
(A nice fresh summer salad!)

2 cups red seedless grapes, halved
2 cups walnuts, coarsely chopped
½ red onion, chopped
3 green onions, chopped
3 radishes, diced
1 cup raisins
1 cup Balsamic Vinaigrette salad dressing

In medium serving bowl, combine the grapes, walnuts, onions, green onion, radishes and raisins. Toss with Balsamic Vinaigrette dressing just before serving.

Pain and suffering are inevitable but misery is optional

"False friends are like our shadow,
keeping close to us while we walk in the sunshine,
but leaving us the instant we cross into the shade."
..... - Christian N. Bovee

CLASSIC WALDORF SALAD

(A Waldorf salad is a salad consisting of apple, nuts (especially walnuts), celery, and mayonnaise or a mayonnaise-based dressing. It was first created around 1893 at the Waldorf Hotel in New York City -the precursor of the Waldorf-Astoria Hotel which opened in 1931. It has survived the test of time and is a classic for good reason — always a hit.)

1 tablespoon sugar
½ teaspoon lemon juice
dash of salt
2 cups apples, diced
1 cup celery sticks, julienned, 1 inch pieces
½ cup walnuts, chopped
¼ cup mayonnaise
½ cup whipping cream, whipped
1 cup mini marshmallows (optional)

Combine sugar, lemon juice and salt. Add apples, celery and walnuts. Fold mayonnaise into whipped cream. Fold gently into apple mixture. Chill. Serve in lettuce lined bowl. Makes 6 servings.

Yesterday is history, tomorrow is a mystery,
today is a gift- that is why it is called 'the present.

HOLIDAY CRANBERRY SALAD
(Great with a turkey dinner!)

1 large package raspberry Jell-O
1 pound raw cranberries, blender ground
1 apple, finely chopped
1 cup crushed pineapple, drained
1 cup sugar
3 cups colored miniature marshmallows
1 large container Cool Whip

Mix Jell-O according to directions. Mix cranberries, apple, and pineapple with sugar. Fold fruit, Cool Whip and marshmallows into Jell-O as it begins to gel. Place in a large glass bowl and allow to set for about 4 hours in fridge before serving.

CREAMY FRUIT SALAD
(A quick and easy fruit salad.)

1 -14 ounce can fruit cocktail, drained
2 medium bananas, sliced
1 medium apple, diced
1 medium orange, peeled and sectioned
2 tablespoons instant vanilla pudding mix
1 -250 ml container vanilla yogurt

In a serving bowl, combine the fruit cocktail, bananas, apple and orange. Combine pudding mix and yogurt until smooth. Add to fruit mixture and stir to coat.

SUMMER SALAD

1 -14 ounce can crushed pineapple, undrained
¾ cup water
½ cup sugar
1 -3 ounce package strawberry Jell-O
1 cup cottage cheese
1 carton Cool Whip

Bring pineapple with juice, water and sugar to a boil for 1 minute. Add Jell-O and let cool to soft set. Fold in cottage cheese and Cool Whip. Refrigerate until firm.

TOMATO AND CHICK PEA SALAD

1 -19 ounce can chick peas, drained
2-4 tomatoes, diced
1 cucumber, diced
1 cup parsley, chopped
5 green onions, sliced
1 cup Feta cheese, cubed
½ cup herbed vinaigrette dressing

Combine chick peas, tomatoes, cucumber, parsley, onions and cheese. Pour vinaigrette dressing over vegetables and toss. Chill 3 hours before serving.

BEET SALAD
(This salad is so nice served with baked ham.)

1 -16 ounce can whole beets
¼ cup red onion, diced
¼ cup white sugar
1 teaspoon prepared mustard
¼ cup white wine vinegar

Drain beets, reserving ¼ cup liquid, and slice into ½ inch slivers. Add onions and toss. In a saucepan over medium heat, cook the sugar, mustard and reserved ¼ cup liquid until dissolved. Add vinegar and bring to boil; remove from heat and cool. Pour over the beet slices and onions, toss and refrigerate for 4 to 6 hours. Remove from refrigerator and serve at room temperature.

"Middle age is when the best exercise is discretion."
Laurence Peter

You need only two tools,: WD-40 and duct tape.
If it doesn't move and it should, use the WD-40.
If it moves and it shouldn't, use the duct tape.

SWEET AND SOUR DRESSING

1 cup sugar
½ cup cider vinegar
1 teaspoon celery seed
¾ teaspoon salt
1 teaspoon paprika
1 cup canola oil
1 head romaine lettuce, chopped (or fresh spinach)

Bring sugar and vinegar to a boil. Put in blender and add spices. Slowly add oil while blending. Serve over lettuce.

SOUR CREAM FRUIT SALAD

1 cup sour cream
1 -11 ounce can mandarin oranges, drained
1 cup pineapple tidbits, drained
1 cup colored miniature marshmallows
1 cup flaked coconut
1 cup green seedless grapes, washed and cut in half

Mix all ingredients together and let stand in fridge overnight.

"Marriage is an alliance entered into by a man who can't sleep with the window shut, and a woman who can't sleep with the window open." .....George Bernard Shaw

PRETZEL SALAD

2 cups pretzel crumbs
¼ cup sugar
¾ cup margarine

Mix together and bake in a greased 9 x 13 pan for 15 minutes at 350° F. Cool.

1 -250 ml package cream cheese, softened
1 cup sugar
2 cups Cool Whip

Mix and spread over cooled cooked crumb mixture.

2 -3 ounce packages strawberry Jell-O
2 cups hot pineapple juice (water may be used)
2 -10 ounce packages strawberries, partially thawed

Dissolve Jell-O in juice and let partially set, add strawberries. Pour over above mixture. Let set for several hours.

Take the time to live!!
Life is too short. Dance naked.

TOMATO SHRIMP ASPIC SALAD

(This salad can be made the day before. Spray mold pan
with non-stick cooking oil for easier removal.)

2 ½ cups tomato juice
1 small bay leaf
½ teaspoon onion powder
2 -¼ ounce packages unflavoured gelatin
½ cup cold water
3 tablespoons sugar
¾ teaspoon salt
¼ teaspoon paprika
¼ cup celery, finely chopped
½ cup small shrimp, drained and rinsed

Put tomato juice, bay leaf, and onion powder in saucepan. Heat
and simmer for 5 minutes. Discard bay leaf. Sprinkle gelatin
over water in small saucepan. Let stand for a minute. Heat and
stir to dissolve. Add to tomato juice. Stir in sugar, salt and
paprika until sugar dissolves. Chill, stirring and scraping down
sides often until mixture shows signs of thickening. Fold in celery
and shrimp. Turn into 3 cup mold or a 9 x 9 inch pan. Chill
until firm. Serves 6-8.

Don't take guilt trips. Take a trip to the mall, even to
the next country; to a foreign country, but not
to where the guilt is.

147

COBB SALAD

(The Cobb salad was a signature menu item of the legendary Brown Derby in Hollywood, a landmark restaurant in Los Angeles, California. Variations of the salad are now served in restaurants world-wide. The salad, added to the menu in 1937, was presented to the customer with the ingredients all grouped on a plate, then chopped fine with knives before serving.
The original recipe contained:
lettuce (head lettuce, watercress, chicory, and romaine), tomatoes, crisp bacon, chicken breast, hard-boiled eggs avocado, Roquefort cheese, chives and vinaigrette.)

8 slices bacon
3 eggs
1 head iceberg lettuce, shredded
3 cups chicken meat, cooked and chopped
2 tomatoes, seeded and chopped
¾ cup blue cheese, crumbled
1 avocado, peeled, pitted and diced
3 green onions, chopped
1 -8 ounce bottle Ranch dressing (or another favourite)
Hard boil eggs; cool, peel and chop. Cook bacon over medium high heat until crispy. Drain, crumble and set aside.
Divide shredded lettuce among individual plates. Evenly divide and arrange chicken, eggs, tomatoes, blue cheese, bacon, avocado and green onions in a row on top of lettuce.
Drizzle with your favourite dressing, just before serving.

CHICKEN SPINACH SALAD
(Breast Friends' favourite meal salad!)

3 cups bow tie pasta, cooked and drained

1 cup canola oil

2/3 cup white wine vinegar

2/3 cup teriyaki sauce

1/3 cup sugar

½ teaspoon pepper

2 -11 ounce cans mandarin oranges, drained

2 -5 ounce cans sliced water chestnuts, drained

2 cups cooked chicken, cubed

1 ¼ cups honey roasted peanuts

1 -9 ounce bag fresh spinach

1 cup dried cranberries

6 green onions, chopped

½ cup fresh parsley, minced

Place cooled pasta in a large bowl. In small bowl, combine oil, vinegar, teriyaki sauce, sugar, and pepper. Pour over pasta and toss to coat. Cover and refrigerate for 2 hours. Just before serving, add the remaining ingredients; gently toss to coat. Serves 10 as a complete meal.

RANCH PASTA SALAD

1 pound rotini colored pasta
1 cup bacon, fried crisp and crumbled
1 cup mayonnaise
1 -1 ounce package dry ranch dressing mix
½ cup milk
1 cup celery, chopped
1 red pepper, chopped
1 cup Cheddar cheese, shredded
salt and pepper to taste

Cook pasta according to directions, drain and cool. Mix rest of ingredients. Toss until blended, season with salt and pepper. Cover and chill for at least 1 hour before serving.

The Beauty of a Woman
Is not in the clothes she wears,
Not the figure that she carries,
Or the way she combs her hair
The beauty of a woman
Must be seen from in her eyes,
Because that is the doorway to her heart,
The place where love resides.

PARSNIP SALAD

1 ½ cups raw parsnip, grated
½ cup celery, chopped
¼ cup green pepper, chopped
½ teaspoon parsley flakes
1/3 cup mayonnaise
1 tablespoon canola oil
1 tablespoon vinegar
1 tablespoon lemon juice
½ teaspoon salt

Toss parsnips, celery, green pepper, and parsley flakes in bowl.
Combine mayonnaise, canola oil, vinegar, lemon juice and salt
together. Mix into parsnip mixture. Serves 4-6.

HICKORY TUNA SALAD

1 -213 gram can tuna, drained
1 cup celery, chopped
1 cup carrots, grated
¼ - ½ cup green onion, diced
1 cup mayonnaise or Miracle Whip
1 cup Hickory Sticks

Mix all ingredients; add Hickory Sticks just before serving.

SESAME BROCCOLI SALAD

1 tablespoon sesame seeds
1 pound broccoli, steamed, drained
3 ½ ounces snow peas, steamed, ends removed
1 -10 ounce can baby corn, drained
½ cup green onions, sliced
1 teaspoon sesame oil
2 teaspoons peanut oil
1 tablespoon lemon juice
2 teaspoons soy sauce

Toast sesame seeds in dry frying pan, using moderate heat and stirring constantly until toasted. Set aside. Trim broccoli. On serving dish, toss together broccoli, snow peas, baby corn and green onions. Combine oils, lemon juice and soy sauce. Pour over salad and sprinkle with sesame seeds.

If my body were a car, this is the time I would be thinking of trading it in for a new model. I've got bumps and dents and scratches in my finish. My headlights are out of focus. It takes me hours to reach my maximum speed and my fuel rate burns inefficiently. But the worst of it is - almost every time I sneeze or cough...either my radiator leaks or my exhaust backfires.

VEGETABLE GREEK SALAD

3 large tomatoes, diced
1 English cucumber, diced
1 green pepper, diced
1 red pepper, diced
1 yellow pepper, diced (or orange pepper)
1 cup fresh mushrooms, diced
½ cup black olives, sliced
½ cup red onion, diced
1 cup prepared Greek salad dressing
2 tablespoons vinegar
1 tablespoon sugar

Mix all vegetables in a large bowl. Mix dressing, vinegar and sugar and pour over veggie mixture. Marinate for at least 1 hour before serving.

"Laughter is a tranquilizer with no side effects."
.......Arnold H. Glasgow

"Money will buy you a fine dog, but only love can make it wag its tail." ... *Richard Friedman*

POTATO SALAD
(Plan a picnic, outside or in, and go with this traditional family favorite!)

4 cups potatoes, peeled, cooked (not overdone) and diced
4 eggs, hard boiled, peeled and diced
½ cup cucumbers, peeled and diced
2 green onions, minced
2 or 3 radishes, diced (for color)
3 slices of bacon, fried crisp and crumbled

Dressing:
1 cup mayonnaise
½ cup canned milk or light cream
1 tablespoon vinegar
1 tablespoon prepared mustard
1 teaspoon sugar
¼ teaspoon salt
1/8 teaspoon pepper

Mix dressing ingredients thoroughly in a large bowl. Fold prepared vegetables, eggs and bacon, gently into dressing. Note; A boiled egg is nice reserved for the top. Slice it thinly and garnish the top of the salad with it. Sprinkle paprika over all.

DILL POTATO SALAD

8 cups potatoes, cooked and diced
6 eggs, hard boiled and chopped
2 dill pickles, chopped
1 medium onion, chopped (or ½ cup green onion, chopped)

Dressing:
1 ½ cups Miracle Whip
1 cup sour cream
½ cup sugar
¼ cup vinegar
1 tablespoon prepared mustard
1 ½ teaspoons dill
¼ teaspoon salt
¼ teaspoon pepper

Mix potatoes, eggs, pickles, and onions in large bowl. Mix dressing ingredients in measuring cup. About 1 hour before serving pour dressing over potato mixture and refrigerate until serving.
Options: You can add chopped celery, radishes, cucumber, carrots, or any other vegetable to give your salad more variety.

Keep only cheerful friends. The grouches pull you down.

CREAMED COLESLAW

½ head cabbage, sliced thin
3 carrots, shredded
1 onion, finely chopped
1 cup mayonnaise
4 tablespoons sugar or Splenda
3 tablespoons vinegar
1/8 teaspoon salt and pepper

Mix cabbage, carrots and onion in salad bowl. Blend remaining ingredients in measuring cup, pour over salad mixture and serve.

TUNA PASTA SALAD

2 cups pasta (your choice), precooked and cooled
1 -213 gram can tuna, rinsed and drained
¼ cup green onions, diced (optional)
1 cup mayonnaise
½ cup sour cream
¼ teaspoon salt and pepper

Mix pasta, tuna and onion in large bowl. Blend rest of ingredients in measuring cup and mix into pasta mixture. Note: This salad keeps well overnight in the refrigerator.

HOT CHICKEN SALAD
(Company coming? Make this the night before.)

4 cups cold cooked chicken, cut in chunks
2 tablespoons lemon juice
¾ cup mayonnaise
1 teaspoon salt
1 cup celery, chopped
4 eggs, hard boiled and chopped
1 teaspoon onion, finely minced
1 tablespoon pimiento, finely minced
1 -10 ounce can cream of chicken soup
1 cup Cheddar cheese, grated
1 ½ cups potato chips, crushed
2/3 cup almonds, toasted and finely chopped

In large bowl, combine chicken, lemon juice, mayonnaise, salt, celery, eggs, onion, pimento and soup. Place salad in an ungreased 2 quart casserole. Top with cheese, potato chips and almonds. Refrigerate overnight. Bake in 350° F. oven about 45 minutes. Serves 10-12.

"Never approach a bull from the front, a horse from the rear, or a fool from any direction." ...Danny Saradon

MAKE AHEAD CABBAGE SLAW
(Very tasty, and keeps in the fridge for weeks)

1 head cabbage, shredded
¼ cup green pepper, chopped
¾ cup onion, sliced
2 carrots, shredded
1 cup vinegar
1 cup white sugar
2 teaspoons salt
¾ cup canola oil
1 teaspoon celery seed
¼ teaspoon garlic powder
1 teaspoon dried mustard

Mix vegetables together in a large bowl. Bring vinegar, sugar, salt, oil and spices to a boil in a pot, stirring often. Pour hot contents over vegetables. Stir gently. Cool. Put mixture in sealable containers in the fridge.

Throw out all non-essential numbers. This includes age, weight and height. Let the doctors worry about them. That is why you pay them!

Even a turtle makes progress when it sticks out its neck.

MARINATED CARROT SALAD
(Can be made a day or even two ahead, keeps well in the fridge.)

2 pounds carrots, peeled and cut into coins
1 Spanish onion, cut into rings
1 green pepper, cut into rings or slices

Cook carrots in boiling water until just tender. Drain and cool quickly. (Carrots look nice cut with a crinkle cutter.)

Sauce:
1 -10 ounce can tomato soup
1 cup sugar
1 teaspoon salt
1 teaspoon pepper
½ cup canola oil
¾ cup vinegar

Bring to a boil and pour over carrots, onion and peppers. cool and serve.

Everything is always okay in the end...
if it is not okay, then it is not the end.

SWISS CASHEW SALAD

1/3 cup white vinegar

¾ cup sugar

2 teaspoons prepared mustard

1 teaspoon onion, grated

dash of salt

1 cup canola oil

1 teaspoon poppy seeds

1 head romaine lettuce, torn

1 cup salted cashew halves

4 ounces Swiss cheese, shredded

Combine vinegar, sugar, mustard, onion and salt; whisk or blend until well blended. While mixing, gradually add oil in a steady stream. Stir in poppy seeds. In salad bowl, combine the romaine, cashews and Swiss cheese toss and dress or serve with dressing on the side.

"There is a destiny that makes us brothers,
no one goes this way alone,
All that we send into the hearts of others,
comes back into our own."
...Edwin Markham

Shown on previous page:

❖ Balsamic Grape and Walnut Salad.....page 140

❖ Salmon Skewers with Spicy Thai Coconut
    Sauce.....page 227

❖ Tomato and Chick Pea Salad.....page 143

❖ Cobb Salad.....page 148

❖ Mango Salad.....page 165

❖ Greek Ribs on the BBQ.....page 207

HONEY MUSTARD DRESSING

3 cups mayonnaise
½ cup honey
½ cup sugar
¼ cup prepared mustard
¼ cup vinegar
1 tablespoon parsley
1 small onion, grated
1 cup canola oil
1 head lettuce, chopped or mixed greens
raw vegetables of choice, chopped

Put first 7 ingredients in a blender, blend until smooth, add oil and mix well. Pour over lettuce and vegetables. Toss just before serving.

"Everyone hears what you say.
Friends listen to what you say.
Best friends listen to what you don't say."

CAESAR SALAD DRESSING

(If you want to make your own dressing,
we recommend this one.)

1 tablespoon garlic, crushed
1 can anchovies, drained and chopped
3 dashes Worcestershire sauce
dash of Tabasco
3 tablespoons Dijon mustard
1 egg
1 cup canola oil
salt and pepper

In blender combine all ingredients except oil. Mix at high speed adding oil very slowly in a thin stream. Mix until smooth. Add salt and pepper to taste. Store in fridge for a few hours before using.

"It is not until you have a burning 'yes' inside of you about what is truly important, that you can pleasantly, smilingly, cheerfully, say 'no' to all of that which is urgent, but not truly important.
Our deepest guilt comes from doing the opposite, implicitly saying no, to the truly important and yes, yes, yes, to the urgent that is not important."
...... Stephen Covey,

CRANBERRY SPINACH SALAD

1 tablespoon butter
¾ cup slivered almonds
1 pound spinach, rinsed and torn into bite-size pieces
1 cup dried cranberries
2 tablespoons sesame seeds, toasted
1 tablespoon poppy seeds
½ cup sugar
2 tablespoons onion, minced
¼ teaspoon paprika
¼ cup white wine vinegar
¼ cup cider vinegar
½ cup canola oil

In medium saucepan, melt butter. Cook and stir almonds in butter until lightly toasted. Remove from heat, and let cool. In large bowl, combine spinach with toasted almonds and cranberries. In medium bowl, whisk together sesame seeds, poppy seeds, sugar, onion, paprika, white wine vinegar, cider vinegar, and canola oil. Toss with spinach just before serving.

The babbling brook would lose its song if you removed the rocks.

FOO YUNG SALAD

1 head romaine lettuce
2 cups fresh bean sprouts
1 -5 ounce can water chestnuts, drained
6 slices bacon, cooked crisp and crumbled
1 can shrimp, drained
Salt and pepper to taste

Dressing:
½ cup canola oil
¼ cup vinegar
2 tablespoons sugar
3 tablespoons soya sauce
¼ teaspoon ginger root, grated

Break lettuce into bite-size pieces. Add sprouts, water chestnuts, shrimp and bacon bits. Mix together dressing ingredients and toss just before serving. Season to taste.

When you make a mistake, make amends immediately.
It's easier to eat crow while it's still warm.

MANGO SALAD

½ cup peanuts, chopped
2 firm mangos, sliced or diced
1 red pepper, diced
2 carrots, grated
¼ cup green onions, chopped
1 large head of romaine lettuce, chopped

Dressing:
¼ cup canola oil
2 tablespoons lime juice
1 teaspoon lime rind
1 tablespoon soy sauce
2 teaspoons sugar
¼ teaspoon hot sauce
¼ teaspoon salt
¼ teaspoon pepper

Roast peanuts in oven at 325° F. for 10 minutes or until browned. Toss mangos, pepper, carrots, onions and lettuce in large salad bowl. Mix dressing ingredients in order given and pour over salad mixture. Top with roasted peanuts.

"There is no use worrying about things over which you have no control, and if you have control, you can do something about them instead of worrying."..........Stanley C. Allyn

MANDARIN ORANGE CRANBERRY SALAD WITH CARAMELIZED ALMONDS

½ cup slivered almonds
3 tablespoons sugar
1 head romaine lettuce, chopped
1 cup celery, chopped
½ cup green onions, chopped
1 -11 ounce can mandarin oranges, drained
¼ cup dried cranberries
vinaigrette dressing (below)

Cook almonds and sugar in a skillet over medium heat until sugar is dissolved and almonds are coated. Transfer to wax paper and let cool. Break cooled almonds apart. Combine lettuce, celery and green onions in medium bowl. Add mandarin oranges, cranberries and vinaigrette, (below) tossing to coat. Add almonds and serve immediately.

Vinaigrette Dressing:
Whisk the following together and chill for 1 hour.
¼ cup canola oil
2 tablespoons cider vinegar
2 tablespoons sugar
2 tablespoons fresh parsley, minced
½ teaspoon salt
¼ teaspoon pepper

A lecturer was giving a lecture to his students on stress management. He raised a glass of water and asked the audience, "How heavy do you think this glass of water is?" They answered anywhere from 20g to 500g.
The lecturer replied, "It does not matter on the absolute weight. It depends on how long you hold it.
If I hold it for a minute, it is OK.
If I hold it for an hour, I will have an ache in my right arm.
If I hold it for a day, you will have to call an ambulance. It is the exact same weight, but the longer I hold it, the heavier it becomes."
The lecturer continued, "If we carry our burdens all the time, sooner or later, we will not be able to carry on, the burden becoming increasingly heavier. What you have to do is to put the glass down, rest for a while before holding it up again. We have to put down the burden periodically, so that we can be refreshed and are able to carry on."
So tonight, put the burden down for awhile. It is not easy but work at it - don't carry it tonight. You can pick it up tomorrow. Let it down for a moment if you can. Pick it up again later when you have rested... Rest and relax.

A Woman of Strength.

She walked in, resolute and smiling. I remembered her as a sweet, pretty, promising little girl. Here she was -a beautiful young mother with three active children in tow. I mused – time goes by so quickly!

"Thank you ladies for all the good work you are doing for cancer causes", she said warmly.

"How are you?" I questioned her, noticing her pensive and somewhat solemn blue eyes.

Those eyes brimmed over suddenly with tears. We gently hugged each other as she haltingly informed me; "I have breast cancer... I've just had a breast removed". Pain and fear so apparent, so raw ... in all facets of her person. I tried to mutter some consoling words. Words ring hollow at times. She collected herself, straightening up stoically, as she chatted purposefully. In this poignant encounter the painful reality of Cancer has taken on yet another familiar face. Yet.....here is a survivor, she is a woman of strength, a woman of faith and a woman who is sustained daily by a tenacious hope. Hope that "they got it all". Hope that the Almighty will see fit to arrest this evil disease that has become such a plague on our human condition. Hope that the intelligence and motivation that has allowed us to travel through space may figure out the causes and the cures for this often relentless ill that seems too common among us. However, it wasn't about her, she was focused beyond herself. She verbalized her concern for her children, her husband, and others. She expressed her gratitude to Breast Friends. I was so humbled and somehow ashamed. How could I ever open my mouth and complain about anything, ever? I'm a grandma, I've raised my kids. I am mostly preoccupied with my own life. I am certainly no hero. She is my hero, and women like her. These are our role models. Those who are walking the walk as cancer survivors, and walking it with courage, faith, hope and love. She lives with quiet determination and grace as she continues unselfishly to be at the service of her family, and even folks beyond them. She seizes and celebrates each day as a gift. Through her anguish she's thanking us? .... I thought about how helpless we all are, when faced with our pending mortality. How this disease tends to rip us and rob us, in so many ways. What can we do for her and for the many others facing similar circumstances? Is there anything we can do? I hoped and prayed there was something that someone could do. Individually and collectively however, there needed to be the will to do it! Her prognosis is hopeful; we've come a fair way. Together we all need to continue to engage in the cause and the struggle.

Thank God she is a survivor. Bless her!

Entrees

A strong woman has faith that she is strong enough for the journey, but a woman of strength has faith that it is in the journey that she will become strong.

BEEF BURGUNDY
(A slow cooker recipe)

2 pounds round steak, cut in 1 ½ - 2 inch cubes
2 teaspoons canola oil
2 medium onions, sliced thin
2 cloves garlic, crushed
3 large carrots, cut into ½ inch rounds
1 -10 ounce can stems and pieces mushrooms, drained
1 bay leaf
½ teaspoon salt
½ teaspoon pepper
¼ teaspoon thyme
1 teaspoon tomato paste
1 ½ cups French Burgundy wine
¼ cup fresh parsley
¼ cup flour
½ cup water

In a large skillet heat oil and brown beef. Add onion, garlic, carrots and stir for a few minutes. Pour into a crock pot and add remaining ingredients except flour and water. Cook on low for 6-8 hours. Drain juices into a large saucepan, mix flour and water to make a paste and whisk into juices over med-high heat to make gravy. Add to stew, stir and serve.
Serve with a salad and French bread and of course the remaining Wine!!

BEEF PEPPER QUESADILLAS
(Try these with left over roast beef, they'll become very popular!)

2 teaspoons canola oil
1 red pepper, cut into ¼ inch strips
1 green pepper, cut into ¼ inch strips
1 small onion, slivered
6 -8 inch tortilla shells
2 cups roast beef, thinly sliced
1 ½ cups Cheddar or Monterey Jack Cheese, shredded
chili flakes (optional)
salsa
light sour cream

Heat oil in a medium frying pan over medium heat. Sauté peppers and onion. Remove from heat and divide in 6 portions. Lay tortillas on a flat surface. Place 1/3 cup of beef on each of the tortillas. Spoon a portion of peppers and onion over beef. Top each with ¼ cup grated cheese. Sprinkle with chili flakes to taste. Fold tortillas in half to form a semicircle. Heat a large frying pan coated with canola oil over medium to medium-low heat. Place 2 quesadillas in the frying pan. Cook for 1- 2 minutes on each side. Cut in half crosswise on a serving plate. Repeat process with the remaining tortillas. Serve with salsa and sour cream.

GRANDMA'S CABBAGE ROLLS
(A family favourite!)

1 head cabbage

2 pounds lean ground beef

1 cup long grain rice, uncooked

1 medium onion, chopped

salt and pepper to taste

2 -10 ounce cans tomato soup

water

Steam cabbage in a large pot or the microwave, until leaves get soft and peel easily. Take off a few leaves at a time and return to steam. Mix ground beef, rice, onions, salt and pepper. Roll a medium size handful of meat mixture in each leaf, and place edge down in a medium roaster. Pour soup over the top and fill the roaster ½ full with water. Bake at 350° F. for about 2 hours. Makes about 10 good size cabbage rolls. Serve with tomato sauce.

Tomato Sauce:
(We called it Red Gravy, when we were kids.)

1/3 cup margarine

2 tablespoons flour

1 -1 litre bottle tomato juice

salt and pepper

Sauté onions in margarine, stir in flour, add tomato juice and salt and pepper. Bring to boil and simmer until thickened. Serve over cabbage rolls.

LEFTOVER ROAST BEEF FAVOURITE
(This simple recipe will become such a favourite you will make roasts just to have leftovers.)

¼ cup butter
½ medium head cabbage, grated coarsely
½ medium green pepper, diced
1 medium onion, diced
3 stalks celery, diced
1 cup short grain rice, cooked according to instructions
2-3 cups leftover roasted beef, cubed
3 tablespoons soya sauce
salt and pepper

Sauté all vegetables in a large skillet in butter until tender. When vegetables are done add beef cubes and cooked rice. Stir in soya and salt and pepper to taste.

"When we were young, you made me blush, go hot and cold and turn to mush. I still feel all these things, it's true......
but is it menopause or you?"................Susan D. Anderson

LIVER, BACON and ONIONS
(Raised rurally? Liver may be a favourite, here's
a traditional popular recipe.)

½ cup milk   ¼ cup cornmeal
1 tablespoon soya sauce   ½ teaspoon paprika
1 tablespoon Worcestershire sauce   ½ teaspoon seasoning salt
1 garlic clove, crushed   ¼ teaspoon granulated garlic
1 pound sliced beef liver   ¼ teaspoon black pepper
4 slices bacon, cut in half   1 medium onion, sliced
1/3 cup flour

In a 7 x 11 inch baking dish, combine milk, soya sauce,
Worcestershire sauce and garlic. Cut liver slices to make 4 equal
portions. Add the liver to the milk marinade, marinate for 1-8
hours in the refrigerator. Cook bacon in a frying pan, over
medium low heat, until crisp. Combine flour, cornmeal, paprika,
seasoning salt, garlic and pepper, in a pie plate. Remove liver
from marinade; discard marinade. Coat both sides of liver in the
flour mixture. Remove bacon from frying pan and set aside. Fry
liver slices in the bacon fat for 6 minutes, or until the top is wet.
Turn over, lay onion slices on top. Cook for 6 minutes. Remove
liver to warm serving plate. Keep warm. Continue cooking
onions for 5 minutes or until soft, stirring frequently. Arrange
onions and bacon on liver. Serves four.

173

MOZZARELLA SPAGHETTI SKILLET

1 pound lean ground beef
2 cups mushrooms, sliced
1 cup onion, chopped
1 cup green pepper, chopped
1 -28 ounce can tomatoes, diced
1 cup water
1 ½ cups spaghetti, broken
1 ½ teaspoons Italian seasoning
1 ½ teaspoons salt
2 cups Mozzarella cheese, shredded

Combine beef, mushrooms, onion and green pepper in a large fry pan or Dutch oven. Sauté over medium heat until meat is browned and vegetables are tender. Drain fat. Add tomatoes and juice to pan. Stir in water, spaghetti, Italian seasoning and salt. Bring to boil. Reduce heat; cover and simmer 15-20 minutes or until pasta is cooked, stirring occasionally. Add cheese; stir until melted.
Makes 5 or 6 servings.

"One of the most important things you can do is remember the power of girlfriends, your family is there for you, but they get emotional. Girlfriends saved my day." ....Jaclyn Smith

NO FUSS STROGANOFF
(A different twist-made with ground beef rather than round steak)

2 tablespoons butter or margarine

1 cup onion, finely chopped

1 pound lean ground beef

2 tablespoons flour

1 teaspoon salt

¼ teaspoon pepper

1 -10 ounce can sliced mushrooms, drained

1 -10 ounce can cream of chicken soup

½ cup sour cream

¼ cup Cheddar cheese, grated

Melt butter in frying pan. Add onions and sauté slowly until clear. Add beef, stirring to break up lumps. Drain off fat. Sprinkle flour, salt and pepper over meat mixture; stir. Add mushrooms and cook uncovered for 10 minutes. Add soup, stir and cook, uncovered for an additional 10 minutes. Stir in sour cream and cheese. Heat through. Can be served immediately or poured into a casserole, covered and held in a warm oven. Serves 4.

Friends are the chocolate chips in the cookie of life.

POLYNESIAN SATAY

1 ½ pounds sirloin steak (thick)
¾ cup soya sauce
½ cup brown sugar
2 tablespoons canola oil
¼ teaspoon garlic, minced
½ teaspoon ginger powder

Slice steak 1/8 inch thick. Mix above ingredients and marinate meat for ½-1 hour. Thread on wooden skewers (which have been soaked in water) and broil until medium-rare. You can also place meat in one layer on a broiling pan and broil until medium-rare.

Peanut Sauce:
¼ cup peanut butter
½ cup water
2 tablespoons brown sugar
1 tablespoon soya sauce
2 teaspoons lemon juice
½ teaspoon red chili peppers
1 clove garlic, minced
Mix in saucepan. Simmer 5 minutes. Pour over Satay. Serve with rice.

PORCUPINE MEATBALLS

(This is an old fashioned recipe but so tasty. My sister-in-law always makes these at Christmas and serves with her turkey. We all know we can never have enough food at our Christmas dinner!!)

1 ½ pounds lean ground beef
2/3 cup long-grain rice, uncooked
½ cup water
½ cup onion, finely chopped
2 teaspoons garlic powder
1 teaspoon seasoned salt
¼ teaspoon pepper
1 -15 ounce can tomato sauce
1 cup water
2 teaspoons Worcestershire sauce

Mix ground beef with rice, water, onion, garlic powder salt and pepper. Shape mixture by tablespoons into 1 ½ inch meatballs. Place meatballs in ungreased shallow casserole dish. Mix remaining ingredients and pour over meatballs. Cover and bake at 350° F. for 45 minutes. Uncover and bake an additional 15-20 minutes.
Serves 4 - 6.

"Each of us are like angels with only one wing—we can fly only by embracing another.".......*Barbara Johnson*

RULLAPYLSA
(An old Icelandic recipe that is great served
with fresh brown bread.)

3 pounds beef flank, trimmed
2 tablespoons salt
¼ teaspoon saltpeter
1 teaspoon allspice
½ teaspoon pepper
½ teaspoon cloves
1 large or 2 small onions, chopped fine

Mix all seasonings and onion together in a bowl or in food
processor and spread over meat. Roll tightly, like a jelly roll,
and place in fine mesh netting. Place in cooled brine.

Brine:
4 litres water
2 cups salt
1 cup brown sugar
2 level teaspoons saltpeter
Boil above ingredients for 20 minutes. Cool and place meat in
brine. Put a plate over meat to hold meat down and keep
covered in brine. Leave in a cool place for one week.

Boil meat gently in fresh water for 2-2 ½ hours. Cool and
refrigerate.

SLOPPY JOE'S

1 pound lean ground beef
1/4 cup onion, chopped
1/4 cup green bell pepper, chopped
1/2 teaspoon garlic powder
1 teaspoon prepared yellow mustard
3/4 cup ketchup
3 teaspoons brown sugar
salt and pepper to taste
2 cups Cheddar cheese, grated

In a medium skillet over medium heat, brown the ground beef, onion, and green pepper; drain off liquids. Stir in the garlic powder, mustard, ketchup, and brown sugar; mix thoroughly. Reduce heat, and simmer for 30 minutes. Season with salt and pepper. Serve on half buns, topped with grated Cheddar cheese.

"Most of us will miss out on life's big prizes; the Pulitzers, the Heismans, the Oscars. But we're all eligible for a pat on the back, a kiss on the cheek, a thumbs-up sign!"
.....Barbara Johnson

SPAGHETTI AND MEATBALLS
(A basic recipe you can spice up if you wish.)

2 pounds lean ground beef
¾ cup oatmeal
1 egg
1 small onion, diced
½ teaspoon garlic powder
1 teaspoon salt and pepper
1 -1.89 litre tomato or clamato juice
3 -10 ounce cans tomato soup
3 -10 ounce cans mushroom stems and pieces, drained

Mix ground beef, oatmeal, egg, onion, and spices. Shape into small meatballs. Fry or bake on a cookie sheet sprayed with non-stick spray in oven at 400° F. until browned. While these are baking, pour juice, soup and mushrooms into a large Dutch oven. When meatballs are done put them into tomato mixture and simmer everything for an hour before serving.
NOTE: For a spicier sauce use spicy clamato juice.
Add: (optional)
1 tablespoon chili peppers
1 teaspoon chili powder

Friendship isn't a big thing... it's a million things.

STEAK IN FOIL

1 ½ pounds round steak
½ cup brown sugar
1 cup ketchup
1 package onion soup mix
1 onion, chopped
1 teaspoon lemon juice
1 green pepper, chopped (optional)

Brown steak and place in foil-lined pan. Mix other ingredients
and pour over steak. Fold foil over steak. Bake at 350° F. for
1 ½-2 hours. Can also be cooked in slow cooker for 8-10
hours on low.

THIRTY MINUTE CASSEROLE

1 pound lean ground beef, fried and crumbled
½ package frozen hash browns
1 -12 ounce can kernel corn
1 -10 ounce can mushroom soup
½ can water

Layer ground beef, hash browns, and corn in a lightly greased
or sprayed 3 quart casserole dish. Mix soup and water and
pour over layers. Bake at 350° F. for 30 minutes or place in
microwave for 10 minutes. <u>Variation</u>: Use prepared Kraft
dinner instead of hash browns.

STUFFED STEAK

1 round steak, cut into 6 pieces
6 cups dried bread, cubed
1 egg
1 teaspoon sage
½ teaspoon poultry seasoning
1 teaspoon salt
½ teaspoon pepper
1 cup water
1 -10 ounce can mushroom soup
1 -10 ounce can mushroom stems and pieces
1 -10 ounce can water

Tenderize steak by pounding it with a mallet, or purchase meat that is already tenderized. Mix bread and water until slightly pasty. You may need to add more water. Add the egg and seasonings, and mix again. Into the center of each piece of meat place a couple tablespoons of bread mixture, roll the meat around mixture and fasten with a toothpick. Place in the bottom of a small roaster. Mix the soup, mushrooms and water in a separate container and pour over the meat mixture. Cover and bake at 300° F. for about 2 hours or until done. Serve with mashed potatoes.

SWEET AND SOUR BEEF STEW

1 ½ pounds stewing beef, cut into 1 inch cubes
2 tablespoons canola oil
2 medium carrots, shredded (1 cup)
2 onions, sliced (1 cup)
1 -8 ounce can tomato sauce
½ cup water
¼ cup brown sugar, packed
¼ cup vinegar
1 tablespoon Worcestershire sauce
1 teaspoon salt
1 tablespoon cold water
2 teaspoons cornstarch

In a saucepan, brown meat in hot oil. Add next 8 ingredients.
Cover and cook over low heat until meat is tender (about 1 ½
hours). Blend 1 tablespoon water with cornstarch, add to stew
and stir until thickened and bubbly. Serve over rice.

Note: I like to double the sauce.

"What is the best way to have your husband remember your
anniversary? Get married on his birthday."...........Cindy Garner

BASIL & PIMENTO CREAM CHICKEN BREASTS

1/3 cup bread crumbs

1/3 cup milk

4 chicken breasts, skinless, boneless

3 tablespoons butter

½ cup chicken broth

1 cup whipping cream

1 -4 ounce jar sliced pimentos, drained

½ cup Parmesan cheese, grated

¼ cup fresh basil, minced

1/8 teaspoon pepper

Place bread crumbs and milk in separate containers. Dip chicken breasts in milk and then coat with crumbs. Place butter and chicken in a medium skillet over medium heat and cook 5-6 minutes on each side or until juices run clear. Remove chicken from heat and keep warm. Add broth to the skillet and bring to a boil over medium heat. Stir in the cream and pimentos; boil and stir for one minute. Reduce heat. Add Parmesan cheese, basil and pepper; cook over low heat for another few minutes until heated through. Pour sauce over the chicken. Serves four.

"Forget injuries, never forget kindness.".........*Confucius*

CHICKEN CACCIATORA

4 pounds chicken, cut into pieces
½ cup flour
1 teaspoon salt
1 teaspoon pepper
½ cup canola oil
¼ cup onion, finely chopped
½ cup carrots, chopped
1 tablespoon parsley, dried
1 bay leaf
1 teaspoon basil, dried
½ teaspoon garlic, crushed
4 cups plum tomatoes, strained
¼ cup red or white wine

Coat chicken in flour, sprinkle with salt and pepper and brown in
hot oil until golden brown on all sides. Place in covered dish
and keep warm. Brown onions, garlic, carrots, parsley, bay
leaf and basil in oil left in pan. Add tomatoes to onion mixture.
Bring to a boil. Add chicken and wine and simmer for 30
minutes or until chicken is tender. Serve with rice or angel hair
pasta.

"How beautiful a day can be when kindness touches it."
George Ellison

CHICKEN STIR FRY

300 grams angel hair pasta
2 cups broccoli florets
1 pound boneless chicken breasts, cut into thin strips
½ cup Asian sesame dressing
2 tablespoons soya sauce
½ teaspoon ground ginger
½ teaspoon garlic powder
½ teaspoon crushed red pepper
1/3 cup dry roasted peanuts, chopped

Cook pasta as directed on package, adding broccoli to the boiling water for the last 3 minutes of the pasta cooking time. Spray a large nonstick skillet with cooking spray and heat on medium-high. Add chicken and cook 6-8 minutes or until chicken is cooked through, stirring occasionally. Stir in dressing, soya sauce, ginger, garlic and red pepper. Cook 1 minute stirring occasionally. Drain pasta mixture and place in large bowl. Add chicken mixture and mix lightly. Sprinkle with peanuts and serve immediately. Makes 4 servings.

"Nine words often heard on second honeymoons:
"What do you think the kids are doing now?"
...Linda Fiterman

CHICKEN WITH FETA
AND RED PEPPER SAUCE

1 egg
½ cup dry bread crumbs
¼ teaspoon salt
¼ cup Parmesan cheese
4 chicken breasts, boneless, skinless
2 tablespoons canola oil
1 jar roasted red peppers, drained
1 teaspoon Italian seasoning
¾ cup Feta cheese, crumbled

In a shallow baking dish, lightly beat the egg. In another shallow bowl combine bread crumbs, salt and Parmesan cheese. Dip chicken in egg, then coat with the crumb mixture. In a large skillet, cook the chicken with oil over medium heat for 6-8 minutes on each side or until juices run clear. Meanwhile in a blender or food processor combine the red peppers and Italian seasoning. Cover and process until pureed. Transfer to a microwave safe bowl. Cover and microwave on high for 1-2 minutes or until heated through, stirring once. Spoon over the chicken breasts and sprinkle with Feta cheese.

"Life is too short to be small.".......*B. Disraeli*

CLASSY CHICKEN
(This is a delicious entrée, served with rice and Monterey Bread, found in *For the Breast of Friends* under Breads.)

3 large chicken breasts, chopped
pepper
3 bunches broccoli, cooked and chopped
canola oil

Sauce:
1 -10 ounce can cream of chicken soup
1 tablespoon lemon juice
¼ - 1 teaspoon curry powder
½ cup mayonnaise

1 cup Cheddar cheese, grated

Pepper chopped chicken breasts and fry in oil until slightly brown. Set aside. In saucepan, heat the cream of chicken soup, lemon juice, curry (to taste), and mayonnaise. In an ungreased 9 x 13 inch pan, layer broccoli then chicken. Pour heated sauce over all. Top with Cheddar cheese. Bake at 375° F. for 30 minutes. Serves 4-6.

"Nothing great was ever achieved without enthusiasm."......Aristotle

EASY CHICKEN DINNER
(One of our husbands, who shall remain nameless, invented this little chicken dish and yes, his wife loved it!)

6 boneless, skinless chicken breasts
¼ cup canola oil
1 medium onion, chopped into eighths
1 cup fresh mushrooms, quartered
1 celery stalk, chopped
1 cup Dole vegetable fruit blend, any flavour

Coating:
1 ½ cups bread crumbs
1 teaspoon paprika
3 teaspoons garlic powder
1 teaspoon ground coriander
1 cup milk.

Mix coating ingredients except milk in a dish. Place chicken in milk and then coat with bread crumb mixture. Heat oil in large skillet. Sauté chicken breasts until golden brown. Add onion to chicken making sure they fit around breasts. Sauté for 5 minutes. Add mushrooms, celery and juice. Transfer to baking dish and place in preheated 350° F. oven for 20-25 minutes. Serve with rice, pasta or potatoes.

GRILLED CHICKEN BREAST IN MANGO-CURRY MARINADE
(This recipe can be done in the oven with the marinade.)

4 chicken breasts, boneless, skinless
1/3 cup mango chutney
3 tablespoons honey
2 tablespoons lemon juice
1 tablespoon soya sauce
1 teaspoon curry powder
1 teaspoon ground cumin

Arrange chicken breasts in baking pan. Combine remaining ingredients in a small bowl and pour over chicken. Turn pieces to coat both sides with marinade. Cover and marinate in the refrigerator for 1 hour. Prepare grill. Remove chicken from marinade and grill for 5 minutes on both sides. Baste often with the leftover marinade. If using oven, bake for 1 hour 350° F.

"When you are a mother, you are never really alone in your thoughts. A mother always has to think twice, once for herself and once for her child."......Sophia Loren

JAMAICAN CHICKEN

4 boneless, skinless chicken breasts, cut into serving pieces
1 cup flour
2 eggs, well beaten
2 cups dry bread crumbs
1 teaspoon salt
½ teaspoon pepper
½ teaspoon garlic powder
½ teaspoon basil
½ cup oil
6 green onions, chopped fine
3 celery stalks, chopped fine

1 -14 ounce can tomato sauce
1 cup water
2 tablespoons vinegar
2 tablespoons brown sugar
1/8 teaspoon salt
1/8 teaspoon pepper
1/8 teaspoon garlic powder
12-16 Mozzarella slices

Coat chicken pieces with flour, then dip into egg mixture.
Combine bread crumbs with salt, pepper, garlic powder, basil
and coat chicken. Heat skillet with ½ cup oil. Brown coated
chicken until golden brown. Place in a 9 x 13 inch casserole
dish. Sprinkle with chopped green onion and celery. Mix
tomato sauce, water, vinegar, sugar, and remaining seasonings.
Pour over chicken and bake at 350° F. for 30-40 minutes.
Ten minutes before serving place Mozzarella cheese slices over
cooked chicken and return to oven until cheese is melted.

*"As long as you keep a person down, some part of you has
to be down there to hold him down, so it means you cannot
soar as you otherwise might."*........*Marian Anderson*

LEMON CHICKEN BREASTS

3 tablespoons olive oil
4 chicken breasts, skinless
1 cup dry white wine
1 teaspoon parsley flakes
½ teaspoon thyme, dried, whole
¼ teaspoon salt
3 tablespoons lemon juice
¼ teaspoon pepper
¼ teaspoon paprika

Heat olive oil in heavy skillet until hot. Add chicken and cook for 5 minutes on each side and drain. Place the drained chicken in an 8 x 8 inch baking dish. Bring the wine, parsley flakes, thyme and salt to a boil in the skillet and pour over the chicken. Sprinkle with lemon juice, pepper and paprika. Bake, covered, at 375° F. for 35 minutes.

"You grow up the day you have your first real laugh at yourself."........Ethel Barrymore

LEMON CHICKEN PASTA TOSS
(Love that flavour, and quick to prepare!)

2 tablespoons cornstarch
1 ¾ cups chicken broth
2 tablespoons lemon juice
1 tablespoon Dijon mustard
1 pound chicken breasts, skinless, boneless, cut in strips
2 cloves garlic, minced
3 tablespoons chopped fresh parsley or 1 tablespoon dried parsley flakes
4 cups hot, cooked spaghetti (cooked without salt)

Mix cornstarch, broth, lemon juice and mustard. Cook chicken and garlic in non-stick skillet until browned, stirring often. Remove chicken, add cornstarch mixture. Cook and stir until mixture boils and thickens. Return chicken to skillet and heat through, stir in parsley, toss with spaghetti. Enjoy!

"Sometimes one little spark of kindness is all it takes to reignite the light of hope in a heart that's blinded by pain."
....Barbara Johnson

LETTUCE CASHEW CHICKEN WRAPS
(Great in the summer when you need something light!)

12 Iceberg lettuce leaves
3 tablespoons hoisin sauce (also known as Peking sauce)
2 tablespoons rice vinegar
1 tablespoon water
2 chicken breasts, boneless, skinless, cut into thin strips
1 teaspoon Kosher salt
2 tablespoons canola oil
1 tablespoon fresh ginger, peeled and finely chopped
1 medium carrot, cut into 2-inch pieces and julienned (about
1 cup)
2 green onions, chopped
½ cup roasted, salted cashews

Stir hoisin sauce, vinegar and water in a small bowl until well blended and set aside. Season chicken with salt and set aside. Heat wok over high heat until hot. Add oil and swirl to coat sides. Add ginger, stir until fragrant about 10 seconds. Add chicken and stir-fry for 1 minute. Add carrot and stir fry another 2 minutes or until chicken is just cooked and carrots are tender. Add hoisin mixture and green onions and toss gently until heated through. Remove from heat and add cashews. Arrange chicken mixture on a platter along with lettuce leaves. Spoon mixture into lettuce leaves. Wrap and enjoy!!

MANDARIN ORANGE CHICKEN

1 pound boneless chicken breasts
1 tablespoon canola oil
½ cup green onions, thinly sliced
2 cups fresh mushrooms, sliced
2 teaspoons flour
1 -6 ounce can frozen orange juice concentrate, thawed
2/3 cup water
2 chicken bouillon cubes
1 -11 ounce can mandarin orange sections, drained

Cut chicken into 1 inch chunks. Heat oil in large skillet and cook chicken until browned and cooked inside. Remove chicken from pan. Cook mushrooms and green onions. Sprinkle flour over mushrooms and onions, stirring quickly to combine. Gradually stir in orange juice concentrate, water, and bouillon cubes, stirring constantly. Bring to boil. Reduce heat, add chicken and simmer 3-4 minutes. Stir in orange segments and heat.
Serve over rice.

"We are continually faced with great opportunities which are brilliantly disguised as unsolvable problems."
Margaret Mead

PAD THAI

(What makes pad thai, in addition to the noodles, is the sauce.
The general mix of flavors is sweet, salty, sour, and hot.)

3 ½ tablespoons white vinegar

2 tablespoons water

2 ½ tablespoons fish sauce or soya sauce

3 tablespoons tomato paste

2 ½ tablespoons sugar

½ tablespoon dried shrimp, pounded into a powder

9 ounces flat rice stick noodles, 1/8 inch wide

2 ½ tablespoons canola oil

2 red Serrano chili peppers, seeded and very finely minced

4 cloves garlic, minced

1 ½ chicken breast halves, cut into very thin slices

½ pound small shrimp, shelled

2 eggs, lightly beaten

2 cups fresh bean sprouts, beans removed

¼ cup unsalted peanuts, roasted and coarsely ground

cherry tomatoes, halved
lime wedges
sliced green onions
cucumber slices

Combine vinegar, water, soya sauce, tomato paste, sugar, and

Continued on next page.......

PAD THAI continued.....

dried shrimp in a small bowl; mix until well blended and reserve.
In a large bowl, soak the noodles in enough warm water to cover.
Drain and rinse them well. Heat about 2 ½ tablespoons of oil
in a wok or large sauté pan. Fry peppers about 10 seconds, add
garlic and chicken, stir-fry until chicken is opaque. Stir in
shrimp and sauce mixture. Make a well in center of mixture and
pour in the eggs. When they are almost set, scramble them
evenly. Add half the noodles, thoroughly incorporating them
into the mixture; stir in the remaining noodles and half the bean
sprouts. Cook just until the bean sprouts are nearly wilted.
Heap the meat and noodles onto a large platter. Cover one half
with ground peanuts and the other half with uncooked bean
sprouts. Ring the noodles with lime wedges, cherry tomatoes,
sliced green onions and or sliced cucumbers.

SLOW COOKER ORANGE CHICKEN

8 chicken thighs
3 tablespoons flour
1/3 cup orange marmalade
1/3 cup barbeque sauce
2 tablespoons soya sauce
1 tablespoon fresh gingeroot, grated
Toss chicken with flour in slow cooker. In small bowl mix rest of
ingredients and pour over chicken. Cover and cook on low for
6-8 hours or high for 3-4 hours. Serves 4.

PINEAPPLE CHICKEN CURRY
(Easy to prepare, delicious chicken dish!)

4 boneless chicken breasts halves (2 whole breasts)
1 cup crushed pineapple with juice
2 tablespoons honey
1 tablespoon prepared mustard
1 teaspoon curry powder
½ teaspoon salt
½ teaspoon ginger
1/8 teaspoon black pepper

Preheat oven to 350° F. Lightly spray an 8 x 12 inch baking dish with cooking oil. Lay chicken breast halves in dish.
In a bowl combine pineapple, honey, mustard, curry, salt, ginger, and pepper. Pour over chicken, cover and bake for 30 minutes. Remove the cover and bake for another 30 minutes, or until the chicken is no longer pink in the center. Enjoy!

"Try to do to others as you would have them do to you, and do not be discouraged if they fail sometimes. It is much better that they should fail than that you should."......Charles Dickens

ROAST TURKEY, GRAVY AND STUFFING

(Everyone has their own style but this is just
some "Mom advice" to get you started!)

Heat the oven to 400° F. Remove the giblets and neck from the cavity. Wash the turkey with cold water and blot dry, inside and out, with a paper towel. Place the neck, giblets (or discard if you are not going to eat them) and onion in a large roasting pan. Insert a roasting rack (if you don't have a rack, place some whole carrots in the bottom of the roaster) and arrange the turkey on top, breast-side up. Loosely pack the stuffing in the neck cavity and inside the body. Fold the skin under to enclose the stuffing and secure with poultry picks or sew shut with string. Tie the legs together and cover the tips with foil. Season the turkey with salt. Add one cup of broth into the roasting pan. Cover with lid or foil tent and roast according to chart below, basting frequently. When you hear the turkey beginning to cook (about 30 minutes) turn oven down to 325° F. For the last 30-40 minutes of the cooking time uncover to allow for browning and crispness of the skin. Test for doneness with a meat thermometer. Internal temperature should be 180° F. Remove the stuffing, let sit for 10 min. before carving.

Approximate table for Roasting Unstuffed Turkey at 325° F. Add 15-30 minutes to these times when roasting a stuffed turkey.

		These times are approximate depending on oven and turkey. Always use a thermometer to ensure doneness.
8 to 12 pounds	2 3/4 to 3 hours	
12 to 14 pounds	3 to 3 3/4 hours	
14 to 18 pounds	3 3/4 to 4 1/4 hours	
18 to 20 pounds	4 1/4 to 4 1/2 hours	
20 to 24 pounds	4 1/2 to 5 hours	

GRAVY

Remove turkey and vegetables from the pan. Strain the pan juices from the roasted turkey and pour off the fat. Measure 4 cups of the juices and place back in the roaster. If you have less than four cups, add chicken broth to make up the difference. Place roaster over two burners set to medium, and stir drippings to get all the brown bits off the pan. If you don't have a lot of brown bits in the pan you may add some gravy browner at this point. In a separate bowl or shaker mix ½ cup + 2 tablespoons flour with 1 cup water and stir or shake until smooth. Whisk flour mixture into hot drippings. Simmer for 5 to 8 minutes. If gravy is too thick add some boiling water, chicken broth or vegetable water drained from potatoes, carrots or other vegetables. Season with salt and pepper.

MOIST POULTRY STUFFING

8 cups bread crumbs, dried
2 cups water
½ pound ground pork or beef
1 teaspoon poultry seasoning
1 onion, chopped
1/3 cup margarine, melted

1 egg
½ teaspoon sage
1 egg
1 teaspoon salt
½ teaspoon pepper

Mix crumbs and water until pasty — add more water if necessary. Add remaining ingredients, mix and stuff your turkey or chicken. Note: Chestnuts or celery can also be added.

* To complete this meal — make the cranberry sauce on page 235 of this book. The only problem may be, that you will have to host Thanksgiving every year!!!!

SALSA CHICKEN

6 chicken breasts, boneless, skinless, thawed
2 cups salsa
4 cups Mozzarella cheese, grated

Preheat oven to 350° F. Place chicken breasts in a 9 x 13 inch pan. Pour salsa over breasts. Bake for 30 minutes. Sprinkle cheese on top and bake for an additional 15 minutes. This goes well with rice.
Note: For a faster meal, cut up chicken breasts and place in a sauce pan with salsa. Cook on your stove top at medium heat and add cheese just before serving.

APRICOT CHICKEN

2 chickens, cut into pieces
1 cup apricot jam
1 cup Russian salad dressing
1 package onion soup mix
1 teaspoon salt
½ teaspoon pepper

Arrange chicken pieces in a roaster or 9 x 13 inch pan. Mix remainder of ingredients and pour over chicken. Bake at 350° F. for 1 ½ hours. Serve with rice.

SOY GINGER CHICKEN
(A slow cooker recipe)

½ cup soya sauce

2 tablespoons brown sugar

5 garlic cloves, thinly sliced

2/3 cup fresh cilantro, chopped, plus sprigs for garnish

1 piece fresh ginger, peeled and cut into thin strips

5 scallions, thinly sliced on the diagonal (about 1 cup packed)

1 tablespoon balsamic vinegar

1 teaspoon ground coriander

½ teaspoon ground pepper

4 chicken drumsticks and 4 thighs, skin removed

2 medium carrots, thinly sliced crosswise

1 tablespoon cornstarch

1 tablespoon water

In a slow cooker, stir together soya sauce, sugar, garlic, cilantro, ginger, ½ cup scallions, vinegar, coriander, and pepper. Add chicken and carrots; toss to coat. Cover and cook on low until chicken is tender, about 6 hours. Using a large spoon, skim off and discard any fat from surface of cooking liquid. In a 2 cup glass measuring cup, whisk cornstarch with water. Ladle 1 cup cooking liquid into measuring cup; whisk to combine. Pour into a small saucepan, and bring to a boil; cook until thickened, about 1 minute. With slow cooker turned off, stir in cornstarch mixture. Serve chicken with white rice, and garnish with cilantro sprigs and remaining ½ cup scallions.

SPICY PEANUT CHICKEN

½ cup chicken broth
2 tablespoons cornstarch
2 tablespoons sugar
4 tablespoons soya sauce
2 tablespoons white vinegar
¼ teaspoon cayenne pepper
1 tablespoon canola oil
1 pound chicken thighs, boneless, cut into pieces
1 clove garlic, minced
1 teaspoon gingerroot, grated
1 red pepper, cut into ¾ inch pieces
1/3 cup roasted peanuts
2 green onions, chopped

Mix broth, cornstarch, sugar, soya sauce, vinegar and cayenne pepper in a bowl. Heat wok or 12-inch skillet over high heat. Add oil, rotate wok to coat side. Add chicken, garlic, and gingeroot. Stir fry until chicken is no longer pink. Add red pepper to wok. Stir fry 1 minute. Add cornstarch mixture to wok. Cook and stir about 1 minute until sauce thickens. Stir in peanuts. Garnish with onions.

"I love Thanksgiving turkey...it's the only time in Los Angeles that you see natural breasts". Arnold Swartznegger

BAKED PORK TENDERLOIN

4 whole pork tenderloins
2 tablespoons margarine
3 tablespoons flour
1 -10 ounce can condensed beef consommé
Sauce:
3 tablespoons butter
3 tablespoons onion, chopped
3 tablespoons flour
1 -10 ounce can condensed beef consommé
1 ¼ cups water
2 teaspoons vinegar
2 teaspoons prepared mustard

Brown tenderloins in margarine in frying pan. Transfer to
baking pan or small roaster.
Sauce: Melt butter in frying pan. Add onion and sauté until
softened. Remove from heat. Mix in flour. Stir in consommé
until smooth. Heat until mixture boils and thickens, loosening
any bits in pan. Add water, vinegar and mustard. Pour sauce
over pork and cover. Bake at 350° F. until no pink remains,
about 1-1 ½ hours. Remove tenderloins from sauce and slice into
medallions, ¼ inch slices, to serve. Pour sauce into container
and serve as accompaniment to pork tenderloin.
Serves 8 to 10.

BARBEQUED PORK RIBS
(These will have the whole family licking their fingers.)

2-3 pounds pork ribs, cut into single ribs
1 ½ teaspoons seasoning salt
½ teaspoon garlic powder
Barbeque sauce (to your liking)

Place ribs in a large Dutch oven. Sprinkle salt and garlic over ribs. Pour 1 cup water into pan and bring to a boil. Cook over medium heat for about 1 hour or until the ribs just start to come away from the bone. Take off heat. About 20 minutes before you are ready to eat: Preheat barbeque. Drain extra liquid from ribs and place ribs on the barbeque on low-medium setting. Spread barbeque sauce over ribs. Cook for about 10 minutes on each side, spreading sauce over ribs one more time. Serve hot.

"When you get into a tight place and everything goes against you till it seems as though you could not hang on a minute longer, never give up then, for that is just the place and time that the tide will turn."............Harriet Beecher Stowe

GINGER SPICED PORK

2 tablespoons flour
1 ½ teaspoons salt
dash black pepper
1 teaspoon ground ginger
1 ½ pounds shoulder pork, cubed
2 tablespoons canola oil

Sauce:
¼ teaspoon Tabasco
1 -397 gram can tomatoes
100 grams fresh mushrooms
1 tablespoon Worcestershire sauce
2 tablespoons brown sugar
2 tablespoons vinegar
2 cloves garlic, crushed
1 bay leaf

Mix flour, salt, pepper, and ginger; use to coat pork. Heat oil in a large frying pan, fry pork quickly until browned, turning frequently. Transfer to a 4 litre baking dish. Combine sauce ingredients and remaining flour mixture. Pour over the meat. Cover and bake at 325° F. for about 2 hours, until meat is tender. Remove the bay leaf and serve with rice or potatoes.

GREEK RIBS ON THE BBQ
(Barbecuing always takes 10 more minutes from the time one asks, "are the ribs ready yet?!")

4 racks pork back ribs
seasoning salt
ground oregano
leaf oregano

1 cup butter, melted
1 teaspoon ground oregano
1 tablespoon leaf oregano
1 tablespoon lemon juice

Remove membrane from the back of the ribs. Easier done if partially frozen. (This will make for more tender ribs.) Sprinkle both sides generously, with seasoning salt, ground and leaf oregano. In small saucepan, melt butter, add oregano's and lemon juice for basting. Barbecue ribs on low, basting with butter mixture each time you turn the ribs. Takes about 30-40 minutes. Serves 6-8 or 4 hungry people!

"Opinions expressed by the man in this house should not be confused with those held by his spouse."........Susan Anderson

HAM BEAN BAKE
(Easy, easy!! A one-dish meal using on-hand ingredients.)

1 pound ham, cut into ½ inch cubes
1 -19 ounce can white kidney beans, drained
1 -14 ounce can pork 'n beans in molasses
1 -10 ounce can mushroom, stems and pieces
1 -8 ounce can pineapple tidbits, with juice
1 -5 ½ ounce can tomato paste
½ teaspoon garlic powder
¾ cup water
2 tablespoons brown sugar
2 tablespoons barbecue sauce
1 medium onion, chopped
1 celery stalk, chopped
½ red pepper, diced

In a large Dutch oven, combine all ingredients. Cover and bake at 350° F. for 1 ½ -2 hours. Remove lid for last 15 minutes. Serves 6-8.

"I can always find my husband. I just follow the trail of his dirty clothes."........Babs Bell Hajdusiewicz

HOMEMADE SAUSAGE
(Secret recipe that has finally been shared!)

16 ½ pounds ground pork
3 ½ pounds lean ground beef
¼ cup pepper, coarsely ground
3/8 cup coarse pickling salt
¼ cup Morton's Tenderquick salt
1/8 cup brown sugar
¼ teaspoon garlic powder
3 cups boiling water

Mix all the spices in the boiling water and pour over meat. Mix meat and spices thoroughly by hand until specks of red from the beef and specks of black from the pepper are no longer prominent. Squeeze mixed meat into sausage casings using a sausage press, or make patties. If you make sausage, hang them overnight in a cool place. Be sure that the links are not touching each other. Smoke the sausage if desired — it is good either way.

Continued on next page...........

"Snuggle: an act of warmth that your husband will inevitably interpret as foreplay."..........Tom Carey

HOMEMADE SAUSAGE, continued.....

Notes:

- Grind the meat at 5 mm, twice. The texture is important. If the grind is too fine, the sausage is also too fine — like garlic ring or baloney. Grinding the beef twice prevents "rubbery" sausage.
- DO NOT use pork scraps. The butcher may try to sell you this, because it is very cheap, and it is used commercially for making sausage. However, you are guaranteed to have "rubbery" sausage if you buy pork scraps.
- It is important to mix by hand, because if you mix with a machine; it will have the effect of pulverizing the meat, and the texture will be too fine, or if you stop before it is pulverized, the meat won't be mixed thoroughly.
- Hanging the sausage overnight is very important. If you don't, the sausage will go "sour". When you hang it, the casings have a chance to dry somewhat, and the meat "sets". Some of the water you used in the mixing process will drip out onto the floor, or evaporate. It is important that the links not touch each other, because where they touch, you will get drying of the casing and some "sourness".
- Have fun and enjoy! We always had a fried patty with a bun, when we were finished.

HONEY MUSTARD GLAZED PORK TENDERLOIN

2 -1 pound pork tenderloins, fat trimmed off

Marinade:
½ cup Worcestershire sauce
1 teaspoon hot pepper sauce
1 clove garlic, minced

Glaze:
1 cup chicken stock
2 tablespoons honey
2 tablespoons Dijon mustard
pinch of salt and pepper

In a baking dish, whisk together marinade ingredients. Add tenderloin, turning to coat. Marinate in fridge for 1 hour turning once. Preheat oven to 350° F. Heat a skillet over medium heat. Remove tenderloins from marinade, shaking off excess; reserve marinade. Put tenderloins in skillet and cook, turning often for about 3 minutes or until browned on all sides. Transfer tenderloin back to baking dish. Reserve browning liquid.

Continued on next page..........

A friend is someone who knows all about you,
but loves you anyway.

HONEY MUSTARD GLAZED PORK TENDERLION, continued.....

Bake for about 30 minutes or until done. Remove tenderloin to cutting board. Cut each tenderloin diagonally into ½ inch slices and arrange on a warm platter. Whisk together glaze ingredients and 2 tablespoons of reserved marinade. Add to skillet and boil over high heat, stirring to scrape up any brown bits from skillet. Boil for 5-7 minutes until it has reduced to about ¾ cup and has thickened slightly. Drizzle over cut tenderloin. Serves about 6.

BARBEQUED PORK CHOPS

8 pork chops
3 tablespoons canola oil
½ cup ketchup
1 teaspoon salt
½ cup celery, chopped
½ teaspoon nutmeg
1/3 cup vinegar
1 cup water
1 bay leaf

Brown pork chops in hot oil. Combine remaining ingredients and pour over browned pork chops.
Cover and bake at 325° F. for 1 ½ hours. Serves 8.

PORK CHOPS IN SPICY ORANGE SAUCE

4-6 pork chops
2 tablespoons canola oil
¼ teaspoon lemon pepper
¼-1/3 cup red pepper jelly
1 cup orange juice
½ teaspoon cinnamon
¼ teaspoon allspice
dash HP sauce
1 tablespoon cornstarch
¼ cup water

Brown pork chops in canola oil with lemon pepper. Remove pork chops and set aside. Add jelly and orange juice to pan and mix well. Season with cinnamon and allspice. Add dash HP sauce. Add chops back into pan and simmer for 30 minutes. Remove chops. Add cornstarch mixed with water to thicken sauce. Add chops back into pan and coat with sauce. Serve with your favourite pasta or rice.

If you want your spouse to listen and pay strict attention to every word you say, talk in your sleep.

PORK CUTLETS WITH APPLE RAISIN SAUCE OR MUSHROOM CREAM SAUCE

2 -1 pound pork tenderloins
1 cup fine breadcrumbs
2 eggs, whisked
2 tablespoons canola oil

Raisin Apple Sauce:	Mushroom Cream Sauce
¾ cup apple juice	1 cup heavy cream
2 tablespoons brown sugar	2 cups fresh mushrooms, sliced
2 apples, peeled and chopped	

1/3 cup raisins

Cut tenderloins into rounds 1 ½ inches thick. Flatten rounds with a meat mallet until they are the desired thickness (approximately ½ inch thick). Place eggs into shallow bowl and spread breadcrumbs onto a sheet of waxed paper. Dip cutlets into egg and then breadcrumbs.
In a large skillet, over medium heat; fry cutlets in canola oil for 4-5 minutes on each side or until done. Choose one of the sauces below:
Raisin Apple Sauce: When done remove rounds from heat and cover with foil to keep warm. Bring apple juice, brown sugar, chopped apples and raisins to boil in a small saucepan. Let simmer for 8 to 10 minutes to reduce liquid and thicken a bit. Serve cutlets on a platter and top with sauce. OR
Mushroom-Cream Sauce: Add mushrooms to the pan just before cutlets are done. When they have started to brown add cream in pan to cutlets and mushrooms. Simmer 4-5 minutes for cream to thicken.

SAGE STUFFED PORK TENDERLOIN

2 pork tenderloins
1 tablespoon lemon juice
2 tablespoons canola oil
1 onion, finely chopped
1 cup fresh breadcrumbs
1 teaspoon sage
1/4 teaspoon lemon pepper
1/2 teaspoon salt
1 egg
flour to coat
1 tablespoon flour
1 cup water
1 cube chicken bouillon or 1 tablespoon chicken broth powder

Split tenderloin along length, but not to separate. Lay flat and rub with lemon juice. Cook onion in 1 tablespoon canola oil and add breadcrumbs, sage, lemon pepper and salt. Mix well. Beat egg separately and blend into stuffing mixture. Place stuffing on 1 tenderloin, cover with 2nd and tie with string. Roll in flour. Cook in 1 tablespoon of canola oil until browned on both sides. Cover and simmer for 1 hour. Remove meat, add 1 tablespoon flour and brown in drippings. Add water and chicken bouillon for gravy.

A friend is a person who says nice things about you behind your back.

SWEET AND SOUR COUNTRY RIBS
(A slow cooker recipe)

3-4 pounds spare ribs, cut in serving size
salt and pepper
1 can pineapple chunks, undrained
2 -8 ounce cans tomato sauce
½ cup onions, sliced thin
½ cup green pepper, sliced thin
½ cup brown sugar, packed
¼ cup cider vinegar
¼ cup tomato paste
2 tablespoons Worcestershire sauce
1 garlic clove, minced
salt and pepper

Place ribs in slow cooker and season with salt and pepper. In a bowl combine remaining ingredients. Pour over ribs, cover and cook on low for 8 to 10 hours or until ribs are cooked through and tender. Serves 6 to 8.

"To reach our goal we must sail sometimes with the wind and sometimes against it. But we must sail and not drift, not lie at anchor.".........Oliver Wendell Holmes

216

BAKED SALMON STEAKS

3 salmon steaks
3 pats butter (1 tablespoon each)
garlic and onion powder
salt and pepper, to taste
½ cup Ritz crackers, crumbled
1 tablespoon fresh parsley, minced
lemon juice
lemon wedges

Spray a shallow sided aluminum baking pan with olive oil spray.
Place fish steaks on pan, each with a pat of butter on top.
Sprinkle evenly with garlic and onion powder and a pinch each
of salt and pepper. Crumble the crackers over the top of the fish.
Sprinkle with parsley. Broil (on the top rack), without turning,
until the edges of the fish are browned and the flesh is a whitish
pink (no longer clear) and it starts to look flaky when touched
with a fork. This will take about 10-15 minutes, depending on
your oven and the size of the fish steak. Squeeze lemon juice over
top before serving. Garnish with a sprig of fresh parsley and
lemon wedges.

*"The difference between the impossible and the possible
lies in a person's determination."......Tommy Lasorda,*

217

BAKED TROUT

2 fresh or thawed trout, each about 12 inches long
1 onion, sliced
pinch of curry powder
pinch of salt
pinch of cayenne pepper
1 tablespoon butter
1 lemon or lime, thinly sliced

Arrange washed trout on a cookie sheet. Place onion on top of trout and sprinkle with seasonings. Dot bits of butter on top of fish and arrange lemon or lime slices over that. Cover with foil and bake at 450° F. for 30 minutes.

SALMON or TUNA CASSEROLE

2 cups macaroni, cooked
1 -213 gram can tuna or salmon
1 -10 ounce can cream of mushroom soup
1 cup frozen peas
1 -10 ounce can mushrooms, stems and pieces, drained
½ cup of whole wheat cracker crumbs
Cook macaroni according to package instructions. Mix macaroni, salmon or tuna, soup, peas and mushrooms together. Put in a greased casserole. Put cracker crumbs on top and bake uncovered at 375° F. for 30 minutes.

CAESAR SALMON

4 -8 ounce salmon fillets

¼ cup creamy Caesar salad dressing

½ teaspoon pepper

1 cup garlic salad croutons, crushed

½ cup Parmesan cheese, grated

2 teaspoons dried basil

2 tablespoons canola oil

Place salmon in a greased 15 x 10 inch baking pan. Spoon salad dressing over the fillets and sprinkle with pepper. Combine the croutons, Parmesan cheese and basil; sprinkle over fillets and press into dressing. Drizzle with oil. Bake, uncovered, at 350° F. for 20 minutes or until fish is flaky and done. Makes 4 servings.

Some exercises for seniors

Jump on the band wagon
Run around in circles
Toot my own horn
Pull out all the stops
Add fuel to the fire
Open a can of worms
Put my foot in my mouth
Start the ball rolling

FISHERMAN'S PIE

1 ½ pounds white fish, any type
salt and pepper
2 ¼ cups milk, divided
½ cup butter
½ cup flour
110 grams shrimp
2 eggs, hardboiled and chopped
1 tablespoon capers, drained
3 tablespoons fresh parsley, chopped
1 tablespoon lemon juice
Topping:
2 pounds freshly cooked potatoes
¼ cup butter
¾ cup sour cream
pinch of nutmeg

Arrange fish in a baking pan and season well with salt and pepper.
Pour 1 cup milk over fish. Bake at 400° F. for 15-20 minutes.
Pour off and reserve the cooking liquid. Remove any bones and skin.
Flake into fairly large pieces. Melt butter in a saucepan, stir in flour,
gradually add the reserve liquid, stirring well after each addition. Add
the remaining milk and season again with salt and pepper. Add fish,
shrimp, hardboiled eggs, capers, and parsley. Stir in lemon juice.
Pour into a 4 litre buttered baking dish. Mash potatoes with butter
and sour cream, add nutmeg. Spread over fish mixture. Bake for
35-40 minutes or until heated through and brown.

GLAZED SALMON

1 salmon fillet, skin on
2 tablespoons olive oil
2 cloves garlic, minced
2 teaspoons lemon juice
2 tablespoons dried basil
2 teaspoons Dijon mustard
¼ teaspoon rosemary
¼ teaspoon thyme
¼ teaspoon parsley
¼ teaspoon lemon pepper
¼ teaspoon salt

Mix all ingredients except salmon in a blender, spread on the skinless side of salmon and allow to sit for at least ½ hour, covered in fridge. Place salmon, skin side down, on a lightly greased cookie sheet and bake at 400° F. until fish flakes with a fork (approximately 15-20 minutes).

"Motherhood has a very humanizing effect. Everything gets reduced to essentials.".......Meryl Streep

GRECIAN BAKED FISH
(Healthy and delicious)

2 pounds fish fillets
2 tablespoons lemon juice
1/3 teaspoon seasoning salt
2 tomatoes, diced
3 garlic cloves, minced
2 teaspoons crushed oregano
2 teaspoons olive oil
½ cup Feta cheese, crumbled

Preheat oven to 350° F. Lightly grease a 9 x 13 inch pan.
Place fillets in pan and sprinkle with lemon juice and seasoning
salt. Sprinkle with tomatoes, garlic and oregano. Drizzle olive
oil over the tomato topping. Top with crumbled Feta cheese.
Bake for 40 minutes, or until the fish flakes with a fork.
Serves four.

*"Your present circumstances don't determine where you can go;
they merely determine where you start."*...........*Nido Qubein*

"The future you see is the future you get."..........*Robert G. Allen*

MANICOTTI OVERBOARD

8-10 manicotti shells, uncooked
1 ½ tablespoons butter
1 garlic clove, minced
3 tablespoons flour
1 ½ cups 2% milk
1 -19 ounce can tomatoes, drained and chopped
1 cup Swiss cheese, shredded
1 tablespoon fresh dill, chopped or ¾ teaspoon dried dill
½ teaspoon red pepper flakes, crushed
¼ teaspoon salt
¼ teaspoon pepper
1 -10 ounce can crab meat or lump crabmeat, chopped
1 cup cottage cheese
½ -10 ounce package frozen spinach, thawed, drained &
chopped
2 tablespoons Parmesan cheese
1 egg white

Prepare manicotti to package directions but undercook slightly.
Rinse in cold water twice and drain very well. Melt butter, add
garlic and cook 1 minute. Mix flour and milk together until
smooth and add to garlic. Cook until thick (7 minutes). Stir in
tomatoes, ½ of the Swiss cheese, dill, red pepper flakes, salt,
and pepper. When cheese is melted, remove from heat.

Continued on next page........

MANICOTTI OVERBOARD continued....

Set aside. In bowl, combine crab, cottage cheese, spinach, and other ½ of the Swiss cheese, Parmesan cheese and egg white. Mix well. Spoon this filling into the manicotti shells and place in a 9 x 13 inch greased pan. Pour sauce evenly over top. Bake at 350° F. for 30 minutes. Serves 5-6.

Note: This also works well with shrimp or both shrimp and crab.

MAPLE GLAZED SALMON

4 salmon fillets
3 tablespoons maple syrup
2 tablespoons soya sauce
1 tablespoon fresh ginger, grated
1 ½ teaspoons cornstarch
1 tablespoon water
1 scallion, sliced thin
1 tablespoon sliced almonds, toasted (optional)

In a small bowl whisk together, maple syrup, soya sauce, ginger, cornstarch and water until smooth. Place fillets, skin side down, in shallow baking pan. Pour syrup mixture evenly over all. Bake uncovered at 450° F. for 15-18 minutes. Baste with glaze halfway through. Sprinkle with scallions and almonds before serving.   Serves 4.

PASTA WITH SHRIMP IN TOMATO CREAM

1/3 cup sun-dried tomatoes packed in oil
1 clove garlic, minced
1 pound medium-large raw shrimp
¼ cup green onions, thinly sliced
1 ½ tablespoons basil, chopped
¼ teaspoon white pepper
1 cup chicken broth
¾ cup dry vermouth
1 cup whipping cream
10 ounces linguine
Parmesan cheese

Drain tomatoes, reserving 2 tablespoons of the oil. Sliver tomatoes; set aside. Heat oil from tomatoes in a pan over medium-high heat. Add garlic and shrimp. Cook, until shrimp are opaque, about 5 minutes. Lift out and set aside. Cook pasta according to directions.

Place tomatoes, onions, basil, pepper, broth, vermouth and cream in pan. Bring to boil over high heat; boil, stirring occasionally, until reduced to about 1 ½ cups. Return shrimp to pan and stir until heated through. In a large pasta dish layer linguini and shrimp mixture; sprinkle with Parmesan. Serve immediately.

SALMON LOAF
(Salmon, so tasty they won't notice how nutritious it is!!)

2 eggs

1 cup milk

2 cups canned salmon, mashed

1 cup cracker or fine bread crumbs

2 teaspoons lemon juice

1 tablespoon fresh parsley or 1 teaspoon dried parsley

2 tablespoons onion, finely chopped

1 stalk celery, finely chopped

½ teaspoon salt

1/8 teaspoon pepper

In a medium bowl, beat eggs, add milk and salmon. Add crumbs, lemon juice, parsley, onion, celery, salt and pepper. Mix well. Pour into a greased loaf pan and bake for 1 hour at 350° F.

"A really strong woman accepts the war she went through and is ennobled by her scars."........*Carly Simon*

SALMON SKEWERS WITH SPICY THAI COCONUT SAUCE
(Not as spicy as the cook who served this!)

1 pound fresh salmon filet, not the tail section
fresh lime, cut into wedges

Sauce:
2 tablespoons ginger, finely grated
½ cup coconut milk
2 tablespoons soya sauce
2 tablespoons rice wine
2 teaspoons Asian chili sauce
1 teaspoon curry powder
¼ cup fresh cilantro sprigs

Skin and remove pin bones from salmon. Cut into ½ inch strips and weave on bamboo skewers and place in deep dish. Combine ginger, coconut milk, soya sauce, rice wine, chili sauce, and curry powder. Pour the coconut sauce over the salmon skewers and marinate for 15 minutes. Place skewers on a baking tray lined with foil or parchment paper. Bake at 350° F. for 10-15 minutes. Sprinkle on cilantro. Serve at once with lime wedges. Serves 4.

When you're too busy for friends....you're TOO busy!

227

SEA LOAF
(Rich in Vitamin D and omegas! Try these as sea burgers!)

1 -170 gram can tuna, drained
1 -213 gram can salmon, drained
1 green onion, minced
1 small stalk celery, finely chopped
½ red sweet pepper, finely chopped
2 teaspoons teriyaki sauce
¼ cup sweet pickle relish
¼ cup Miracle Whip
2 eggs, beaten
½ cup quick-cooking oatmeal
1/3 cup Cheddar cheese, grated

Mash fish with a fork in a medium bowl. Add onion, celery, red pepper, teriyaki sauce, relish, Miracle Whip, eggs and oatmeal. Mix well. Pack mixture into a sprayed loaf pan. Sprinkle cheese evenly over top. Bake at 325° F. for 40 minutes. Let sit for 10 minutes, serve in slices.

For <u>Sea Burgers</u>: Divide mixture evenly into 8 portions, form into plump patties. Pan fry in a sprayed frying pan until golden, turning once. Serve in burger buns or pita bread.

Friends are like wine, they get better with age.

SHRIMP AND SAUSAGE PENNE

1 -16 ounce package penne pasta
1 pound bulk mild Italian sausage
½ cup onion, chopped
1 ½ teaspoons garlic, minced
½ teaspoon crushed red pepper flakes
2 -14 ounce cans Italian stewed tomatoes, drained and chopped
1 ½ cups heavy whipping cream
½ teaspoon salt
¼ teaspoon dried basil
½ pound shrimp, cooked, peeled and deveined
1 cup Parmesan cheese, shredded

Cook pasta according to package directions. In a large pot, cook sausage, onion, garlic and pepper flakes over medium heat for 4-5 minutes or until meat is done; drain. Stir in the tomatoes, cream, salt and basil. Bring to a boil over medium heat. Reduce heat; simmer, uncovered, for 6-8 minutes or until thickened, stirring occasionally. Add shrimp and cook for 1 more minute. Drain pasta; toss with sauce. Sprinkle with Parmesan.

"Worry is as useless as a handle on a snowball."
Mitzi Chandler

229

SPICY SHRIMP WITH ASPARAGUS

1/3 cup freshly squeezed orange juice
2 tablespoons oyster sauce
2 tablespoons hoisin sauce
1 tablespoon sesame oil
2 teaspoons cornstarch
2 teaspoons Asian chili sauce

1 pound raw shrimp, shelled and deveined
6 stalks fresh asparagus
3 cloves garlic, finely minced
3 tablespoons canola oil

Combine orange juice, oyster sauce, hoisin sauce, sesame oil, cornstarch, and chili sauce. Stir well and set aside. Split shrimp in half. Set aside. Snap off and throw away tough asparagus stems and cut diagonally into 1 inch lengths. Place wok or sauté pan over highest heat, when hot add half the cooking oil. Stir in shrimp and toss until orange, transfer to plate. Return wok to high heat and a bit more oil; stir fry asparagus and garlic until it brightens. Pour in orange mixture, add shrimp and stir until the sauce glazes the food. Serve at once with rice. Serves 2-4.

LEMON DILL SAUCE on FISH
(Grilled or barbecued fish is good with this sauce
lathered on it. Cod is an excellent choice.)

2 tablespoons butter
1 ½ tablespoons flour
2 cups milk or creamilk
2 ½ tablespoons lemon juice
1 teaspoon dill, dried or 1 tablespoon fresh dill, chopped fine
¼ teaspoon salt
1/8 teaspoon pepper

In skillet, over medium heat, melt butter, add flour. Mix well
until combined. Gradually add milk whipping gently with a fork
until it is the consistency of sauce. Add lemon juice, dill, salt and
pepper. Mix well. Pour over baked or grilled fish.

*"The most important trip you may take in life is
meeting people halfway."......Henry Boye*

*"Hope perches in the soul and sings the tune without
the words and never stops at all."......Aristotle*

MEAT MARINADES

Chili Garlic Marinade
¼ cup Worcestershire Sauce
2 tablespoons olive oil
2 teaspoons chili powder
2 teaspoons garlic, crushed

Red Wine Marinade
2 tablespoons olive oil
6 tablespoons red wine
1 clove garlic, chopped
1 teaspoon brown sugar
2 teaspoons Worcestershire Sauce
dash of black pepper

Herb Marinade
2 tablespoons olive oil
4 tablespoons lemon juice
2 teaspoons Worcestershire Sauce
1 clove garlic, crushed
1 onion, finely sliced
½ teaspoon each: thyme, marjoram and parsley

Pour combined ingredients over meat in a sealable plastic bag or covered container. Let sit in refrigerator for 1 to 24 hours.
Brush marinade on meat, grill as usual, discard the rest.

Keeping Abreast

There is some good news in Breast Cancer statistics.

Breast cancer is one of the most feared diseases of all women. In 2007, an estimated 22,300 Canadian women will be diagnosed with breast cancer. However, many women are alive and well today because their breast cancer was detected and treated early.

The breast cancer death rate is declining significantly and more women are surviving longer, according to a special report in _Canadian Cancer Statistics 2007_ The declining death rate is due to more and better screening, as well as more effective treatments.

According to the report, the age-standardized death rate for breast cancer for Canadian women has fallen 25 per cent since 1986. The five-year relative survival rate is 86 percent. Better quality mammography and increased participation in organized breast screening programs (by women aged 50-69 in particular) have led to more breast cancers being detected earlier, which means successful treatment is more likely.

The breast cancer special report identifies four key ways to ensure progress continues against this disease so that fewer women are diagnosed with the disease and fewer die from it:

-Through research identify additional modifiable risk factors for breast cancer, such as occupational and environmental exposure, and vitamin D;

-Increase research to identify further genetic factors so that women at high risk can take appropriate actions;

-Increase participation in organized breast screening programs among women aged 50-69 by developing more effective methods for recruitment and retention;

-Continue to use the best treatment options, and develop and test new treatments.

Although not a screening method, something you can do on your own is to be breast aware. Being breast aware means knowing how your breasts normally look and feel. That way, if there are any significant changes, you'll be more likely to notice them and can have them checked by a doctor. 75% of all breast growths, whether malignant or benign are discovered during breast self examination. 9 out of 10 growths are detected by women themselves

Although breast cancer is primarily a women's disease and our book is dedicated to Women of Strength, We have to remember that male incidence of breast cancer accounts for 2% of all cases. In 2005 an estimated 150 men in Canada will be diagnosed with breast cancer and 45 of them will die from it.

.....Facts and Statistics from Canadian Cancer Society, 2007

Vegetables and Side Dishes

A strong woman can tell you what she expects of you, but a woman of strength awakens your own expectations.

AWESOME APPLESAUCE

12 apples, peeled, cored, and diced
½ cup raisins
½ cup water
1 teaspoon cinnamon

In a 4 litre saucepan, combine the apples, raisins, and water. Cover and cook over low heat for 30 minutes, adding more water as needed to maintain desired thickness and to avoid sticking. Stir frequently. Remove from the heat and blend in a food processor until smooth. Add cinnamon once blended.

CELEBRATION CRANBERRY SAUCE
(A new twist on cranberries, to go with that turkey, delicious!)

1 teaspoon cornstarch
1 ½ cups sugar
½ cup water
3 cups fresh or frozen cranberries
1 medium orange, peeled and sectioned
1 teaspoon orange zest

Combine cornstarch, sugar and water in medium saucepan, stir until dissolved. Add cranberries, orange sections, and orange zest, bring to a boil, stirring constantly over medium heat. Reduce heat and simmer, stirring often until cranberry skins begin to pop and mixture begins to thicken (about 5 minutes). Set aside to cool. Cover and chill at least 3 hours.

BEANS, SUMPTUOUS and SLOW COOKED
(Plump full of protein, and perfectly delicious!)

8 bacon strips, diced
2 medium onions, halved and thinly sliced
1 cup brown sugar, packed
½ cup vinegar
1 teaspoon salt
1 teaspoon dry mustard powder
½ teaspoon garlic powder
1 -28 ounce can baked beans, undrained
1 -16 ounce can kidney beans, drained and rinsed
1 -28 ounce can chick peas, drained
1 -16 ounce can lima beans, drained

In a large skillet, cook bacon until crisp. Remove to paper towels. Drain and reserve 2 tablespoons bacon drippings. In the drippings, fry onions until tender, add brown sugar, vinegar, salt, mustard, and garlic powder. Bring to a boil. In a slow cooker gently combine beans and peas, add onion mixture and bacon, mix well. Cover and cook on high for 3-4 hours. Serves 15-20.

"The hardest arithmetic to master is that which enables us to count our blessings." .....*Eric Hoffer*

Shown on previous page:

❖ Copper Pennies.....page 244

❖ Awesome Applesauce.....page 235

❖ Spaghetti Squash Casserole.....page 266

❖ Stuffed Tomatoes.....page 269

BEAN WRAPS
(The colored wraps look great on a platter.)

1 large onion, chopped
3 cloves garlic, minced
1 tablespoon olive oil
1 -19 ounce can kidney beans, rinsed
1 -19 ounce can black beans, rinsed
1 teaspoon salt
1 teaspoon pepper
1 tablespoon brown sugar
1 ¼ cups salsa (medium or hot)
½ cup water
1 green pepper, chopped
1 tomato, chopped
3 green onions, chopped
2 cups Cheddar cheese, grated
12 tortilla wraps (spinach, tomato, plain)

Cook onion and garlic in olive oil. Add beans, salt and pepper. Cover and cook for 5 minutes on medium heat. Add brown sugar, ¼ cup of the salsa and water. Cook 5 more minutes; mash with potato masher. Lay out 12 wraps. Place 3 tablespoons of bean mixture closer to the edge of wrap. Add vegetables, 1 tablespoon salsa, and handful of cheese to each wrap and roll up. Line a baking sheet with tinfoil, spray with oil. Place wraps, seam side down, cover with tinfoil and bake at 350° F. for 20 minutes. Turn wraps over and bake another 10 minutes, uncovered. Serve with sour cream. Freezes well.

BEET LEAF ROLLS
(Something to do with beet leaves... and is so delicious!)

1 onion, chopped fine (set aside ¼ cup)

½ cup margarine

2 cups water

1 teaspoon salt

1 cup rice

½ cup chopped fresh or frozen dill

dash pepper

3 to 4 dozen beet leaves

1 cup cream

Sauté ¾ cup onions in margarine. Bring water and salt to a boil. Add rice, sautéed onion and 2 tablespoons dill. Turn heat to low, cover tightly and simmer for approximately 15 minutes. Cool.

Choose young fresh beet leaves. Wash well. Wilt the leaves in the microwave for 1 minute or in hot water. Place a spoonful of rice mixture onto each beet leaf, roll and tuck in ends. Place rolls in layers into a greased casserole dish. Sprinkle each layer with remaining ¼ cup onion and dill. Pour cream over the beet leaf rolls. Cover. Bake in 300 ° F. oven for 45 minutes. Beet Leaf Rolls may be made ahead, frozen separately on cookie sheets and then placed in zip lock bags for a delicious side dish to be served at a later date.

BROWN RICE ALMONDINE

1 medium onion, chopped
2 tablespoons canola oil
2 ½ cups water
1 ½ tablespoons chicken bouillon
1 tablespoon lemon juice
1 ½ cups brown rice
½ teaspoon dill
1 cup frozen green beans
2 tablespoons almonds, sliced and toasted

Place all the ingredients except beans and almonds in a 3 quart baking dish. Bake at 350° F. for 1 hour. Take out of oven and mix in green beans and sprinkle almonds on top. Place back in oven for another 15 minutes or until beans are done.

BAKED RICE

3 ½ cups water
2 cups rice, uncooked
1 -10 ounce can sliced mushrooms, undrained
4 tablespoons soya sauce
¼ cup canola oil
1 package dry onion soup mix.

Put water in a large, greased casserole dish. Add remaining ingredients and stir. Bake at 350° F. for 1 ½ hours in a uncovered casserole. Serves 8.

CARROTS AND SPROUTS ALMONDINE

10 ounces fresh or frozen Brussels sprouts
2 cups carrots, sliced diagonally
¼ cup butter or margarine
1/3 cup slivered almonds, roasted
2 teaspoons lemon juice

Cook sprouts and carrots together in boiling salted water 10-15 minutes, just until tender. Drain, turn into serving dish and keep warm. (If using frozen sprouts, cook as directed on package.) Heat butter until bubbly, add roasted almond slivers and continue heating until butter is golden brown. Remove from heat, stir in lemon juice and pour over vegetables. Serve at once. Makes 4-6 servings.

<u>Note</u>: To roast almonds, spread in single layer in pan. Place in 350° F. oven and leave about 10 minutes. Remove when they start browning. They turn a little darker once out of the oven.

"When one door of happiness closes, another opens; but often we look so long at the closed door, that we do not see the one which has been opened for us"....Helen Keller

"I know God doesn't give me more to bear than I can handle.....but sometimes I wish he didn't trust me so much." ...Mother Theresa

CAULIFLOWER AND BROCCOLI WITH LEMON CHEESE SAUCE

¾ pounds broccoli
¾ pounds cauliflower
Cut broccoli and cauliflower into small florets. Cook in boiling salted water for approximately 5 minutes and drain.

LEMON CHEESE SAUCE

½ cup milk
½ -250 gram package cream cheese, cubed
½ teaspoon lemon peel, grated
1 teaspoon lemon juice
¼ teaspoon ginger, ground
1/8 teaspoon salt

Heat milk in small saucepan until hot. Add cream cheese and cook on low heat, stirring until melted and smooth. Stir in lemon juice, ginger and salt. Pour over the broccoli and cauliflower.

"Life expectancy would grow by leaps and bounds if green vegetables smelled as good as bacon."......Doug Larson

CHEESY GREEN BEAN BAKE

½ cup onion, chopped
1 tablespoon margarine
2 tablespoons flour
2 cups sour cream
4 cups green beans
1 cup Cheddar cheese, shredded
Brown onions in margarine and sprinkle flour into mixture. Add sour cream and mix well. Place beans in a 1 ½ quart lightly greased, uncovered baking dish and pour liquid mixture over beans. Sprinkle cheese on top and bake at 350° F. for 20 minutes or until beans are done.

TURNIP BAKE

2 turnips, peeled and diced
1 cup applesauce or 2 fresh apples, peeled and diced
4 teaspoons sugar
1 teaspoon salt
2 eggs, beaten
1 ¾ cup bread crumbs, reserve ½ for topping
6 tablespoons butter, melted
Cook turnip and fresh apple until tender. Mash and add applesauce (if using), sugar, salt and ½ bread crumbs, and eggs. Pour into a 2 quart casserole dish. Mix butter and remaining crumbs and pour over top of turnip mixture. Bake at 350° F. for 30-35 minutes.

CLASSIC ITALIAN RISOTTO
(This dish is worth the extra effort in preparation)

4 cups stock (chicken, fish or vegetable)
1 tablespoon butter
2 tablespoons olive oil
1 large onion, finely chopped
2 cloves garlic, minced
1 stalk celery, chopped
2 cups rice, Arborio (or another Italian rice)
¾ cup dry vermouth or dry white wine
salt and pepper to taste
4 tablespoons butter
½ cup Parmesan cheese, grated

Heat stock. In separate pan, heat olive oil and butter, add onions, garlic and celery and fry for about 15 minutes. Add rice and turn up the heat. Slightly fry rice until it is slightly translucent. Add vermouth or wine and keep stirring. Once wine has cooked into the rice, add your first ladle of stock and some salt and keep stirring. Turn down heat and keep adding ladlefuls of stock, and keep stirring. Stir for about 15 minutes. Add rest of stock until rice is cooked. Add more salt and pepper to taste. Remove from heat and add butter and Parmesan. Stir well. Place lid on pot and allow to sit for 2 minutes. This will make the rice creamy.

COPPER PENNIES

2 pounds carrots, sliced
1 cup tomato sauce
¼ cup margarine, melted
1/8 teaspoon salt
1/8 teaspoon pepper
½ teaspoon dry mustard
1 green pepper, sliced thin
1 cup sugar
½ cup vinegar
½ teaspoon Worcestershire sauce
1 medium onion, diced

Cook carrots until tender and drain. In a saucepan, combine remaining ingredients and cook 5 minutes over medium heat. Pour over carrots. This dish can be served hot or cold, as a vegetable side dish.

The trouble with being punctual is that
nobody's there to appreciate it.

Mammography Machine: the only known equipment
that can make a cup into a saucer.

CORN CASSEROLE

1 medium onion, chopped
1 tablespoon butter
1 -15 ounce can creamed corn
1 -15 ounce can whole kernel corn, drained
1 cup sour cream
2 eggs
½ cup butter, melted
1 -8 ounce package corn muffin mix (Jiffy is a good one)
1 cup Cheddar cheese, grated

Preheat oven to 350° F. In a medium pan, sauté onion in butter. Grease a 9 x 13 inch baking dish. Mix together onions, corn, sour cream, eggs, and melted butter. Mix in muffin mix. Pour into greased baking dish. Bake, uncovered for 35 minutes, sprinkle with cheese and bake another 5-10 minutes, or until a knife inserted midway into pan comes out clean.

"If you haven't got charity in your heart you've got the worst kind of heart trouble." ..... Bob Hope

"The heart ages last."...Sylvester Stallone

CREAMY POTATOES

4 large potatoes, peeled and sliced
½ cup onions, diced
½ cup milk
¼ cup cream cheese, softened
2 tablespoons margarine, softened
½ cup Cheddar cheese, shredded
1 teaspoon paprika

Boil potatoes, drain and place in a shallow 2 quart greased baking dish. Mix onions, milk, cream cheese, and margarine and pour over potatoes. Top with Cheddar cheese and paprika. Bake at 350° F. for 25 minutes. Serve hot.

EASY POTATOES

10 medium potatoes, cut into one inch cubes
½ cup margarine, melted
1 large onion, sliced
1 package onion soup mix
Mix all ingredients in a 2 quart lightly greased baking dish and bake at 350° F. for 45 minutes.

By the time you make ends meet, they move the ends.

CREAMY SCALLOPED POTATOES
(This recipe never boils over, and is a great side dish with pork.)

5 pounds potatoes, thinly sliced
1 large onion, chopped
1 -10 ounce can mushroom soup
1 pint whipping cream
½ teaspoon salt
¼ teaspoon pepper
¾ cup Cheddar cheese, grated

Spray large casserole dish with non stick cooking spray. Mix all ingredients together and bake uncovered at 350° F. for 1 hour. Note: You can substitute the whipping cream with 4 cups milk, 2 tablespoons flour and 2 tablespoons margarine. If using milk bake at 300° F. for 2 hours, so milk doesn't curdle.

OVEN-BAKED FRIES
(Children love these dipped in ketchup!)
potatoes, washed and cut into fries or wedges
¼ cup canola oil
½ teaspoon seasoning salt

Place potatoes on a large cookie sheet. Pour oil over fries and toss. Sprinkle seasoning salt over, and place in 400° F. oven for about 30 minutes, or until done.

FRIED GREEN TOMATOES
(These taste best when you are watching this great movie!)

fresh green tomatoes, washed, sliced in ¼ inch slices
salt
1 cup flour
1 teaspoon seasoning salt or
1 teaspoon salt and pepper
4 tablespoons canola oil

After slicing tomatoes sprinkle with a bit of salt and place at room temperature or in fridge to eliminate extra liquid from tomatoes. After about 6 hours blot tomatoes on paper towel. Mix flour and seasoning salt and coat each tomato slice with mixture. Let sit an additional 30 minutes. Coat again and place in skillet with oil and fry on medium heat until each side is golden brown. Serve immediately.

One evening a Cherokee told his grandson about
a battle that goes on inside people.
He said, "My son, the battle is between 2 wolves inside of us all.
One is Evil. It is anger, envy, jealousy, sorrow, regret, greed,
arrogance, self-pity, guilt, resentment, inferiority, lies, false pride,
superiority, and ego. The other is Good. It is joy, peace, love, hope,
serenity, humility, kindness, benevolence, empathy, generosity,
truth, compassion and faith." The grandson thought about it for a
minute and then asked his grandfather: "Which wolf wins?"
The Cherokee simply replied, "The one you feed."
Author Unknown

HOMEMADE CREAMED VEGETABLES
(There is nothing like home-creamed vegetables and so,
after consulting with grandmas who are great cooks,
we have some recipes to share.)

CREAMED CORN

1 can niblets corn, undrained
1 tablespoon cornstarch, dissolved in 1 tablespoon water
1/3 cup heavy cream (or coffee cream to make a lighter version)

In medium saucepan, over medium heat, bring corn to a boil.
Mix cornstarch and cream until smooth and add slowly to corn.
Bring mixture back to a boil. Makes four servings.

CREAMED PEAS OR CARROTS
(Or peas and carrots together if you wish.)

2 tablespoons onion, minced
2 tablespoons butter
1 cup carrots, sliced
½ cup heavy cream
1 tablespoon sour cream

Sauté onions in butter. Cook carrots in a pot of boiling water
until tender. Drain off the liquid. Add sautéed onion. Mix cream
and sour cream and pour over carrots. Simmer until cream
thickens. Enjoy!

LEMON RISOTTO

1 tablespoon canola oil

1 ½ cups fresh mushrooms, sliced

2 shallots, thinly sliced

2 garlic cloves, minced

pepper to taste

1 cup short grain rice

2 cups chicken broth

½ cup water

1 large carrot, cut into matchstick slices

1 bunch asparagus spears, chopped

¼ cup Parmesan cheese

2 teaspoons grated lemon zest

In a large saucepan, heat oil and cook mushrooms, shallots, garlic and pepper until vegetables are tender. Add rice and cook and stir 2 minutes more. Stir broth and water into rice mixture and bring to a boil. Reduce heat, cover and simmer for 30 minutes ensuring not to lift cover. Remove from heat. Stir in carrots, asparagus, cheese, and lemon zest. Cover and let stand for 5 minutes. Add additional water if necessary for desired consistency. Serves 8.

"When you get cancer, it's really time to look at what your life was and is, and I decided that everything I've done so far is not as important as what I'm going to do now."... Herbie Mann

NEW POTATOES IN CREAM
(There is no better fare — than new potatoes cooked in cream!)

2 pounds small early potatoes, skinned* (or 8 medium)
6 carrots, quartered (optional)
1 medium onion, whole
1 tablespoon dill weed (if you have fresh dill from the garden just add 2 or 3 sprigs to the pot)
2 cups cream
3 tablespoons white vinegar (or more to taste)
½ teaspoon salt

In large heavy saucepan place potatoes, carrots, onion and dill. Add cream, vinegar and salt. Bring to a boil over medium high heat and then turn heat down to medium low — just enough to keep cream simmering. Watch carefully so cream does not boil over. Cook until fork tender, about 30-35 minutes. Remove onion and dill sprigs. Serve potatoes and cream in a bowl with a ladle so sauce can be served with potatoes.
*There is no need to peel new potatoes as the peeling will just rub off or can be easily scraped off with a knife.

You ain't gonna learn nothing with your mouth open.

ORIENTAL RICE
(Wonderful as a side dish, especially with fish.)

1 small onion, finely chopped
1 celery rib, diced
2 tablespoons canola oil
1/8 teaspoon cinnamon
1/8 teaspoon cardamom
1/8 teaspoon turmeric
¾ teaspoon salt
1 cup Basmati rice, rinsed well and drained
1 -14 ounce can light coconut milk
1/8 cup water

Sauté onion and celery in oil in a large saucepan until soft.
Add cinnamon, cardamom, turmeric and salt. Stir.
Add rice to onion mixture. Heat and stir on medium heat for
about 2 minutes until rice is well coated and turning golden. Add
coconut milk and water. Heat and stir until boiling. Reduce heat
to low. Cover. Simmer for about 20 minutes, without lifting the
lid, until liquid is absorbed and rice is tender. Makes about 4
cups.

"A leader is one who knows the way, goes the way, and shows the way." .....John C. Maxwell

ORZO RICE PILAF

¼ cup butter
½ cup uncooked long-grain rice
¼ cup uncooked orzo pasta
½ cup fresh mushrooms, sliced
½ cup onion, chopped
¼ cup celery, finely chopped
2 cups chicken broth
2 tablespoons fresh parsley, chopped
¼ teaspoon dried marjoram
¼ teaspoon ground black pepper
½ cup pine nuts, chopped and toasted

In a large skillet over medium-low heat melt butter, and sauté
rice, orzo, mushrooms, onion, and celery. Stir constantly until
rice is lightly browned. Add chicken broth, parsley, marjoram,
pepper, and pine nuts. Bring to a boil, then reduce heat to low,
cover skillet, and allow to simmer 15 minutes. Remove from heat
and let stand 10 minutes before serving.

*"The function of leadership is to produce more leaders,
not more followers."* ......*Ralph Nader*

PASTA VEGETABLE SCRAMBLE

½ cup zucchini, thinly sliced

2/3 cup green onions with tops, chopped

1/3 cup red bell pepper, julienned

2 eggs

4 egg whites

2 tablespoons Parmesan cheese, grated

1 tablespoon garlic salt

¾ cup Italian seasoning

1/8 teaspoon red pepper, ground

4 ounces fettuccini, cooked and drained

4 cherry tomatoes, halved

Spray a 10 inch skillet with nonstick cooking spray. Add zucchini, green onions and red pepper. Cook covered, over medium heat for 3 minutes. Beat eggs, egg whites, cheese, garlic salt, Italian seasoning and red pepper in a bowl until smooth. Pour over vegetables. Add pasta and tomatoes. Cook until the egg mixture begins to set, gently turning with a spatula. Continue cooking until egg mixture is thickened, but still moist. Stir occasionally.

Laugh as much as you breathe and love as long as you live.
Laughter is the shock absorber that eases the blows of life.

PERFECT STEAMED RICE
(When more rice is required, simply add same proportional amount of water.)

1 cup long grain rice
1 ½ cups water

Wash rice by rubbing it between palms of hands. Drain all water. Place rice in saucepan; add water. (Any temperature of water can be used.) (Do not add salt or butter to cook rice as it will destroy the sweet flavour of good steamed rice.) Cook rice over high heat, uncovered, until tiny holes or craters form over the surface of the rice. Turn heat to low and cover tightly with a lid. Simmer rice for 15-20 minutes. Do not take lid off until time is up. This is the most critical time, as the rice is steam-cooked under pressure. When done, stir and serve.
Yields 3 cups.

Note: Try to cook rice ahead of time if you need cooked rice for frying. Fluff up the cooked rice before refrigerating. This makes it easier to handle and improves the final result giving it a more professional appearance.

"To say my fate is not tied to your fate is like saying, 'your end of the boat is sinking'." ...Hugh Downs

POTATO PUFFS

(These make a great side dish at a fondue. Dipped in a sweet and sour sauce, ranch dressing, or ketchup, they're appealing to your palette, as a snack. Use up those leftover potatoes!)

½ cup flour
1 teaspoon baking powder
¼ teaspoon salt
1 cup mashed potatoes, room temperature
1 egg, slightly beaten
1 teaspoon dried parsley
canola oil for deep frying

In bowl, combine flour, baking powder and salt. Add and mix in mashed potatoes. (If potatoes are not soft, add a little hot milk or water and beat.) Stir in egg and parsley. Drop by spoonfuls into deep oil heated to 365° F. Fry to a golden brown. Drain on paper toweling. Serves 3-4. These also freeze well.

Forcing positive thoughts drives away our negatives. We can't think two opposite thoughts at the same time. By changing our thoughts, you change your attitude and your feeling. Even the Bible says: Let the weak say I am strong.

RED CABBAGE
(An Austrian dish served with roast beef, turkey or wild game.)

1 medium head red cabbage, sliced
1 medium sweet onion, sliced
2 large apples, peeled and quartered
1 tablespoon bacon fat
1 teaspoon salt
½ cup sugar
1 ½ cups water
1 cup vinegar
1 bay leaf
6 peppercorns

2 teaspoons cornstarch, dissolved in ¼ cup water

In large sauce-pan combine, red cabbage, onion, apples, bacon fat, salt, sugar, water, vinegar, bay leaf and peppercorns. Cover and simmer for 1 ½ hours. Add cornstarch to thicken. Remove bay leaf and peppercorns before serving. Serves 12 or more.

"A man who has committed a mistake and doesn't correct it, is committing another mistake." ..... *Confucius*

RICE CABBAGE ROLLS IN TOMATO SAUCE

(A traditional dish that seems time consuming, but well worth the work. The method may be done in stages.)

1 medium onion, finely chopped

½ cup canola oil

4 cups boiling water

1 teaspoon salt

2 cups white rice

½ teaspoon pepper

1 medium sized cabbage

¼ cup vinegar

1 medium onion, chopped finely

¼ cup canola oil

¾ cup tomato juice

1 cup tomato soup with ¼ cup water

Sauté onion in canola oil. Combine water, salt and rice in a saucepan; bring to a boil. Add sautéed onions and pepper. Turn heat to low and cover tightly. Simmer for 20 minutes; cool. Rice must be completely cooked. Remove core from cabbage. Place cabbage in boiling water with vinegar added. Be sure cabbage is completely covered with boiling water. Simmer the cabbage long enough for the leaves to become limp and be easily removed from the head of cabbage. Do not overcook. Remove the leaves from the water; remove the hard center part of each leaf. The cabbage leaves are now ready to use.

Continued on next page . . . .

RICE CABBAGE ROLLS IN TOMATO SAUCE,
continued.......

Add 1 tablespoon of the rice mixture to each cabbage leaf, cut to size and roll tightly. Place the cabbage rolls in a medium sized roaster lined with greased foil. (It is easier to spoon out cabbage rolls if each layer is placed in an opposite direction.)
Turn oven on to 350° F. In a separate pan, sauté onion in canola oil, add; tomato juice, tomato soup and water, mix well. Pour tomato mixture over cabbage rolls.
Foil wrap may be placed on the top to prevent scorching. Half a cup of water may be added to the bottom of the roaster to help steam the cabbage rolls and prevent burning. Bake for 1 ½ - 2 hours or until cabbage leaves are tender when tested with a fork.

My boy", said a father to his son, "treat everybody with politeness, even those who are rude to you; remember, you show courtesy to others, not because they are gentlemen, but because you are one. "

"Science has never drummed up quite as an effective a tranquilizing agent as a sunny spring day."......Earl Hall

ROASTED BUTTERNUT SQUASH & SAGE RISOTTO WITH PINE NUTS
(Having 3 helpings is not uncommon-Yummy!)

1 large butternut squash

2 garlic cloves, chopped

2 tablespoons olive oil, plus extra for drizzling

15 sage leaves, chopped

sea salt and pepper, to taste

3 tablespoons butter

1 large onion, chopped

1 ¾ cups Arborio rice

2 cups white wine

1 litre hot chicken or vegetable stock

¼ cup Parmesan cheese

¼ cup pine nuts

Cut butternut squash into 6-8 wedges; remove seeds and place in a roasting tray. Mix together the garlic, 1 tablespoon olive oil, ½ the sage leaves, sea salt and pepper. Tip into the tray and rub over squash with your hands. Roast at 400° F. for 40-50 minutes until softened and golden in colour. Cool slightly. Scrape the soft flesh into a bowl. Lightly mash with a fork until it is chunky in texture. Scrape any sticky juices left in tray into the bowl and keep warm while making the risotto.

Continued on next page.......

ROASTED BUTTERNUT SQUASH continued....

Heat 1 tablespoon olive oil and 1 tablespoon butter in deep sauté pan. Gently fry the onion until softened. Add rice and stir until the grains are coated with the oil and butter. Pour in the wine and stir continuously until it has cooked into the rice. Add a cup of the stock, remaining sage, salt and pepper. Turn heat down so the stock is simmering gently. Keep adding cups of stock as it cooks into the rice, stirring and moving the rice around pan for 15-20 minutes. Texture should be thick and creamy. Add extra stock if necessary. Remove pan from heat and gently stir in the roasted butternut squash, Parmesan, remaining butter and seasonings to taste. Add any extra stock if the risotto seems particularly thick. Cover with lid for a couple of minutes, this will give the risotto an even creamier texture. During this time, place pine nuts in a fairly hot frying pan and toss until golden. Spoon risotto into warmed bowls and scatter pine nuts and extra Parmesan.

"Our limitations and success will be based, most often, on your own expectations for ourselves. What the mind dwells upon the body acts upon."........*Dennis Waitley*

Rumor is one thing that gets thicker as you spread it.

ROASTED CAULIFLOWER AND GARLIC
(This works great with broccoli too.)

2 tablespoons garlic, minced
3 tablespoons canola oil
1 large head cauliflower, separated into florets
1/3 cup Parmesan cheese, grated
salt and black pepper to taste
1 tablespoon fresh parsley, chopped

Preheat the oven to 400° F. Grease a large casserole dish. Place the oil and garlic in a large bowl or plastic bag. Add cauliflower, and stir or shake to coat. Pour into the prepared casserole dish. Bake for 25 minutes, stirring halfway through. Top with cheese, salt, pepper and parsley, and broil for 3-5 minutes, until golden brown.

A quarrel is like buttermilk, once it's out of the churn, the more you shake it, the more sour it grows. Irish Proverb

"Fear defeats more people than any other one thing in the world."
....Ralph Aldo Emerson

ROASTED YAMS AND POTATOES

2 yams, peeled and sliced
4 large potatoes, cut into chunks
2 large carrots, peeled and sliced
2 bell peppers, 1 green, 1 red, cut into large chunks
1 lemon, cut into wedges
olive oil
fresh rosemary, chopped
salt and pepper

In a roasting pan, place yams, potatoes, carrots and rosemary.
Sprinkle with salt and pepper, drizzle with olive oil. Cook for
30 minutes uncovered at 350° F. Check doneness of potatoes
and yams - if close to being cooked, add peppers and lemons to
pan. Continue to cook for 15 minutes. Serve immediately.

Note: if you have some leftovers, be sure to remove the lemon
wedges and discard before placing in fridge — it will all taste like
lemons by the morning.

Good, to forgive; Best, to forget.

A conclusion is simply the place where you got tired of thinking.

ROMANO RICE
(A must try, delicious!)

1 ¾ cups chicken broth
1 tablespoon Italian seasoning
¾ cup uncooked regular long grain rice
1 cup spinach, chopped
½ cup Parmesan cheese

Heat broth in a 2 quart saucepan over medium to high heat, to a boil. Add seasoning. Stir in the rice. Reduce heat to low, cover the saucepan and cook for 20 minutes, or until rice is tender and most of the liquid is absorbed. Add spinach. Stir in cheese before serving.

COCONUT RICE

1 cup rice
1 -400 ml can coconut milk
1 cup water
Place all ingredients in pot. Bring to boil. Cover. Simmer for about 18 minutes or until rice is cooked.
This recipe goes well with Spicy Peanut Chicken.

Friends may come and friends may go, but enemies accumulate.

A SIDE OF STUFFING

(This makes a great complement for any meat dish or can be used to stuff pork chops, chicken breasts, or actually use as stuffing for a chicken or turkey.)

½ pound bulk Italian sausage, crumbled
¼ cup butter or margarine
½ pound fresh mushrooms, sliced
¾ cup celery, chopped
1 medium onion, chopped
1 teaspoon poultry seasoning
½ teaspoon salt
¼ teaspoon pepper
6 cups unseasoned croutons or dry bread cubes
2 ½ cups chicken broth

In a large skillet, brown sausage; drain. Add to the brown sausage, butter, mushrooms, celery and onion; sauté 2-3 minutes or until onion is tender. Stir in poultry seasoning, salt and pepper. Transfer to a large bowl; add croutons and enough broth to moisten. Place in a greased 2 quart baking dish. Cover and bake at 350° F. for 30 minutes. Remove cover and bake another 10 minutes.

I look within to find my treasures.

"Mammograms are really a sort of gift. You can either catch something early or count your lucky stars because nothing was discovered. Either way you are ahead of the game."....Charlotte Ross

SPAGHETTI SQUASH CASSEROLE

1 medium spaghetti squash
1 cup water
1 tablespoon butter or margarine
1 medium onion, chopped (about 1 cup)
2 garlic cloves, minced
½ pound fresh mushrooms, sliced
1 teaspoon dried basil
½ teaspoon oregano
½ teaspoon salt
¼ teaspoon thyme
¼ teaspoon pepper
2 fresh tomatoes, diced
1 cup cottage cheese
½ cup Mozzarella cheese, shredded
¼ cup parsley, finely chopped
1 cup dry bread crumbs
¼ cup Parmesan cheese

Slice squash in ½ lengthwise; scoop out seeds. Place squash, cut side down in a baking dish. Add water and cover tightly with foil. Bake at 375° F. for 20-30 minutes or until easily pierced with at fork.

Continued on next page...........

266

SPAGHETTI SQUASH continued......

Meanwhile, melt butter in skillet. Add onion, garlic, mushrooms, herbs and seasonings; sauté until onion is transparent. Add tomatoes; cook until most of the liquid has evaporated. Set aside.

Scoop out squash, separating strands with a fork. Combine squash, tomato mixture and all remaining ingredients, except Parmesan cheese. Pour into a greased 2 quart casserole. Sprinkle with Parmesan cheese. Bake, uncovered at 375° F. for 40 minutes or until heated through and top is golden brown. Serves 6.

CORN PUDDING

2 tablespoons flour
2 tablespoons canola oil
1 tablespoon corn meal
2 cans corn
2 eggs, beaten
1 cup milk
½ teaspoon dried dill weed

Combine all ingredients and mix thoroughly. Pour into a greased 9 x 9 inch baking dish. Bake at 350° F. for about 30 minutes or until firm.

STUFFED GREEN PEPPERS
(A simple, but tasty variation.)

6 large green peppers, with tops removed and seeded
1 pound hamburger, browned
2 cups cooked rice
½ can tomato soup
1 teaspoon salt
½ teaspoon pepper
½ teaspoon garlic powder or 1 clove garlic
1 ½ cans tomato soup
1 can water
1 teaspoon mustard powder

Mix browned hamburger, rice, ½ can soup, salt, pepper, and garlic in frying pan. Place peppers upright in casserole dish and fill with hamburger filling. Mix soup, water and mustard in measuring cup and pour over stuffed peppers. Cover and bake for 1 hour at 350° F.

"Rest when you're weary. Refresh and renew yourself, your body, your mind, your spirit. Then get back to work." Ralph Marston

Our attitude determines our attitude.

STUFFED TOMATOES

6 medium tomatoes
1 -10 ounce package frozen chopped spinach
1 tablespoon onion, minced
1 garlic clove, minced
1 tablespoon oregano
¼ tablespoon nutmeg
1 cup Cheddar cheese, grated
Parmesan cheese, grated

Cut off top of tomatoes and scoop out the pulp. Chop and drain the pulp. Thaw spinach and drain well. Combine spinach, pulp, onion, spices and Cheddar cheese. Stuff the tomatoes and top with Parmesan cheese. Bake at 350° F. for 20-30 minutes.

"As we express our gratitude, we must never forget that the highest appreciation is not to utter words, but to live by them."
John F. Kennedy

"The second day of a diet is always easier than the first. By the second day you're off it."   ..... Jackie Gleason

VEGGIE BAKE
(An easy and yummy veggie casserole!)

1 -16 ounce package frozen vegetables; broccoli cauliflower and carrot mix
1 -10 ounce can whole mushrooms
1 -10 ounce can cream of mushroom soup
1 -250 gram package cream cheese
½ teaspoon dill weed
salt and pepper to taste
¾ cup seasoned croutons

Prepare the vegetables according to directions, and drain. Stir in mushrooms, soup, cream cheese, dill weed, salt and pepper. Put vegetable mixture into a greased casserole dish. Sprinkle with croutons. Bake, uncovered at 350° F. for about 30 minutes until bubbly.

"The bad news is; time flies. The good news is; you're the pilot."
.... Michael Alfshuler

"The wisdom you leave your children, is more important than any wealth you might leave them." ...... Helen Keller

"I believe we are living in the midst of a cancer epidemic. Compared to fifty years ago we are living in a sea of chemicals in the soil, the air, our food and water. Perhaps we, who are the cancer warriors and our families, can shine a light into the darkness and lead the search for answers in the war against cancer."

"My friends in the support group for women, those resourceful women who had walked the cancer walk, warned me not to go back to work too soon, to take it gradually, to take time to recover and regain emotional strength. I am grateful for their counsel. It was wise, and it was right. I needed time to build more physical and emotional reserves."

"Amid all the turmoil of cancer, there is a community of people and families who have lived with cancer and understand. This is our community — a community of very special, very real and very empathetic people. It is a community that shared wisdom and strength when I needed it. Sometimes I didn't realize my need until the wise or affirming words had been spoken."

"What is my hope for tomorrow? Well, I hope for a cure so that no one will have to deal with a disease called cancer — or that it is at least beaten down in status to that of a chronic illness. On a more personal level, I hope for spontaneous remission (might as well hope big!) — God, wouldn't that be something? More realistically, I hope that my treatment works to extend my life to the point where I can take advantage of the amazing research that is taking place today."

Cancer is not only the disease of an individual. A cancer diagnosis is a hurricane that affects family and friends as well as the patient in the eye of the cancer's fury. My two daughters were devastated. They had lost their father to cancer when they were six and seven. We have been a very nuclear family. They are strong and realistic women; however, I couldn't expect them to support me emotionally as they dealt with their own turmoil. I joined a support group for women. I have learned that a network of supportive and listening friends is essential for each family member to be able to share and talk outside of the emotional storm in which the family is living.

When you have been diagnosed with cancer, talking to other cancer warriors is sooo important. There are wonderful hope centers and grass roots volunteer organizations that are there for you. The volunteers are dealing with cancer too, either as survivors or in various stages of the illness. They understand where you are coming from. That's so important to me because when I feel a little low on hope, I know that I can get a fill from them. When I feel particularly full of hope, then I know that there might be someone who can benefit from a little of mine. I've learned that's what hope is all about – sharing it with others. The more hope you give, the more hope you receive.

I have been living with cancer for 8½ years. For the past 2½ years I have been at the palliative stage. I tell everyone that I'm long past my "best before date."

Desserts

A strong woman will pull out a weed,
but a woman of strength will pull out
a weed and plant a flower.

Classic dessert recipes are classics for a reason, they have stood the test of time and are still a real treat — 150 years after they were first served. The next three recipes are some of those classics that are still fun to make on a special occasion.

BAKED ALASKA
(The name Baked Alaska originated at Delmonico's Restaurant in New York City in 1876, and was created in honour of the newly acquired territory of Alaska.)

Cake:
Use a good brownie recipe or a heavy pound cake of whatever flavour you prefer.

Filling:
2 pints raspberry sorbet, softened (or any flavour to complement your cake)
1 quart vanilla ice cream, softened

Meringue:
6 large egg whites, room temperature
¾ cup sugar
½ teaspoon vanilla

Line a 4 quart 10 inch diameter bowl with plastic wrap, leaving 8 inch overhang. Spread sorbet in even layer over bottom (not sides) of bowl. Spread ice cream over sorbet. Cut cake to fit shape and place on top of ice cream, pressing slightly to compact.

Continued on next page..........

273

BAKED ALASKA continued..........

Cover with plastic wrap overhang; freeze at least 4 hours or overnight.

For meringue:
Using electric mixer, beat egg whites in large bowl until soft peaks form. Gradually beat in sugar, 1 tablespoon at a time; beat until thick and glossy. Beat in vanilla.

To assemble:
Unfold plastic wrap from over cake at top of bowl. Invert dessert onto a springform cake pan bottom or some other oven safe pan that will accommodate dessert. Remove plastic wrap. Working quickly, spread meringue over dessert, swirling to form peaks and covering completely. Freeze at least 30 minutes. (Can be made 1 day ahead; keep frozen.)

Preheat oven to 500° F. Place dessert on its pan bottom on heavy large baking sheet. Bake just until meringue is light golden, about 5 minutes. Transfer to platter. Serve immediately.

"I am a little deaf, a little blind, a little impotent, and on top of this are two or three abominable infirmities, but nothing destroys my hope." .....Voltaire

PEACH MELBA

(Peach Melba is a French dessert created by Escoffier, the famous French chef of the Savoy Hotel in London at the end of the 19th century. Dame Nellie Melba, an Australian opera singer had so impressed him at a concert that he invented a dessert and named it after her. It is a perfect summer dessert when made with fresh peaches and raspberries.)

4 whole canned peaches or 8 halves
3 tablespoons peach schnapps
Warm peaches and syrup in a medium saucepan, add peach schnapps and bring to a simmer. Refrigerate if making ahead.

Raspberry Sauce: (makes 1 cup)
2 ½ pints fresh raspberries
½ cup sugar
1 tablespoon fresh lemon juice
vanilla ice cream

Rinse berries and place in a small saucepan with sugar. Place pan over medium heat and cook until berries soften and begin to break apart, about 10 minutes. Force mixture through a fine mesh sieve, discarding seeds. Add lemon juice to sauce and refrigerate, covered, up to 3 days.

To assemble dessert: place a scoop of ice cream in a bowl or large goblet. Top with 2 poached peach halves. Spoon some of poached syrup over ice cream, drizzle raspberry sauce over peaches. Serve immediately.

CHERRIES JUBILEE
(Great French chef Escoffier also created Cherries Jubilee to celebrate Queen Victoria's Golden Jubilee in 1887.)

½ cup white sugar

2 tablespoons cornstarch

¼ cup water

¼ cup orange juice

1 pound Bing or other dark, sweet cherries, drained and pitted

½ teaspoon orange zest, finely grated

¼ cup brandy

3 cups vanilla ice cream

Whisk together sugar and cornstarch in a wide saucepan. Stir in water and orange juice; bring to a boil over medium-high heat, whisking until thickened. Stir in cherries and orange zest, return to a boil, then reduce heat, and simmer for 10 minutes. While cherries are cooking, spoon ice cream into serving bowls. Remove cherries from heat, pour in brandy, and ignite with a long lighter. Gently shake pan until blue flame has extinguished itself. Spoon cherries over ice cream. Watch! Initial flame may be quite high. When it has died down, a small blue flame will continue to burn for several seconds as you shake pan - reducing raw alcohol flavor, caramelizing sugars, and entertaining your guests!

Our life cannot always be full of happiness
but it can always be full of life.

276

APRICOT CREAMS

1 egg white, room temperature
¼ cup sugar
¾ cup whipping cream
2 tablespoons brandy or 1 teaspoon almond extract
¼ cup flaked almonds
1 -411 gram can apricots, drained - save juice

Beat egg white until stiff. Beat in sugar a teaspoon at a time.
Set aside. Beat cream until thick; add brandy while continuing to
beat. Fold in egg white and ½ the almonds. Puree apricots in a
blender with a tablespoon of the juice. Toast remaining almonds
and cool.
Spoon a little apricot puree into the bottom of four wine glasses,
then cover with a layer of cream, repeat with another layer of
apricot puree and a final layer of cream. Sprinkle with toasted
almonds.

The Four Stages of Life:
You believe in Santa Claus.
You don't believe in Santa Claus.
You are Santa Claus.
You look like Santa Claus.

BAKED CHOCOLATE PUDDING
(Simple and delicious!)

1 cup flour
2 teaspoons baking powder
1 teaspoon salt
½ cup sugar
2 tablespoons canola oil
1 teaspoon vanilla
½ cup milk
2 tablespoons cocoa
¾ cup brown sugar
1 ¾ cups hot water
2 tablespoons cocoa

Mix together: flour, baking powder, salt, sugar, oil, vanilla, milk and first 2 tablespoons cocoa. Pour into a greased 9 x 12 inch pan.
Mix brown sugar, hot water and final 2 tablespoons of cocoa, and pour over the batter in pan. Bake at 350° F. for about 45 minutes. Serve with ice-cream, frozen yogurt or table cream.
This recipe can be doubled.

I've learned that even when I have pains,
I don't have to be one.
I've learned that everyday you should reach out and touch
someone. People love that human touch—holding hands, a warm
hug, or just a friendly pat on the back.

BLACK FOREST CAKE

8 egg yokes
4 tablespoons water
2/3 cup sugar
2 teaspoons vanilla
½ teaspoon almond flavouring
1 teaspoon cinnamon
2/3 cup flour
2 tablespoons cocoa
6 tablespoons cornstarch
1 teaspoon baking powder
6 egg whites, room temperature
1/3 cup sugar

Beat egg yokes and water until foamy. Gradually add sugar, vanilla, almond flavouring, cinnamon, flour, cocoa, cornstarch and baking powder. In a separate bowl beat egg whites until soft peaks form. Continue to beat and add 1/3 cup sugar 2 tablespoons at a time. Fold the yoke mixture into the egg white mixture. Pour into 2 -9 inch greased spring form pans. Bake 20-25 minutes at 350° F.

To assemble:
¼ cup cherry brandy
1 can cherry pie filling
Continued on next page.......

BLACK FOREST CAKE continued.......

3 cups whipping cream, whipped

4 tablespoons icing sugar

1 teaspoon vanilla

When cakes have cooled cut each in half. Drizzle brandy on bottom layer. Top with pie filling and whipped cream that has been flavoured with sugar and vanilla. Place second cake layer on top. Continue with brandy, filling and cream layers until all layers are in place. Ice cake with whipped cream and garnish with cherries and chocolate shavings.

Refrigerate 2-3 hours before serving.

LEMON FLUFF DESSERT

1 ½ cups graham wafer crumbs

¼ cup sugar

1/3 cup butter, melted

1 small package lemon Jell-O

1 ½ cups boiling water

¾ cup sugar

¼ cup lemon juice

1 -370 ml tin evaporated milk, chilled

Mix crumbs, sugar and butter and press into greased 9 x 13 inch pan. Dissolve Jell-O powder in boiling water. Add sugar and lemon juice. Chill until syrupy. Beat chilled milk until like whipped cream. Fold jelly mixture into cream and pour over graham wafer crust. Chill before serving.

CARAMEL GRAPES
(These are always one of the first desserts to
disappear on a dessert table.)

4 to 5 cups red seedless grapes, washed and dried

Mix and toss over grapes:
1 cup sour cream
½ cup white sugar
1 teaspoon vanilla

In a saucepan mix:
½ cup butter
½ cup brown sugar
Bring to a boil and pour over grapes and cream mixture.

This dessert works well when served in individual glasses.
A parfait glass or a small champagne flute looks very nice. Just
prior to serving, top with a swirl of whipped cream.

Monday I made angel food cake. The recipe said beat 12 eggs
separately. The neighbors were nice enough
to loan me some extra bowls.
Tuesday Tom wanted fruit salad for supper. The recipe said
serve without dressing. So I didn't dress. What a surprise
when Tom brought a friend home for supper.
Wednesday is a good day for rice. The recipe said wash
thoroughly before steaming the rice. It seemed kind of silly but
I took a bath anyway. I can't say it improved the rice any.

CHEESE CAKE WITH ORANGE GLAZE
(Oh ma cherie, this is so good!)

Crust:

1 ½ cups graham wafer crumbs

¼ cup brown sugar

1 teaspoon cinnamon

½ cup butter, melted

Filling:

3 -250 gram packages cream cheese, softened

4 eggs

¾ cup sugar

1 teaspoon vanilla

Topping:

1 cup sour cream

¼ cup sugar

Glaze:

4 cans mandarin oranges in juice, drained (reserve 2 cups)

2 cups of the reserved orange juice

¼ cup sugar

¼ cup cornstarch

1 teaspoon lemon juice

1 teaspoon orange extract

Mix together wafers, sugar, cinnamon and butter. Press into 9 x 13 inch greased pan. Beat cream cheese, eggs, sugar and vanilla until smooth. Pour over crust and bake at 350° F. for Continued on next page.....

CHEESECAKE WITH ORANGE GLAZE continued...

25-30 minutes, or until set. Mix sour cream and sugar, spread over hot cheesecake. Return to oven for 5 minutes. Remove and set aside to cool.

Glaze:
Arrange drained oranges on cake. In saucepan combine reserved juice, sugar, lemon juice and cornstarch until smooth. Place on medium-high heat, stirring constantly until thick. Remove from heat; stir in orange extract and pour over cooled cake. Refrigerate until set.
Note: Mangos or peaches also work well.

CHERRY CRUNCH
(Serve warm topped with ice cream.)

1 cup quick cooking rolled oats
1 cup flour
¾ cup brown sugar
½ teaspoon cinnamon
½ cup margarine
1 -22 ounce can cherry pie filling (or any filling)
Combine oats, flour, sugar, and cinnamon. Cut in margarine until it forms fine crumbs. Pat half mixture into a greased 9 x 9 inch pan. Cover with filling and sprinkle with remaining oat mixture. Bake at 375° F. for 40 minutes.

Conceit is the quicksand of success.

CHERRY TRIFLE

12 maraschino cherries, drained and dried
¼ cup brandy
1 -113 gram package instant chocolate pudding
1 -500 ml whipping cream
1 teaspoon vanilla
1 tablespoon sugar
1 package of 4 Swiss rolls
1 large jar pitted sour red cherries
chocolate sprinkles

In large bowl, pour brandy over red cherries. Let sit 30 minutes. Make pudding according to directions and set in fridge. Whip cream into peaks, adding vanilla and sugar. Cut Swiss rolls into 4 slices each. In trifle bowl, put half of rolls on bottom, then half of brandy/cherry mixture, then half of chocolate pudding, and then half of whipped cream. Repeat layers ending with whipped cream. Decorate with maraschino cherries and chocolate sprinkles. Cover tightly and refrigerate.

"Be thankful for what you have; you'll end up having more. If you concentrate on what you don't have, you will never, ever have enough." ....*Oprah Winfrey*

CHOCOLATE CARAMEL PECAN CHEESECAKE
(Proven to be a favourite at coffee parties!)

1 ½ cups graham wafer crumbs
6 tablespoons butter, melted
¾ cup caramel flavoured topping sauce
1 cup pecans, chopped
3 -250 gram packages cream cheese, softened
1 cup sugar
1 teaspoon vanilla
3 eggs
8 squares semi sweet chocolate, melted

Preheat oven to 325° F. Mix crumbs and butter and press into
the bottom and 1 inch up the sides of a 9 inch greased, spring
form pan. Bake for 10 minutes. Cool. Pour caramel sauce
over cooled crust. Top with pecans. Combine cream cheese,
sugar and vanilla until smooth. Beat in eggs, one at a time,
until blended. Stir in slightly cooled melted chocolate and pour
over pecans. Bake for 50 minutes or until centre is set.
Remove from oven and run a knife around sides of pan to
loosen. Cool at room temperature and chill overnight. Serve
with whipped cream topping and sifted cocoa.

Today is the future I created yesterday.

285

CHOCOLATE JELLY ROLL

4 egg whites, room temperature
¾ cup sugar
4 egg yolks
1 teaspoon vanilla
6 tablespoons flour
6 tablespoons cocoa
1 ½ teaspoons baking powder
pinch of salt
1 cup whipping cream, whipped

In large bowl, beat egg whites until stiff but not dry. Beat in sugar, a tablespoon at a time, until quite stiff. In separate bowl, beat egg yolks and add to egg whites. Stir in vanilla. Mix flour, cocoa, baking powder and salt in a separate bowl and slowly fold into egg white mixture. Pour into greased 10 x 15 inch jelly roll pan lined with wax paper. Bake at 400° F. for 10-15 minutes. Turn out immediately onto clean tea towel covered heavily with sifted icing sugar. Remove wax paper. Roll up towel with cake and cool. Fill cooled jelly roll with sweetened whipped cream.

"Money often costs too much." … Ralph Waldo Emerson

Shown on previous page:

❖ Strawberry Shortcake Trifle.....page 303

❖ Lemon Snowball.....page 298

❖ Merry Berry Cheese Bars.....page 299

❖ Raspberry Dessert.....page 300

CHOCOLATE PAVLOVA

6 egg whites, room temperature

¼ teaspoon salt

¼ teaspoon cream of tartar

1 ½ cups sugar

1 tablespoon cornstarch

2 teaspoons vinegar

2 teaspoons vanilla

3 tablespoons unsweetened cocoa powder

2 ounces bittersweet chocolate, finely chopped

<u>Topping:</u>

3-4 cups hulled strawberries, sliced

1 ½ cups whipping cream

1 teaspoon sugar

1 ounce bittersweet chocolate, melted

Line baking sheet with parchment paper or lightly greased foil.
Trace 9 inch circle on paper, turn paper over. In bowl, beat
egg whites, salt, and cream of tartar until soft peaks form.
Gradually beat in sugar (2 tablespoons at a time) until stiff
glossy peaks form, 10 minutes or longer. Beat in cornstarch,
vinegar, and vanilla. Sift cocoa over top; gently fold in. Gently
fold in chopped chocolate. Mound onto circle on prepared
baking sheet. Bake at 275° F. for 1 ½ hours or until crispy
outside but still soft in centre. Transfer to rack and cool
completely.

Continued on next page....

CHOCOLATE PAVLOVA continued....

Topping:

Just before serving, whip cream; beat in sugar. Spoon half of the strawberries onto meringue; cover with whipped cream. Garnish with remaining berries. Drizzle melted chocolate over berries. Serves 6-8.

Note: If you have no bittersweet chocolate to drizzle over the berries, just sieve some unsweetened cocoa powder over top for a dazzling effect.

HALF HOUR PUDDING

(This is sometimes called Hasty Pudding — delicious served warm with a little cream or ice cream.)

1 cup flour

1 teaspoon baking powder

1 teaspoon baking soda

½ teaspoon salt

1/3 cup brown sugar

2 tablespoons margarine, softened

1 egg

1 cup raisins

½ cup milk

Sauce:

1 cup brown sugar

2 cups boiling water

1 tablespoon butter

¼ teaspoon nutmeg

In a 1 ½ quart ungreased casserole dish mix dry ingredients. Cut in margarine. Add egg and milk. Mix until moistened and add raisins. Mix sauce and boil for 1 minute. Pour over batter and bake at 375° F. for 30-35 minutes.

CROWN JEWEL DESSERT
(An old favourite that brings back special memories.)

1 package orange, cherry and lime Jell-O
1 cup boiling water for each package
½ cup cold water for each package
1 package lemon Jell-O
1 cup boiling water
1 ½ cup graham wafer crumbs
¼ cup margarine, melted
2 envelopes Dream Whip
1 cup cold milk

Separately mix each package of Jell-O in boiling water. Once dissolved, add cold water. Pour each flavour into a 9 x 9 inch pan and refrigerate until set. Mix next cup of boiling water with lemon Jell-O. Once dissolved, place in fridge until partially set. Mix crumbs and margarine and place in greased 9 x 13 inch pan. Whip Dream Whip and milk until soft peaks form. After the orange, cherry and lime Jell-O are set, cut into cubes. Mix the partially set lemon Jell-O, set Jell-O cubes and Dream Whip and pour over crumb crust. Chill for 5 hours before serving.

> "The only way to keep your health is to eat what you don't want, drink what you don't like, and do what you'd rather not."........*Mark Twain*

GREAT GRANDMA'S FAMOUS APPLE STRUDEL
(This grandma was famous for miles around because of this strudel.)

Dough:
3 cups flour

1 teaspoon salt

1 ½ cups lukewarm water

¾ cup butter, softened

Mix flour, salt and water into a soft dough. Place on floured tea towel in warm place for ¾ hour. Flour large tablecloth. Stretch and pull out dough by hand (being careful not to put holes in it) until it is paper thin. Brush dough with soft butter.
*Phyllo sheets can be substituted for pastry.

Filling:
4 pounds apples, peeled and sliced

3 cups dry bread crumbs

¾ cup white sugar

¾ cup brown sugar

3 teaspoons cinnamon

1 cup raisins

Mix bread crumbs with sugar, cinnamon and raisins and sprinkle over dough; cover with apples. Roll, using tablecloth to help. Cut into lengths that will fit on a cookie sheet. Lift carefully. Place on greased cookie sheet (with sides), brush with butter and bake at 350° F. until apples are done, and pastry is golden brown, approximately 1 hour.

FRUIT FLAX CRISP
(Sure to please with whichever fruit you choose!)

4 cups fruit, chopped (apples, apricots, peaches or pears)

1 cup sugar

2 tablespoons fresh lemon juice

3 teaspoons cornstarch

2 cups cornflakes, crushed to make 1 cup

1/4 cup flax seed

2 tablespoons butter

Lemon Cream:

1 cup light sour cream

1/3 cup icing sugar

3 tablespoons lemon juice

rind of one lemon

Preheat oven to 350° F. Lightly grease an 8 cup baking dish. Place prepared fruit evenly in baking dish. In a small bowl, mix sugar, lemon juice and cornstarch. Pour mixture over fruit and stir gently to coat. In a medium bowl, mix cornflakes, flax seed and melted butter. Sprinkle crumb mixture over fruit. Bake 30 minutes or until juice bubbles and is clear.

In a medium bowl, mix sour cream, icing sugar, lemon juice and lemon rind. Chill until serving time. To serve, spoon 2 tablespoons of lemon cream over each serving.

Dare to colour outside the lines.

HEAVEN IN A PAN

1 cup pecans, finely chopped
1 cup flour
½ cup butter
1 -250 gram package cream cheese
1 cup icing sugar
1 large tub Cool Whip
1 package instant chocolate pudding
1 package instant vanilla pudding
3 cups milk
1 milk chocolate bar, shaved

Combine pecans, flour and butter and press into a greased
9 x 13 inch pan. Bake at 350° F. for 20 minutes. Cool.
Combine cream cheese and icing sugar and spread on cooled
base. Spread ½ the Cool Whip over cream cheese. In a bowl
beat chocolate and vanilla puddings with milk. Spread over Cool
Whip. Spread remaining ½ Cool Whip over pudding layer.
Sprinkle with chocolate bar. Cool several hours or overnight.

*"In oneself lays the whole world and if you know how to look and
learn, the door is there and the key is in your hand. Nobody on
earth can give you either the key or the door to open,
except yourself." - Jiddu Krishnamurti*

LEMON ANGEL DELIGHT

¼ angel food cake, cubed
1 -113 gram (large package) lemon pie filling
2 egg whites, room temperature
1/3 cup sugar
2 ½ - 3 cups mini marshmallows
1 package prepared Dream Whip or 2 cups whipped cream

Spread cubed cake in bottom of 9 x 13 inch greased pan.
Prepare lemon pie filling according to package directions. Cool
slightly. Beat egg whites until stiff, add sugar, and continue
beating until blended. Fold egg white mixture and marshmallows
into lemon pie filling. Spread mixture over cake in pan. Spread
prepared Dream whip or whipped cream on top. Refrigerate for
a few hours to set. Enjoy!

*I believe that our background and circumstances may have
influenced who we are, but we are responsible for who we become.*

*I believe that true friendship continues to grow, even over the
longest distance. Same goes for true love.*

*I believe that just because someone doesn't love you the way you
want them to, doesn't mean they don't love you with all they have.*

*I believe that no matter how good a friend is, they're going to hurt
you every once in a while and you must forgive them for that.*

LEMON LIME CHEESECAKE

Toasted Coconut Crust:
2 cups shredded coconut
2 tablespoons sugar
2 tablespoons butter, melted
½ teaspoon lemon rind, grated

Lightly grease a 10 inch spring form pan. Mix coconut, sugar,
butter and lemon rind. Spread evenly in pan, patting down
lightly. Bake at 350° F. for 10-12 minutes or until lightly
toasted around edges.

Cream Cheese Filling:
2 -250 gram packages cream cheese
1 cup sugar
4 eggs
2 tablespoons lemon juice
2 tablespoons lime juice

Blend cream cheese until fluffy and smooth. Add sugar, eggs,
one at a time, add juices. Pour over crust and return to oven
and bake at 350° F. for 35 minutes or until set. Remove from
oven and run knife around edges of cheesecake. Cool, cover and
refrigerate.
Continued next page.......

294

LEMON LIME CHEESECAKE continued ....

Lemon Lime Curd Topping:

2 eggs
¾ cup sugar
1 ½ teaspoons lemon rind, grated
1 ½ teaspoons lime rind, grated
2 tablespoons lime juice
¼ cup lemon juice
2 tablespoons butter

Whisk eggs until foamy. Combine in heavy saucepan with sugar, rinds, juices and butter. Cook over low heat, stirring frequently or whisking if necessary until smooth and thickened. This usually takes about 6-8 minutes. Remove from heat to cool. Spread over top of cooled cheesecake.

The only thing that unites all human beings, regardless of age, gender, religion, economic status or ethnic background, is that, deep down inside, we ALL believe that we are above average drivers.

LEMON SEMIFREDDO WITH RASPBERRY COULIS

(A refreshing lemony dessert, excellent choice for entertaining
since it can be made up to two weeks ahead.
Semi-freddo means half frozen in Italian.)

4 eggs, separated and room temperature

1 cup sugar

3 tablespoons lemon rind, grated

½ cup lemon juice

1 ½ cups whipping cream

Raspberry Coulis:

2 cups unsweetened raspberries, fresh or thawed

1 tablespoon lemon juice

3 tablespoons sugar

Line 2 litre loaf pan with waxed or parchment paper to extend
1 inch above edge. Set aside. In large glass or Pyrex bowl,
combine egg yolks, ¼ cup of the sugar, lemon rind, and juice;
place bowl over saucepan of simmering water and cook, whisking
constantly, for about 8 minutes or until thickened. Place plastic
wrap directly on surface; refrigerate until cold (30 minutes). In
bowl, whip cream; fold into cold lemon mixture. In separate
bowl, beat egg whites until soft peaks form; gradually beat in
remaining sugar, 2 tablespoons at a time, until stiff glossy peaks
form. Fold ¼ into lemon mixture; fold in remaining egg whites.
Turn into prepared pan, smoothing top. Freeze for about 6
Continued on next page.......

LEMON SEMIFREDDO WITH RASPBERRY COULIS continued......

hours or until firm. Wrap in plastic wrap or foil and freeze overnight. To serve, run knife between paper and pan of semifreddo; turn out onto cutting board and remove paper. Slice and arrange on chilled plates. Drizzle with Raspberry Coulis. Serves 10.

Raspberry Coulis:
In blender, puree raspberries and lemon juice until smooth; strain through fine sieve into airtight container. Stir in sugar. This can be refrigerated for up to 3 days. Makes 1 cup.

BRANDIED PEACHES

1 -28 ounce can peach halves, drained
2 tablespoons syrup from peaches
4 tablespoons butter
½ cup brown sugar
¼ teaspoon cinnamon
¼ cup brandy

Place peaches in shallow baking dish. Combine rest of ingredients and spoon over peaches. Bake at 350° F. for 25-30 minutes, basting occasionally.
Serve over vanilla ice cream.

LEMON SNOWBALL

2 envelopes unflavoured gelatin
¼ cup cold water
1 cup boiling water
1 cup sugar
1 -355 ml can frozen orange juice, thawed
2 tablespoons lemon peel, grated
1 tablespoon lemon juice
dash of salt
3 cups whipping cream, divided
1 angel food cake, cubed
¼ cup icing sugar
½ cup shredded coconut

In large bowl, sprinkle gelatin over cold water. Let stand 5
minutes. Add boiling water. Stir until gelatin is dissolved. Add
sugar, orange juice, lemon peel, lemon juice, and salt. Mix well.
Refrigerate, stirring occasionally until mixture begins to thicken;
about 1 ½ to 2 hours. Whip 2 cups of cream; fold into lemon
mixture. Line 12 cup bowl with plastic wrap. Spoon 1 cup of
lemon filling into lined bowl. Sprinkle with layer of cake.
Alternate filling and cake, ending with filling. Cover and
refrigerate 6 hours or overnight. To serve; invert bowl onto large
serving platter. Remove plastic wrap. Beat remaining cream and
icing sugar, frost entire cake, and sprinkle with coconut.
Yield: 16-20 servings.

MERRY BERRY CHEESE BARS
(Cut into large squares and serve warm with
ice cream for dessert. Oh so yummy!)

1 cup margarine or butter, softened

2 cups flour

1 ½ cups oatmeal

¾ cup & 1 tablespoon brown sugar, firmly packed

1 -250 gram package cream cheese, softened

1 -300 ml can sweetened condensed milk

¼ cup concentrated lemon juice

1 -16 ounce can whole berry cranberry sauce

2 tablespoons cornstarch

Preheat oven to 350° F. Beat margarine, flour, oats, and ¾ cup sugar until crumbly. Set aside 1 ½ cups of this mixture. Press remaining mixture on bottom of a greased 9 x 13 inch pan. Bake for 15 minutes or until lightly brown.
With mixer, beat cheese until fluffy. Gradually beat in condensed milk and lemon juice until smooth. Spread over baked crust. Combine cranberry sauce, cornstarch, and remaining 1 tablespoon of sugar. Spoon over cheese layer. Top with reserved crumb mixture. Bake for 45 minutes or until golden brown.

*"Expect trouble as an inevitable part of life and repeat to yourself
the most comforting words of all: 'This too, shall pass'."*
.....Ann Landers

RASPBERRY DESSERT
(So easy, so good!)

<u>Crust:</u>
1 cup graham wafer crumbs
¼ cup butter, melted
¼ cup sugar

<u>Filling:</u>
1 -3 ounce package of raspberry Jell-O
¾ cup sugar
1 ½ cups cold water
¼ cup cornstarch
2 cups raspberries, fresh or frozen
2 cups whipped topping, prepared

Mix crust ingredients together and press into a lightly greased 8 x 8 inch pan. Combine dry Jell-O powder, sugar, water and cornstarch in a saucepan and bring to a boil. Boil gently, stirring continually until the mixture thickens. Remove from heat and add raspberries. Cool slightly and pour evenly over base. Refrigerate until set. Spread whipped topping over raspberry layer. Refrigerate for 2-3 hours. Enjoy!

It's easy enough to be pleasant, when life flows along like a song, but the man worthwhile is the man with a smile, when everything goes dead wrong.

RHUBARB CRUNCH DESSERT

4 cups flour

1 cup sugar

2 cups butter, softened

1 -250 gram package cream cheese

2 cups sugar

5 tablespoons flour

1 cup whipping cream

3 eggs

1 teaspoon vanilla

1 cup icing sugar

5 cups fresh rhubarb, finely chopped

Preheat oven to 350° F. Mix flour, 1 cup sugar and butter until crumbly. Press all but 2 cups of mixture into 9 x 13 inch ungreased baking dish. Bake 10 minutes.

Beat cheese, 2 cups sugar, flour, whipping cream, eggs, vanilla, and icing sugar until smooth. Add rhubarb and pour over baked base. Sprinkle remaining 2 cups of crumbs on top. Return to oven for an additional 45 minutes.

Note: You can use 7 cups frozen rhubarb instead of fresh. Mix rhubarb, 2 cups sugar and ¼ cup water in sauce pan. Bring to a boil and cool. Mix cheese, whipping cream, eggs, vanilla and icing sugar ingredients until smooth. Add the rhubarb mixture and pour over crust. Sprinkle with remaining crumbs and bake for 45 minutes.

SASKATOON CREAM CHEESECAKE
(If you aren't lucky enough to have Saskatoons, fresh blueberries taste great too!)

¼ cup cornstarch

¼ cup sugar

½ cup water

3 cups Saskatoon berries or blueberries

3 cups graham wafer crumbs

¾ cup margarine

1 ½ -250 gram packages cream cheese

1 cup sugar

2 teaspoons vanilla

1 large container Cool Whip

Combine first four ingredients in saucepan and cook over medium heat until thick. Cool. Combine wafer crumbs and margarine. Spray 9 x 13 inch pan with light coating of canola oil. Press ½ of crumb mixture into pan. Cream cheese and add sugar and vanilla. Fold in Cool Whip. Spread ½ of cheese mixture over crumbs in pan. Top with fruit mixture, then other half of cheese mixture. Sprinkle with remainder of crumbs. May be frozen.

Never be afraid to try something new.
Remember that a lone amateur built the Ark.
A large group of professionals built the Titanic.

STRAWBERRY SHORTCAKE TRIFLE

4 pints fresh strawberries or equivalent frozen strawberries

1/3 cup sugar

2 ounces Grand Mariner

4 cups heavy cream

3 tablespoons icing sugar

1 teaspoon vanilla

1 angel food cake or pound cake

Slice strawberries and gently mix in a bowl with sugar and Grand Marnier. Let sit for 20 minutes. Whip heavy cream, icing sugar and vanilla until you have soft peaks. Dice cake into 1 inch cubes and place in bottom of a trifle or glass bowl. Add strawberry mixture over the top of cubed cake. Top with whipped cream. Decorate with chocolate shavings and fresh whole strawberries.

"Blessed is the generation in which the old listen to the young, and double-blessed is the generation in which the young listen to the old."....The Talmud

I've learned that you can tell a lot about a person by the way he/she handles four things: a rainy day, the elderly, lost luggage and tangled Christmas tree lights.

TAPIOCA CUSTARD
(So good, just like your grandma made it!)

⅓ cup tapioca, not instant
¾ cup cold water
1 ½ cups milk
2 eggs
⅓ cup sugar
¼ teaspoon salt
½ teaspoon vanilla

Soak tapioca in water 6 hours, or overnight in covered container. Add milk. Cook in covered double boiler over simmering water for 2 ½-3 hours, or until tapioca is clear and tender. Stir occasionally. Beat eggs with sugar and salt. Add a little of the hot mixture to the eggs, blend. Add the egg mixture into the hot tapioca, stirring well to blend. Continue cooking until mixture thickens (about 15 minutes); stir frequently. Remove from heat and add vanilla. Serve warm or chilled. Makes 4 servings.

"The truth is that our finest moments are most likely to occur when we are feeling deeply uncomfortable, unhappy, or unfulfilled. For it is only in such moments, propelled by our discomfort, that we are likely to step out of our ruts and start searching for different ways or truer answers." .... Scott Peck

TRADITIONAL GERMAN CHEESECAKE

<u>Crust:</u>
2 1/3 cups flour
¼ teaspoon baking powder
¾ cup butter or margarine
½ cup sugar
½ teaspoon salt
1 teaspoon vanilla
2 eggs
2 tablespoons milk
<u>Filling:</u>
4 eggs
¾ cup sugar
500 grams creamed cottage cheese
1 -250 gram package cream cheese
2 tablespoons lemon juice
4 tablespoons flour

Mix flour, baking powder, butter, sugar, salt, vanilla, eggs and milk in food processor to make crust. Press into the bottom of 2 -9 inch spring form pans, sprayed with non-stick cooking spray. For filling mix eggs, sugar, cottage cheese, cream cheese, juice and flour in processor and blend until smooth. Pour into one of the crusts. Freeze the other crust for another time.
Bake 1 hour at 350° F.
To serve, top with berries and whipped cream.

In 2002 they found a lump in my left breast near the nipple and I had to have a mastectomy. I thought I may be the only man in North America to have had a mastectomy for breast cancer. I didn't really understand what breast cancer was or that men could be diagnosed with it. Now, everywhere I go, I carry a "poster" I made to increase men's awareness. If there's one thing that would improve things now, it would be more information for and about men with breast cancer. We need to tell women that their spouses can develop it. We need more encouragement for men to pay attention and to remember that early diagnosis is important.

Gradually I grasped the need to face the monster (cancer diagnosis) head on, due to the ongoing support of my husband and young son, and encouragement from colleagues at school. . . I enrolled in a program titled: Relaxation and Stress Management. I learned numerous coping strategies such as; the use of affirmations pasted throughout our home, audio tapes with subliminal affirmations, the use of a pillow speaker when my sleep was disrupted during the night, reflective-type books, interacting with others through sharing and questioning, and exploring visualization techniques – all of the strategies helped to brighten my journey.

My journey of healing and hope, commenced with the absence of hope brought about largely due to the predetermined belief that a cancer diagnosis is a death sentence. However, with treatment options, time, love and support, hope gently unfolded in my presence and nudged me along the healing pathway to empower me and others living with the disease.

Cakes and Pastries

A strong woman treads familiar territory, but a woman of strength risks the unchartered.

APPLESAUCE SPICE CAKE

6 tablespoons shortening

1 1/3 cups sugar

1 egg

¾ cup applesauce

2 cups flour

1 teaspoon baking powder

¼ teaspoon cinnamon

½ cup walnuts, coarsely chopped

1 cup raisins, chopped

Cream shortening; beat in sugar and egg. Stir in applesauce. Fold in flour and rest of ingredients. Put in a greased 8 inch round or square cake pan. Bake at 350° F. for 45-50 minutes, or until a toothpick inserted in the centre comes out clean. Cool to lukewarm, sprinkle with icing sugar and serve with ice cream or whipped cream.
Option: Ice with cream cheese icing.

"The perfect man? A poet on a motorcycle."
.....Lucinda Williams

BUTTER TART SQUARE

Base:
1 ¼ cups flour
¼ cup brown sugar
½ cup margarine

Mix and press in a 9 x 9 inch pan. Bake at 350° F. for 15 minutes.

Topping:
1/3 cup margarine
1 egg, beaten
1 cup brown sugar
2 tablespoons cream
1 teaspoon vanilla
1 cup raisins

Mix and spread over base. Return to oven and bake for about 20-30 minutes until light brown.

"In primitive society, when native tribes beat the ground with clubs and yelled, it was called witchcraft;
In civilized society, it is called golf."
..... Edgar Watson Howe

CHOCOLATE BANANA CAKE
(Great combination!)

2/3 cup buttermilk

½ cup canola oil

1 cup sugar

2 eggs

1 teaspoon vanilla

1 ¼ cups bananas, mashed

2 cups flour

¾ cup cocoa

1 ½ teaspoons baking powder

1 teaspoon baking soda

¾ teaspoon salt

Cream together; oil, sugar and eggs. Stir in bananas and vanilla. In a separate bowl mix together; flour, cocoa, baking powder, baking soda and salt. Add dry ingredients to creamed mixture alternately with buttermilk. Divide batter between two greased 9 inch round cake pans. Bake at 350° F. for 40-45 minutes. Cool. Ice with Chocolate Banana Frosting.

CHOCOLATE BANANA FROSTING

¼ cup butter, melted

½ cup cocoa

¼ cup bananas, pureed

2 tablespoons milk

½ teaspoon vanilla

3 cups icing sugar

Combine: butter, cocoa, bananas, milk, vanilla and sugar. Mix until smooth. Spread between and over layers.

"Kindness is ever the begetter of kindness."
......Sophocles

CHOCOLATE CAKE
(So easy yet so delicious!)

2 cups flour

1 1/3 cups sugar

2/3 cup canola oil

1 teaspoon salt

1 teaspoon vanilla

½ teaspoon cinnamon

½ cup cocoa

2 teaspoons baking powder

1 teaspoon baking soda

3 eggs

2 cups milk

Combine all ingredients into a mixing bowl. Beat thoroughly for 2 minutes. Bake at 375° F. for 30 minutes.

"A successful team is a group of many hands but of one mind" ....Bill Bethel

CHOCOLATE FLECK CAKE

(This delicious cake, although takes a little time to make, has been known to sell at auctions for ninety dollars!)

2 squares semi-sweet chocolate
1 cup sugar
½ cup butter, softened
1 cup milk
1 teaspoon vanilla
2 cups cake flour, sifted
3 teaspoons baking powder
2 eggs, separated
pinch of salt

Frosting:
½ cup butter
1 ¾ cups sugar
2 egg yolks
2 squares semi-sweet chocolate, melted

Shred or chop chocolate and keep cold until ready to use. Beat egg whites until stiff, add ½ cup sugar gradually and beat until stiff glossy peaks form. Set aside. In large bowl, cream butter and remaining ½ cup sugar until light. Add vanilla to milk. Sift flour, baking powder, and salt together. Add milk/vanilla

Continued on next page.......

CHOCOLATE FLECK CAKE continued...

mixture alternately with the flour mixture to the butter mixture. Starting and ending with flour. Mix well. Fold in egg whites gently, then fold in chocolate. Pour into 2 greased and floured 9 inch layer tins and bake at 325° F. for 45 minutes. When cool, remove from pans. To make frosting: cream together butter, sugar and egg yolks. Use 1/3 for the middle and the rest for the top and sides. Melt chocolate and pour over top and let it dribble down the sides.

CHOCO CARAMEL BARS

1 small package caramels
3 tablespoons milk
1 box German chocolate cake mix
1 cup margarine
½ cup nuts, chopped (your choice)
1 cup chocolate chips

Melt caramels and milk in microwave and keep warm. Mix cake mix, margarine, and nuts and press ½ of mixture into 9 x 13 inch greased pan. Bake 6 minutes at 350° F. Take out of oven and spread caramel syrup and chips over baked cake. Sprinkle remaining crumb mixture on top and bake an additional 25 minutes.

CHOCOLATE TOFFEE SQUARE

1 cup margarine

2 cups flour

2/3 cup sugar

2 tablespoons margarine

1 can sweetened condensed milk

1 -300 gram package chocolate chips

1 -200 gram package Skor bits

Mix margarine, flour, and sugar and press into 9 x 13 inch greased pan. Bake 15 minutes at 350° F. In a medium sauce pan, heat margarine and milk, until thick. Pour over shortbread base and bake in oven until golden brown - about 30 minutes. Remove from oven and sprinkle chips on top. Return to oven for 2 minutes, take out and spread melted chips like an icing. Sprinkle Skor bits on top and let cool. Cut into squares and serve.

"Great things are not done by impulse, but by a series of small things brought together." ....Vincent Van Gogh

CINNAMON BARS

2 cups flour
1 ¼ cups white sugar
¼ cup brown sugar, packed
1/3 cup margarine, softened
½ cup walnuts, chopped
1 teaspoon baking soda
1 teaspoon cinnamon
1 teaspoon vanilla
1 egg
¾ teaspoon salt

Mix flour, sugars and margarine until crumbly. Press 2 cups into ungreased 9 x 13 inch pan. To the rest of crumbs add walnuts, baking soda, cinnamon, vanilla, egg and salt. Mix well and pour over base. Preheat oven to 350° F. and bake for about 20 minutes.

Icing:
2 cups icing sugar
3-4 tablespoons milk or cream
¼ teaspoon almond extract
¼ cup walnuts, chopped
Mix icing sugar, milk and almond extract together and spread on cooled cake. Sprinkle with walnuts.

COCONUT PECAN CAKE
WITH COCONUT PECAN FROSTING

Cake:
1 white cake mix
1 -102 gram package vanilla instant pudding
4 eggs
1 cup sour cream
½ cup canola oil
1 ½ cups flaked coconut
¾ cup pecans, chopped

Frosting
1 -250 gram package cream cheese, softened
½ cup margarine, softened
4 cups icing sugar, sifted
1 teaspoon vanilla
2/3 cup pecans, chopped
1/3 cup flaked coconut, toasted

Cake method: In large mixing bowl, combine cake mix, pudding mix, eggs, sour cream and oil. Beat on medium speed for 2 minutes. Stir in coconut and pecans. Mix well. Spread batter evenly in greased 9 x 13 inch pan. Bake at 350° F. for 45-50 minutes. Cool completely in pan on a wire rack.

Continued on next page ......

COCONUT PECAN CAKE continued ....

Frosting Method: In a large mixing bowl; beat cream cheese and margarine until smooth. Gradually add icing sugar and mix on low speed until smooth and creamy. Add vanilla, pecans and coconut. Mix well. Spread over cooled cake. Chill until serving. Store leftover cake in the refrigerator.

PUMPKIN DUMP CAKE

1 -19 ounce can pumpkin pie filling
1 -13 ounce can evaporated milk
1 cup sugar
3 eggs, beaten
4 teaspoons pumpkin pie spice
1 yellow cake mix
¾ cup margarine, melted

Mix together; pumpkin, milk, sugar, eggs and pumpkin pie spice. Put in a greased 9 x 13 inch pan. Shake cake mix evenly over the base. Pour margarine over cake mix. (If you like, sprinkle any choice of nuts on top at this point). Bake at 350° F. for 50-60 minutes. Serve cake topped with whipped cream or ice cream.

"Ever notice how irons have a setting for permanent press?
I don't get it!".....Steven Wright

CRANBERRY ALMOND COFFEE CAKE

Cake:
2 cups fresh cranberries
¼ cup flour
1 white cake mix
3 eggs
1 ¼ cups water
1/3 cup canola oil
½ teaspoon almond extract

Toss cranberries in flour to coat well. In a large bowl, combine cake mix, eggs, water, oil and almond extract. Beat for 2 minutes on medium speed. Stir in floured cranberries. Spread batter evenly in a 9 x 13 inch greased cake pan.

Topping:
¾ cup slivered almonds
1/3 cup brown sugar, packed
½ teaspoon cinnamon, ground

Combine almonds, brown sugar and cinnamon. Mix well. Sprinkle evenly over batter. Bake at 350° F. for 30-40 minutes or until center comes out clean when tested. Cool 30 minutes in pan on a wire rack. Serve warm or cool.

"Children's children are the crown of old men."
.....Proverbs 17:6

DAD'S CHOCOLATE SLICE

<u>Crust:</u>
24 Dad's coconut cookies, crushed (2 ½ cups)
¼ cup butter, melted

Reserve half crumbs for top. To remaining crumbs, add melted butter. Press in an ungreased 8 x 8 inch pan and bake at 300° F. for 10 minutes.

<u>Filling:</u>
1 ½ cups icing sugar
1 egg, beaten
½ cup butter, melted
1 teaspoon vanilla
2 squares semi-sweet chocolate, melted
½ cup coconut or ½ cup walnuts, chopped

Whip icing sugar, egg, butter, vanilla, and chocolate until light. Fold in coconut or walnuts. Spread on the crust and sprinkle with reserved crumbs. Refrigerate.

"Life's tough, get a helmet."

"Women complain about PMS, but I think it as the only time of the month when I can be myself."
..... Roseanne Barr

318

ENGLISH TEA CAKES
(These are absolutely delicious. Well worth the effort.)

Prepare your favourite tart pastry.

1 ¾ cups jam, strawberry, raspberry, (your choice)
½ cup butter
1 cup sugar
2 eggs
1 teaspoon vanilla
pinch of salt
1 cup milk
2 cups flour
3 teaspoons baking powder

Line tart tins with pastry. Place 1 teaspoon jam in each tart shell. In bowl, cream together butter and sugar. Beat in eggs, vanilla, and salt. In separate bowl, stir together flour and baking powder. Add flour mixture alternately with milk. Starting and ending with flour. Place 1 tablespoon batter over jam. Bake at 350° F. for 25-30 minutes or until golden brown.
Makes 4 dozen. These freeze really well.

No road is long with good company.
.....Turkish Proverb

319

GERMAN CHEESECAKE SQUARES

Base:
5 tablespoons butter or margarine
1 cup flour
6 tablespoons sugar
1 egg

Lightly spray a 9 x 13 inch pan with cooking spray. Mix all ingredients and press mixture into pan.   Set aside.

Filling:
2 cups creamed cottage cheese
1 cup sugar
¼ teaspoon salt
1 teaspoon vanilla
½ tablespoon cinnamon
½ tablespoon lemon juice
2 tablespoons cornstarch
¾ cup sour cream.

Combine filling ingredients, and then pour over base. Bake 40-50 minutes at 375° F.

"A clear conscience is usually the sign of a bad memory."
....Edgar Watson Howe

Women
working
together
for a cure

Shown on previous page:

❖ Chocolate Banana Cake.....page 309

"HIP PADDER" BARS

1 -385 ml can condensed milk
2 tablespoons margarine
1 teaspoon vanilla
1 cup chocolate chips
½ cup margarine
1 cup brown sugar
1 egg
1 ¼ cups flour
½ cup rolled oats
½ cup walnuts, chopped

Combine milk, margarine, vanilla and chocolate chips in saucepan and heat over low heat until chips are melted. Set aside to cool. Cream together; margarine, sugar and egg. Mix in flour, rolled oats and walnuts. Pat 2/3 of flour mixture into a lightly greased 9 x 13 inch pan. Spread chocolate mixture on top and sprinkle remaining crumb mixture over chocolate. Bake at 350° F. for 30 minutes.

There is nothing wrong with having nothing to say, unless you insist on saying it.

KRISPY PEANUT BUTTER SQUARE
(A quick and easy cookie sheet slice!)

Base:

1 ½ cups graham wafers
1 ½ cups peanut butter
1 pound bag icing sugar
1 cup margarine, melted

Mix and spread in a greased cookie sheet.

Topping:

1 -300 gram package chocolate chips
1 tablespoon margarine
3 tablespoons water
1 package miniature marshmallows
2 cups rice krispies

Melt together; chocolate chips, margarine and water. Add marshmallows and melt again. Add rice krispies. Mix well and spread over base. Let cool before cutting.

If at first you don't succeed,
do as your mother told you.

LEMON CHIFFON CAKE
(Lemony, light and luscious!)

1 ½ cups flour

1 tablespoon baking powder

1 teaspoon salt

½ cup white sugar

½ cup canola oil

6 egg yolks

¾ cup water

1 tablespoon lemon rind, grated

6 egg whites

½ teaspoon cream of tartar

¾ cup white sugar

1 cup whipping cream

2 cups lemon pie filling

Combine flour, baking powder, salt and ½ cup sugar in large mixing bowl. Stir well to blend. Add oil, egg yolks, water and lemon rind. Beat with an electric mixer until smooth. Beat in small mixing bowl; egg whites and cream of tartar to form stiff but moist peaks. Gradually add ¾ cup sugar and continue beating until stiff and shiny peaks are formed. Fold egg whites into the egg yolk mixture gently but thoroughly. Turn batter into ungreased 10 inch tube pan. Bake at 350° F. for 60 minutes. Invert pan and cool completely. When cool loosen edges and shake pan to remove cake.

Filling:

Beat cream to stiff peaks. Fold in lemon filling. Chill until stiff. To assemble, slice cake horizontally into 3 equal layers. Fill layers with 1/3 of filling. Spread remaining filling on top layer.

"The soul would have no rainbow, had the eye no tears."
….. John Vance Cheney

323

PEANUT BUTTER BROWNIES

½ cup margarine
2 eggs
½ cup peanut butter
1 cup brown sugar
1 teaspoon vanilla
1 cup flour
1 teaspoon baking powder
½ teaspoon baking soda
½ teaspoon salt
1 cup chocolate chips
2 tablespoons icing sugar

Mix margarine, eggs, peanut butter, and sugar. Add rest of ingredients, except icing sugar. Spread in greased 9 x 9 inch pan. Bake at 350° F. for 30 minutes. Sprinkle cake with icing sugar when cooled.

One generation plants the trees; another gets the shade.
.....Chinese Proverb

PINEAPPLE SLICE

2 cups flour
2 tablespoons sugar
1 cup margarine
¼ teaspoon salt
1 -19 ounce can crushed pineapple, undrained
½ cup sugar
3 tablespoons cornstarch
¼ cup cold water
¾ cup red maraschino cherries, chopped
2 egg whites
1 tablespoon sugar
½ teaspoon vanilla
¼ cup flaked coconut

Blend flour, 2 tablespoons sugar, margarine and salt until crumbly. Pat into an ungreased 9 x 13 inch pan. Bake at 350° F. until light brown. Put pineapple, ½ cup sugar, and cornstarch that has been mixed with cold water, in saucepan and cook until thick. Add cherries and spread over baked crust. Beat egg whites with 1 tablespoon sugar and vanilla until stiff. Spread over filling and sprinkle with coconut. Return to oven and brown lightly.

"One has fear in front of a goat, in back of a mule, and on every side of a fool."
..... Edgar Watson Howe

325

PRALINES 'N CREAM PECAN CAKE

<u>Cake</u>:
1 package white cake mix
1 -102 gram package vanilla instant pudding
4 eggs
1 1/3 cups sour cream
½ cup canola oil
1 ½ cups pecans, chopped

In large bowl, combine cake mix, pudding mix, eggs, sour cream and oil. Beat on medium speed for 2 minutes. Fold in pecans. Spread batter in two greased and floured 9 inch round cake pans, dividing batter evenly. Bake at 350° F. for 30-35 minutes. Cool for 10 minutes in pans on a wire rack, then remove and cool completely on rack.

<u>Pecan Praline Topping</u>:
1 egg white
1 tablespoon water
½ cup brown sugar, packed
1 ½ cups pecans, halved

In a small bowl, beat egg white and water with a fork until foamy. Add brown sugar, mixing until sugar dissolves.

Continued on next page.....

PRALINES 'N' CREAM PECAN CAKE
continued.......

Add pecans, tossing to coat nuts with sugar mixture.
Spread on a greased cookie sheet and bake at 300° F. for 25
minutes, stirring occasionally until nuts are crisp and browned.
Remove from oven. Stir to loosen nuts from cookie sheet. Cool
completely.

<u>Cream Cheese Frosting</u>:
1 ½ -250 gram packages cream cheese, softened
½ cup margarine, softened
2 teaspoons vanilla
4 cups icing sugar, sifted

In a large bowl, beat cream cheese, margarine and vanilla until
light and fluffy. Gradually add icing sugar, beating until
smooth.
<u>Assembly</u>:
Place 1 cake top-side down on serving plate. Spread
1 ½ cups of the frosting over cake. Top with second cake layer,
top-side up. Spread remaining frosting over top and sides of
cake. Arrange pecan praline topping over cake, mounding
slightly in center. Refrigerate until serving. Store cake in the
refrigerator.

RHUBARB CAKE
(Quick, easy and so delicious!)

1 yellow cake mix
1 cup water
1/3 cup oil
3 eggs
4 cups rhubarb, chopped
1 cup sugar
2 cups whipping cream, unwhipped

Beat well; cake mix, water, oil, and eggs. Pour into greased 9 x 13 inch pan. Sprinkle with rhubarb and sugar. Pour cream over top. Bake at 350° F. for 1 hour. Serve warm with ice cream.

"Before you were conceived I wanted you,
Before you were born I loved you,
Before you were here an hour, I would die for you.
This is the miracle of life."
..... Maureen Hawkins

SCRUMPTIOUS ALMOND SQUARES

Base:
1 ½ cups flour
3 tablespoons icing sugar
¾ cup butter, softened

Mix and pat into a greased 9 x 13 inch cake pan. Bake at
350° F. for 10-12 minutes or until golden around the edges.

Topping:
1 cup brown sugar
1 cup slivered almonds
1 teaspoon vanilla
½ cup whipping cream

Mix all ingredients in a saucepan and bring to a boil, stirring
constantly. Boil for 3 minutes. Remove from heat and pour
over base. Return to 350° F. oven and continue to bake for
another 20 minutes.

"You know, when I was diagnosed with breast cancer in 1997, I
realized I had spent too long arranging my attitude."
.... *Carly Simon*

SOUR CREAM CAKE
(A delicious must try cake.)

Crust:
1 ¼ cups graham wafer crumbs
¼ cup sugar
¼ cup butter, melted

Filling:
1 -250 gram package cream cheese
½ cup sugar
1 tablespoon lemon juice
½ teaspoon vanilla
pinch of salt
2 eggs
1 cup sour cream
2 tablespoons sugar
½ teaspoon vanilla

Combine graham crumbs, sugar and butter. Press into a
greased 9 inch square pan. Beat cream cheese until smooth.
Gradually beat in sugar, lemon juice, vanilla and salt. Add
eggs beating very well. Pour onto crumb crust. Bake at
325° F. for 25-30 minutes. During the last few minutes of
baking, mix together in a small bowl; sour cream, sugar, and
vanilla. Spoon over baked cheese cake and bake 10 minutes
longer. Chill before cutting.

BUTTERNUT SQUASH PIE WITH GINGERSNAP CRUST

(This delicious pie always receives great accolades when served!)

Crust:

1 package ginger biscuits

1/3 cup butter

In food processor, whirl biscuits to make 2 ¼ cups. Add butter, whirl until moistened. Press into bottom and sides of a 9 inch pie plate. Bake at 350° F. for 15 minutes or firm to the touch. Let cool.

Filling:

1 -2 pound butternut squash

1/3 cup sugar

2 tablespoons fancy molasses

1 teaspoon vanilla

¼ teaspoon cinnamon

¼ teaspoon allspice

¼ teaspoon nutmeg

pinch of salt

3 eggs, beaten

½ cup whipping cream

½ cup milk

Continued on next page…

BUTTERNUT SQUASH PIE continued....

<u>Topping:</u>
½ cup whipping cream
2 tablespoons icing sugar
20 pecans, toasted (optional)

Cut squash in half lengthwise. Roast, cut side down, on foil lined baking sheet at 375° F. until tender, about 45 minutes. Let cool. With spoon, scoop out enough flesh to make 2 cups. Puree squash until smooth. Whirl in the sugar, molasses, vanilla, cinnamon, allspice, nutmeg, and salt. Scrape into a bowl, and whisk in the eggs, cream, and milk until smooth. Pour into the pie plate. Bake at 375° F. until set and an inserted knife comes out clean. Let cool. Whip the cream with the icing sugar. Serve with the pie. Top with toasted pecans. Hint: You can extend this to 2 pies, by doubling the filling.

**It's not just the jeans that make the bum look fat......
It's the fat!!!**

CAPE COD CRANBERRY VELVET PIE

1 pie crust (crumb or already baked)
1 -250 gram package cream cheese
1 cup whipping cream
¼ cup sugar
½ teaspoon vanilla extract
1 -16 ounce can whole berry cranberry sauce

Beat cream cheese until fluffy. Beat whipping cream, sugar and vanilla until soft peaks form. Gradually add to cream cheese, beating until smooth and creamy. Fold cranberry sauce into whipped mixture. Spoon into pie crust. Freeze for 4 hours or until firm. Remove from freezer 15 minutes before serving. Garnish with chocolate glaze. (optional)

Chocolate Glaze:
1 ½ ounces semi-sweet chocolate
1 tablespoon margarine or butter
½ tablespoon corn syrup
Melt together in double boiler or microwave until melted. Drizzle over pie.

"It is our choices that show us who we truly are, far more than our abilities."..... *J.K. Rowling*

CREAMY CHERRY PIE
(A quick dessert especially for cherry pie lovers.)

Graham Wafer Crust:
1 ½ cups graham wafer crumbs
¼ cup sugar
6 tablespoons butter, melted

Mix together; crumbs, sugar and butter. Press into a greased 9 inch pie plate, covering bottom and sides. Chill well.

Filling:
1 cup whipping cream
1 -250 gram package cream cheese
½ teaspoon vanilla
1 can cherry pie filling

Beat cream and vanilla until it holds peaks. In a separate bowl, beat cream cheese until smooth. Stir in cherry pie filling. Add whipped cream and gently fold in just until blended. Pour into crust. Chill at least 1 hour.

*"I believe I have lots of time. I have to believe that it won't come back, and I'm in good hands.
But I also do live my life by putting nothing off."*
.... Lynn Redgrave

CUPAR RAISIN CREAM TARTS

(These were good enough to beg out of lunch boxes
many years ago - and taste just as great today!)

¾ cup sugar

2 eggs

1 cup evaporated milk

¼ teaspoon salt

cinnamon to taste

¾ cup raisins

16 - 20 tarts shells depending on the size

Heat oven to 400° F. Blend first four ingredients, add
cinnamon. Divide washed raisins among shells; pour mixture over
top. Bake for 10 minutes and then reduce heat to 350° F. and
bake for another 15-20 or until set.

*"When it comes to getting things done, we need fewer
architects and more bricklayers."....Colleen Barrett*

*"The real art of conversation is not only to say the right thing at
the right place but to leave unsaid the wrong thing at the
tempting moment". ...Dorothy Nevill*

IMPOSSIBLE CARROT PIE
(The taste of pumpkin pie made with carrots!)

2 cups cooked carrots
1 cup brown sugar
4 eggs
1 -385 ml can evaporated milk
1 teaspoon cinnamon
½ teaspoon each cloves, allspice, nutmeg and ginger
½ teaspoon salt

Mix all ingredients together in a blender until smooth. Pour into 10 inch pie plate.

Then mix:
1 cup Bisquick
½ cup chopped nuts
⅓ cup sugar
3 tablespoons margarine

Mix ingredients until crumbly. Sprinkle over pie filling. Bake at 350° F. for 45 minutes or until toothpick inserted comes out clean.

If you are happy – you should inform your face!

PERFECT PUMPKIN PIE

1 -15 ounce can pumpkin
1 -14 ounce can sweetened condensed milk
2 eggs
1 teaspoon cinnamon
½ teaspoon ginger
½ teaspoon nutmeg
½ teaspoon salt
1 -9 inch unbaked pie crust
* Or you may substitute 2 teaspoons of pumpkin pie spice
   for the spices above

Preheat oven to 425° F. Whisk pumpkin, milk, eggs, spices and salt in medium bowl until smooth. Pour into crust. Bake 15 minutes. Reduce oven temperature to 350° F. and continue baking 35-40 minutes or until knife inserted 1 inch from crust comes out clean. Cool. Serve warm or cold with whipped cream.

Everyone is kneaded out of the same dough, but not
baked in the same oven. ......Yiddish Proverb

RAISIN BUTTERMILK PIE
(Make more than one, as this pie freezes really well.)

1 -9 inch unbaked pie shell
3 eggs
½ cup brown sugar, packed
¼ teaspoon salt
1 ½ teaspoons cinnamon
1 cup buttermilk
1 cup raisins

In large bowl, beat eggs lightly. Beat in brown sugar until light. Stir in salt, cinnamon and buttermilk until well mixed. Spread raisins in the pie shell. Pour custard mixture into shell. Bake on lowest rack at 375° F. for 40 minutes or until knife inserted in centre comes out clean. Serve warm or cold.

"I don't think a really good pie can be made without children peeking over your shoulder as you stoop to look at it every little while."....John Gould

RUM TARTS

24 small tart shells
4 eggs
½ cup margarine, melted
3 ¼ cup brown sugar
1 tablespoon flour
1 teaspoon vanilla, rum flavouring or rum
1 ½ cups currants, raisins, or nuts

Mix eggs, margarine, sugar, flour, flavouring and fruit. Pour into tart shells. Bake at 350° F. for 15-20 minutes.

PECAN TARTS

½ cup margarine, melted
½ cup corn syrup
1 cup sugar
1 cup pecans
1 teaspoon rum or rum flavouring (optional)
18 tart shells, pre-baked

Mix margarine, syrup, sugar, pecans, and flavouring. Pour into shells. Bake at 350° F. for 7 minutes.

Some days are good, some days are bad. Some days it's all you can do to take care of yourself. It's a journey that can be travelled and completed. I would never wish my situation on anyone, but know that if it does happen to you, you CAN do it.

You need the help and support of friends and family; don't try to go through it alone. Let people help you, let them drive you places, let them bring you meals, let them take the kids places so they can have some fun.

Let yourself rest, let yourself cry, let some things go. This is only a temporary situation and when you are done with treatment, your body will need time to recover, but then you can go back to the way you would normally do things.

Plan ahead, plan for your kids, plan for yourself, plan as though you intend to be around for a loooooooong time. And PLEASE, PLEASE, do your monthly self examinations!!

What Breast Cancer Cannot Do

Cancer is so limited...
It cannot cripple Love
It cannot shatter Hope
It cannot corrode Faith
It cannot destroy Peace
It cannot kill Friendship
It cannot suppress Memories
It cannot silence Courage
It cannot invade the Soul
It cannot steal Eternal Life
It cannot conquer the Spirit

Cookies and Treats

A strong woman strives for goodness
in herself each day, but a woman
of strength strives to see goodness
in each person she encounters.

TURTLE TARTS

48 mini tart shells, baked and cooled
48 pecan halves
¾ cup sweetened condensed milk
2/3 cup brown sugar
½ cup butter or margarine
3 tablespoons corn syrup
½ cup chocolate chips
2 tablespoons margarine

Put a pecan in each shell. Combine milk, brown sugar, butter and corn syrup in a heavy saucepan over medium heat; bring to boil. Stir and boil for 5 minutes - watch that it doesn't stick or boil over. Remove from heat. Slowly beat with a spoon for 2-3 minutes until it starts to thicken - not too long. Spoon mixture over pecans. Melt chocolate chips and margarine together in microwave, then place a dab on each tart. Chill. These are very nice for Christmas!

"I do not seek. I find." ....*Pablo Picasso*

HAZELNUT BISCOTTI

1 package white cake mix
2/3 cup flour
1/3 cup ground hazelnuts
2 eggs
½ cup canola oil
1 tablespoon lemon zest, grated
2/3 cup hazelnuts, coarsely chopped

Preheat oven to 350° F. In a large bowl, combine cake mix, flour, ground hazelnuts, eggs, oil and zest. Beat on low speed for 1 minute or until blended. Work in chopped hazelnuts to form smooth dough. Divide dough in half. On a greased cookie sheet, shape each half into a 10 x 3 inch rectangle, approximately ½ inch thick. Bake, one sheet at a time for 15 minutes. Remove from oven and cool 10 minutes on cookie sheet. Carefully transfer to cutting board and cut each rectangle into ½ inch slices. Place slices on their side on cookie sheets. Return to oven for 10 minutes. Remove from oven and turn. Continue to bake for 5-10 minutes longer or until crisp and golden. Cool on cookie sheet for a few minutes and then transfer biscotti to wire racks and cool completely.

"If you wish to travel far and fast, travel light. Take off all your envies, jealousies, unforgiveness, selfishness and fears."
.......Cesare Pavese

At the **Conexus Arts Centre**
in Regina

★ A BRAND NEW LIVE SHOW!

Care ♥ Bears™
and the
Lost Rainbow

MAY 5, 7PM Interactive musical fun for the whole family!

Tickets are available at the Box Office in Regina
306-525-9999 / 1-800-667-8497 • www.conexusartscentre.ca

PRESENTED BY:

  RAMADA **LEADER-POST** conexus arts centre | AMERICAN GREETINGS

Care Bears™ and related trademarks ©2007. Those Characters From Cleveland, Inc.
Used under license by Sphere Entertainment. American Greetings with rose logo is a trademark of AGC, LLC.

Please Volunteer Today.

1-800-267-WISH   www.childrenswish.ca

Proce
the Sa
EYES
and E

This a

MOMMY'S BREAK TIME BISCOTTI

½ cup butter, softened

2/3 cup white sugar

¼ cup cocoa

2 teaspoons baking powder

2 eggs

1 ¾ cups flour

1 cup white chocolate chips

1 cup chocolate chips

additional chocolate chips and white chocolate chips to decorate
biscotti.

In a large mixing bowl, cream butter and sugar with an electric
mixer until light and fluffy. Gradually beat in cocoa and baking
powder. Beat for 2 minutes. Beat in the eggs one at a time. Stir
in flour by hand. Mix in white chocolate chips and chocolate chips.
Cover dough, and chill for about 10 minutes. Preheat oven to
375° F. Roll dough into a 9 inch long log. Place log on lightly-
greased cookie sheet. Flatten slightly. Bake for 20 to 25 minutes,
or until toothpick inserted in center comes out clean. Cool on cookie
sheet for 5 minutes, then carefully transfer to a wire rack to cool
for one hour. Cut loaf into ½ inch wide diagonal slices with an
electric knife. Place slices on an ungreased cookie sheet, and bake
at 325° F. for 9 minutes. Turn cookies over, and bake for 7-9
minutes. Cool completely. Melt chocolate chips and spread on one
side of biscotti and then drizzle melted white chocolate chips in fine
lines over to decorate. Store in an airtight container.

COFFEE TIME BISCOTTI

2 cups flour
½ cup ground flax
1 teaspoon baking powder
¼ teaspoon salt
½ cup butter, softened
1 cup sugar
2 eggs
zest of one orange
1 teaspoon vanilla
1 cup almonds, coarsely chopped
1 cup semi-sweet chocolate chips (for icing)

Combine flour, flax, baking powder and salt. In another bowl beat butter and sugar until smooth. Beat in eggs, add vanilla and orange zest. Gradually add flour mixture. Fold in nuts. Divide dough in half. Shape into 2 rolls about 10 inches long. Place 2 inches apart on a greased cookie sheet. Flatten logs into 1 inch thick rectangles. Bake at 350° F. for 30 minutes. Cool 10 minutes and carefully transfer to cutting board. Slice both logs into ½ inch thick slices. Return to cookie sheet and bake for 10 minutes or until lightly browned on each side. Immediately transfer to wire racks and cool completely. Melt semi-sweet chocolate and spread on one side of biscotti. Allow chocolate to harden and store in airtight container or cookie jar.

Anyone can be polite to a king. It takes a gentleman to be polite to a beggar.

O'HENRY BARS
(Tastes like the real thing!)

2 cups brown sugar

2 cups corn syrup

1 ½ cups peanut butter

4 cups Special K

4 cups Rice Krispies

1 cup salted peanuts

¼ cup paraffin wax

1 -300 gram package chocolate chips

1 -300 gram package butterscotch chips

Boil sugar and syrup for 1 minute. Add peanut butter and mix well. Pour over cereals and peanuts. Mix and let cool enough to handle. With margarine on hands, roll into balls or small logs and put on wax paper. Melt together; wax and chips. Dip balls into chocolate mixture and put back on wax paper to cool.

Here is what Jeff Foxworthy has to say about Saskatchewanians:
If you've worn shorts and a parka at the same time,
you're from Saskatchewan.
If you carry jumpers in your car and your wife knows
how to use them, you're from Saskatchewan.
If you design your kid's Halloween costume to fit over a snowsuit,
you're from Saskatchewan.
If driving is better in the winter, because the pot holes are filled with
snow, you're from Saskatchewan.
If you are shopping and someone offers you assistance and they
don't work there, you're from Saskatchewan.
If you know several people who have hit a deer more than once,
you're from Saskatchewan.
If you understand these jokes - you're from Saskatchewan.

CHEWY COCONUT NUT BARS
(These are quick to make and a treat to eat.)

Crust:
1 package white cake mix
½ cup butter, melted

In a large bowl, combine cake mix and melted butter. Using a wooden spoon, mix until a soft dough forms. Press firmly into a greased 9 x 13 inch cake pan. Bake at 350° F. for 15 minutes or until golden brown.

Topping:
4 eggs
1 ¾ cups brown sugar, packed
¼ cup flour
2 teaspoons baking powder
1 teaspoon vanilla
1 ½ cups nuts, chopped
1 cup flaked coconut

In a bowl, beat eggs and brown sugar until blended. Stir in flour, baking powder and vanilla. Stir in nuts and coconut. Spread over warm crust. Bake at 350° F. for 25-30 minutes or until golden. Cool completely in pan on wire rack. Cut into bars.

"Take the first step in faith. You don't have to see the whole staircase, just take the first step."
.....Dr. Martin Luther King Jr.

CHEERIO SLICE
(Quick...Easy...Kids of all ages Love It!)

1 cup sugar

1 cup corn syrup

2/3 cup margarine

1 cup peanut butter

4 cups Cheerios

4 cups Corn Flakes

2 cups unsalted peanuts

Boil the first 3 ingredients together for 1 ½ to 2 minutes. Add peanut butter, stirring until smooth. Add the remaining ingredients, mix quickly and press into greased 9 x 13 inch pan. Slice into squares. Freezes well.

For those of you that watch what you eat, here's the final word on nutrition and health. It's a relief to know the truth after all those conflicting medical studies:

1. The Japanese eat very little fat and suffer fewer heart attacks than the Americans, Australians, British or Canadians.

2. The Mexicans eat a lot of fat and also suffer fewer heart attacks than the Americans, Australians, British or Canadians.

3. The Japanese drink very little red wine and suffer fewer heart attacks than the Americans, Australians, British or Canadians.

4. The Italians drink large amounts of red wine and also suffer fewer heart attacks than the Americans, Australians, British or Canadians.

5. The Germans drink a lot of beer and eat lots of sausages and fats and suffer fewer heart attacks than the Americans, Australians, British or Canadians.

6. Ukrainians drink a lot of vodka, eat a lot of perogies and cabbage rolls, and suffer fewer heart attacks than the Americans, Australians, British or Canadians.

Conclusion: Eat and drink whatever you like. Apparently, speaking English is what kills you.   Keep smiling!!!

SELF-ICING CUPCAKES

2 eggs

1 cup canola oil

1 cup sour cream

1 tablespoon vanilla

3 cups flour

2 cups white sugar

½ cup cocoa

1 tablespoon baking soda

2 cups hot water

Filling:

1 egg

1/8 teaspoon salt

1 -250 gram package cream cheese

1/3 cup sugar

2 cups chocolate chips

Mix together; eggs, oil, sour cream and vanilla. Add flour, sugar, cocoa, and soda. Add 2 cups hot water and blend together until smooth. Pour batter into greased muffin tins. Beat together filling ingredients and place 1 heaping teaspoon of filling in the centre of each cupcake. Bake for 20 minutes. Makes about 40 cupcakes.

"If a fellow isn't thankful for what he's got, he isn't likely to be thankful for what he's going to get."....Frank A. Clark

COCONUT ALMOND SLICE
(Easy and delicious!)

1/3 cup margarine

1 -10 ounce bag regular marshmallow

2 ½ cups corn flakes

1 cup sweetened coconut

1 cup sliced almonds, toasted

½ cup maraschino cherries, chopped

Melt together margarine and marshmallows. In a large bowl mix together marshmallow mixture with corn flakes, coconut, almonds and cherries. Pack into a greased 8 x 8 inch pan. Slice into bars while still warm.

Don't worry over what other people are thinking about you. They're too busy worrying over what you are thinking about them. According to all surveys and statistics, your greatest worry won't happen. Happiness is easy - dwell on things that make you glad; expel all thoughts that make you sad. Happiness has little to do with what we have; everything with what we think.

FUDGE BROWNIES

1 cup butter, softened
2 cups brown sugar
2 eggs
2 teaspoons vanilla
3 cups flour
4 tablespoons cocoa
1 cup chocolate chips (optional)
1 cup walnuts (optional)

Mix all ingredients in a large bowl in order given. Pat down in greased 9 x 13 inch pan. Bake for 15 minutes at 350° F. Ice while still warm.

Icing:
2 tablespoons butter, melted
1 teaspoon vanilla
2 tablespoons milk
1 ½ cup icing sugar

Mix above and spread over warm brownies.

"Develop an attitude of gratitude, and give thanks for everything that happens to you, knowing that every step forward is a step toward achieving something bigger and better than your current situation." - Brian Tracy

ANISE COOKIES
(Anise is a licorice flavoured seed used medicinally and in cooking and liquors.)

4 eggs

2 ½ cups icing sugar

1 ½ cups flour

¾ cup cornstarch

1 teaspoon crushed anise seed

1 teaspoon vanilla

Beat eggs until frothy. Add sugar, flour, cornstarch, anise and vanilla. Beat at high speed of electric mixer for 10 minutes. Drop by teaspoons on greased and lightly floured cookie sheets. Let sit uncovered overnight (at least 7 hours). In the morning the cookies should be dry to touch. Bake at 325° F. for 10-15 minutes. The cookies should not brown and should form a "cap" on the top of each cookie. When done, they will have a puffed meringue like top on a soft cookie base. These cookies turn out better when humidity is low.

Be thankful:
For the husband or wife who snores all night, because he or she is at home asleep with me and not with someone else.
For the taxes that I pay because it means that I am employed.
For the mess to clean after a party because it means that I have been surrounded by friends.
For the clothes that fit a little too snug because it means I have enough to eat.
For a floor that needs mopping, and windows that need cleaning because it means I have a home.
For all the complaining I hear about the government because it means that we have the freedom of speech.
For the parking spot I find at the far end of the parking lot because it means I am capable of walking and that I have been blessed with transportation.

BANANA COOKIES
(A nice soft and moist cookie)

2 ¼ cups flour

2 teaspoons baking powder

½ teaspoon salt

¼ teaspoon baking soda

1 cup sugar

2/3 cup margarine

2 eggs

1 teaspoon vanilla

1 cup chocolate chips or raisins

1 cup mashed bananas

Sift flour, baking powder, salt and baking soda together, set aside. Cream sugar and margarine, add eggs and vanilla. Add dry ingredients and mix well, dough will be sticky. Stir in chocolate chips or raisins and bananas. Drop by teaspoonfuls onto greased cookie sheet. Bake at 400° F. for 12-15 minutes.

Two old women were sitting on a bench waiting for their bus.
The buses were running late and a lot of time passed.
Finally one woman turned to the other and said, "You know, I've
been sitting here for so long, my butt fell asleep!"
The other woman turned to her and said,
"I know, I heard it snoring!!!"

CARROT CAKE COOKIES

½ pound unsalted butter
1 cup brown sugar
2 large eggs
½ teaspoon vanilla
½ teaspoon baking soda
1 ½ cups flour
2 cups carrots, coarsely shredded
2 cups fruit and nut granola
1 cup cornflakes
2 tablespoons sugar

Preheat oven to 375° F. Cream butter and sugar. Mix in eggs, vanilla, and baking soda until fluffy. Mix in flour. Stir in carrots, granola, and corn flakes. Drop by heaping tablespoons about 2 inches apart on greased cookie sheets. Sprinkle with sugar and bake until golden, 15-20 minutes.

The best thing to give to your enemy is forgiveness;
to an opponent, tolerance
to a friend, your heart
to a child, a good example
to a father, deference
to your mother, conduct that will make her proud of you,
to yourself, respect, to all man, charity"
.........Francis Maitland Balfour

CHOCOLATE CHIP PEANUT BUTTER COOKIES
(Enjoy this cookie on a rainy afternoon,
with good friends and a cup of coffee.)

1 cup butter

1 cup white sugar

1 cup brown sugar

2 eggs

1 cup peanut butter

1 teaspoon vanilla

3 cups flour

2 teaspoons baking soda

pinch of salt

1 cup semi-sweet chocolate chips

½ cup peanuts, finely chopped (optional)

In large bowl cream butter. Add white and brown sugar and
beat until smooth. Beat in eggs. Add peanut butter and vanilla;
stir until well mixed. Stir together flour, baking soda, salt,
chocolate chips and peanuts (if using). Add to creamed mixture.
Drop by tablespoon on ungreased cookie sheets. Flatten cookie
by criss-crossing with a fork. Bake at 350° F. for 12-15
minutes. Makes 4-5 dozen.

*"People who consider themselves victims of their circumstances
will always remain victims unless they develop a greater vision
for their lives." ...Stedman Graham*

CHOCOLATE CHIP TOFFEE ALMOND COOKIES

(Crunchy toffee bits, almonds and chocolate chips make these cookies a certain favourite.)

1 package white cake mix
2 eggs
½ cup butter, melted
1 teaspoon vanilla
1 cup almonds, chopped
¾ cup crunchy toffee bits
¾ cup milk chocolate chips

Preheat oven to 375° F. In large mixing bowl, combine cake mix, eggs, butter and vanilla. Beat on low speed for 1 minute or until smooth. Stir in almonds, toffee bits and chocolate chips. Mix well. Drop dough by rounded tablespoons, 2 inches apart onto greased cookie sheets. Flatten slightly. Bake for 10-12 minutes or until lightly browned. Cool for 1 minute on cookie sheet or until firm. Transfer cookies to wire rack and cool completely. Makes about 3 ½ dozen cookies.

I've learned that:
Two people can look at the same thing and see something entirely different.
- Money is a lousy way of keeping score.
-Maturity has more to do with what types of experiences you've had and what you've learned from them and less to do with how many birthdays you've had.
-It isn't always good enough to be forgiven by others.
Sometimes you have to forgive yourself.
-No matter how hot and steamy the relationship is at first, the passion fades and there better be something to take its place.

CHOCOLATE PEANUT BUTTER COOKIES
(These cookies are just like peanuts,
you can't stop at just one)

1 package Devil's food cake mix
1 cup creamy peanut butter
2 eggs
¼ cup milk
1 cup peanut butter chips
¾ cup peanuts, chopped

Preheat oven to 350° F. In a large mixing bowl, combine cake mix, peanut butter, eggs and milk. Mix on low speed for 1 minute or until blended. Stir in chips and peanuts. Mix well. Drop by rounded tablespoons, 2 inches apart onto greased baking sheets. Bake for 10-12 minutes or until lightly browned. Cool for a few minutes on baking sheet or until firm, then transfer cookies to wire racks and cool completely. This recipe makes approximately 3 ½ dozen cookies.

LUCK
"The only thing that overcomes hard luck is hard work."
....Harry Golden

"We must believe in luck. For how else can we explain
the success of those we don't like."....Jean Cocteau

"I'm a great believer in luck and I find the harder I work,
the more of it I have."....Thomas Jefferson

COCONUT MANGO MACAROONS
(When you bite into these, you'll do the mango-tango!)

4 egg whites
¼ teaspoon salt
2/3 cup sugar
1 teaspoon vanilla
¼ cup flour
3 cups flaked coconut, lightly packed
½ cup dried mango, diced

In a large bowl beat egg whites until foamy. Add in the salt and sugar in a slow steady stream and continue beating until whites are firm and fluffy. Fold in vanilla and flour gently. Add coconut and mango. Drop the batter by tablespoonfuls on a parchment lined cookie sheet. Space the cookies evenly. Bake at 325° F. for 20-25 minutes or until lightly browned.
Makes 3 dozen.

Chocolate is extracted from the beans of the cocoa plant.
Beans are a vegetable.
Sugar is extracted from sugar beets.
The sugar beet is a vegetable.
Therefore chocolate is a vegetable.
They also contain milk - veggies and milk -
Wow! Eat as much as you like.

COOKIES FOR BREAKFAST
(For those of us that like cookies for breakfast-
here is one that we can enjoy and is good for us!)

¾ cup margarine or butter

½ cup honey

2/3 cup brown sugar

2 eggs

2 teaspoons baking powder

2 teaspoons baking soda

½ teaspoon salt

½ cup ground flax

2 cups whole wheat flour

2 cups rolled oats

1 cup large flake unsweetened coconut

1 cup raisins (chopped)

1 cup grated dates

½ cup pecans, coarsely chopped

½ cup sunflower seeds

½ cup pumpkin seeds

Cream together margarine, honey, brown sugar and eggs. Beat in baking powder, baking soda, salt, flax and flour. Stir in rolled oats, coconut, raisins, dates, pecans, sunflower and pumpkin seeds. Measure out ¼ cup portions and shape into rounds. Place on greased cookie sheet. Bake at 350° F. for 10 minutes. Cool on rack. Enjoy!!

DATE FILLED OATMEAL COOKIES
(Many years ago a grateful and excited bride received a cookie jar of these as a shower gift!)

1 cup butter
1 cup brown sugar
½ cup sour milk (add 2 teaspoons vinegar to sour)
2 cups flour
1 cup rolled oats
1 teaspoon baking soda
¼ teaspoon salt
1 teaspoon vanilla

Date Filling:
½ pound pitted dates, chopped
1/3 cup sugar
2/3 cup water

In small pot over medium-low heat, cook dates, sugar and water until dates are soft enough to be mashed with a fork. The mixture should be of a jam-like consistency. Cool.
In large bowl, cream butter and sugar together well. Slowly mix in milk. Add flour, rolled oats, baking soda, salt, and vanilla. Mix well. Chill dough. Roll out thinly on lightly floured board. Cut into 2 ½ inch rounds. Place on ungreased baking sheets. Bake at 350° F. for 8-10 minutes. Cool. Fill with date filling, to form sandwich cookies. Makes about 4 dozen.

Life is what you make of it - kind of like play dough.

FAMOUS DEPARTMENT STORE COOKIES

(This is the urban legend cookie that has lasted for
years, for very good reason — it is the best!)

1 cup butter, softened (or margarine for a thicker cookie)

1 cup white sugar

2 eggs

1 cup packed brown sugar

1 teaspoon vanilla extract

2 cups flour

2 ½ cups rolled oats

½ teaspoon salt

1 teaspoon baking powder

1 teaspoon baking soda

2 cups semi-sweet chocolate chips

4 ounces milk chocolate, grated

1 ½ cups walnuts, chopped

Preheat oven to 375° F. Measure oats into a blender or food
processor, and then blend to a fine powder. Set aside. In a large
bowl, cream together butter and sugars. Beat in the eggs one at a
time, then stir in the vanilla. In a separate bowl, mix together flour,
oats, salt, baking powder, and baking soda. Stir dry ingredients
into creamed butter and sugar. Add chocolate chips, grated
chocolate, and nuts. Drop by rounded teaspoons onto ungreased
cookie sheets. Bake for 6-8 minutes in the preheated oven.
Cookies should be golden with a little brown around the edge.

Shown on previous page:

❖ Anise Cookies.....page 351

❖ Shortbread Meltaways.....page 368

❖ Prune or Date Pinwheels.....page 369

❖ Coconut Mango Macaroons.....page 357

❖ Self-Icing Cupcakes.....page 348

❖ Date Filled Oatmeal Cookies.....page 359

❖ Chocolate Toffee Square.....page 313

❖ Taffy Q's.....page 376

❖ Pineapple Slice.....page 325

❖ Scrumptious Almond Squares.....page 329

❖ Golden Graham Candy.....page 375

❖ Sesame Wafers.....page 370

❖ Cupar Raisin Cream Tarts.....page 335

❖ English Tea Cakes.....page 319

❖ Chocolate Orange Truffles.....page 374

❖ Buttercrunch Almond Cups.....page 373

❖ Eatmore Bars.....page 375

❖ Easy Pretzel Turtles.....page 377

FLAX PECAN CHOCOLATE CHIP COOKIES

¾ cup canola oil
1 cup white sugar
1 cup brown sugar
2 eggs
1 teaspoon vanilla
1 cup white flour
1 cup whole wheat flour
½ cup ground flaxseed
½ teaspoon salt
1 teaspoon baking powder
1 teaspoon baking soda
1 ½ cups pecans, chopped (optional)
¾ cup chocolate chips

Beat oil and sugars until light and fluffy. Beat in eggs and vanilla. In separate bowl mix flours, flaxseed, salt, baking powder and baking soda. Stir this into creamed mixture. Add pecans and chocolate chips. Form into 1 inch balls and place on ungreased cookie sheets about 2 inches apart. Flatten with a fork if you like a crisp cookie. Bake at 350° F. for about 10 minutes.
Makes about 6 dozen.

I'm not 40, I'm $39.95 plus shipping and handling.

361

GINGER DROP COOKIES

(My brother who did not know his colours called these,
"Green Cookies". The surprising thing the rest of us
(six in all) followed suit..... so they were always
known in our house as Green Cookies!)

½ cup warm water

1 teaspoon baking soda

½ cup margarine

1 ½ cups brown sugar

2 eggs

½ cup molasses

1 cup raisins

1 teaspoon cloves

1 teaspoon ginger

1 teaspoon cinnamon

3 cups flour

Dissolve soda in water. Mix all ingredients in order given. Drop
by teaspoons on a greased cookie sheet. Bake at 375° F. for
7-10 minutes

The trouble with life is you are half-way through it
before you realize it is a do-it yourself thing.

362

GINGERBREAD MEN
(The kids will have fun decorating these cookies!)

1 cup shortening

1 cup sugar

1 teaspoon baking soda

1 ½ cups light molasses

2 tablespoons vinegar

5 cups flour

1 teaspoon salt

1 ½ teaspoons ginger

1 teaspoon cloves

½ teaspoon cinnamon

½ teaspoon nutmeg

Cream shortening and sugar. Dissolve baking soda in molasses and add to creamed mixture along with vinegar. Set aside. Blend flour, salt and spices. Gradually add flour mixture to the creamed mixture and mix well. Roll out on floured surface and cut with cookie cutter. Bake at 350° F. for 8 minutes.

"They say such nice things at people's funerals, that it makes me sad that I'm going to miss mine by only a few days."
.... Garrison Kellor

HALLOWEEN GRANOLA COOKIES
(Great for leftover Halloween chocolate bars.)

1 cup margarine, softened

½ cup white sugar

½ cup brown sugar

2 eggs

1 teaspoon vanilla

1 ½ cups whole wheat flour

2 cups granola

1 cup oatmeal

1 teaspoon baking powder

2 cups chocolate bars, crushed or 1 cup chocolate chips
     and 1 cup raisins

Cream margarine and sugars. Add eggs and vanilla and mix well. Add dry ingredients. Drop by spoonfuls on greased cookie sheets and bake at 350° F. for 10-12 minutes. Makes about 7 dozen.

Note: Peel all chocolate bars, Smarties, raisins, etc. and place them in a plastic bag. Crush by hitting with a mallet or rolling pin. This breaks bars into smaller pieces that can be added to cookies.

It isn't necessary to blow out the other person's light to let your own shine.

LEMON CRISPS
(This is a crisp, lemony cookie to
enjoy with a cup of tea.)

1 package lemon cake mix
1 egg
½ cup butter, melted
1 teaspoon lemon zest
2 tablespoons sugar

Preheat oven to 350° F. In a large mixing bowl, combine cake mix, egg, butter and lemon zest. Mix with wooden spoon until well blended. Shape dough into 1-inch balls. Roll in granulated sugar and place on a greased cookie sheet. Press flat with bottom of a glass dipped in sugar. Bake for 10 minutes or until lightly browned around the edges. Cool 1 minute and then transfer cookies to wire racks and cool completely. You can make these into sandwich cookies by putting 2 cookies together with a lemon frosting or jam filling.

"The secret of health for both mind and body is not to mourn for the past, worry about the future, or anticipate troubles but to live in the present moment wisely and earnestly"....Buddha

MONSTER COOKIES
(A huge cookie that is quickly combined and "dropped" from a cup onto a cookie sheet.)

¾ cup vegetable shortening
1 cup brown sugar, packed
¼ cup water
1 egg
1 teaspoon vanilla
3 cups rolled oats
1 cup flour
¾ teaspoon salt
½ teaspoon baking soda
1 cup candy-coated plain chocolate pieces
½ cup nuts, chopped (optional)

In large mixing bowl, beat at medium speed until well-blended shortening, sugar, water, egg, and vanilla. Add oats, flour, salt and baking soda. Beat at low speed until soft dough forms. Stir in chocolate pieces and nuts. Drop dough by scant cups, 4 inches apart, onto ungreased cookie sheets. Flatten dough to ½ inch thickness with back of spoon. Bake at 350° F. for 18-20 minutes, or until golden brown. Let cool for 5 minutes before removing from cookie sheets. Cool completely before storing. Makes 6 cookies.

ONE HUNDRED BEST COOKIES

(Funny, when we made these we only got 89, was it because we ate some of the dough or were our cookies just too big!!)

1 cup margarine
1 cup white sugar
1 cup brown sugar
1 cup canola oil
1 egg
1 cup Rice Krispies
1 cup coconut
1 cup rolled oats
1 teaspoon baking soda
1 teaspoon salt
1 teaspoon cream of tartar
3 cups flour

Cream margarine and sugars. Beat in oil and egg. Add rest of ingredients in order given making sure to add the flour last. Drop by teaspoon on greased cookie sheet. Bake at 350° F. 12-15 minutes. Enjoy!

"Whatever course you decide upon, there is always someone to tell you that you are wrong. There are always difficulties arising which tempt you to believe that your critics are right. To map out a course of action and follow it to an end requires courage"....Ralph Waldo Emerson

PEANUT CRACKLES

1 cup corn syrup
½ cup sugar
½ cup brown sugar
1 cup peanut butter
3 cups corn flakes

Combine syrup and sugars and just bring to a boil over medium heat. Stir in peanut butter. Remove from heat and stir in corn flakes. Using a heaping tablespoon, drop on a greased cookie sheet. Chill until firm. Yields about 48 cookies.

SHORTBREAD MELTAWAYS

1 cup butter, softened
½ cup icing sugar
2 teaspoons vanilla
1 ¾ cups flour
½ cup cornstarch
¾ teaspoon baking powder
1 cup Skor bits
icing sugar

Mix butter, icing sugar and vanilla until creamy. Add flour, cornstarch, and baking powder. After mixed well, add Skor bits. Roll into 1 heaping tablespoon balls. Place on ungreased cookie sheets and bake for 15 minutes at 350° F. Dust with icing sugar after baking.

PRUNE or DATE PINWHEELS
(Easy and elegant, an old family favourite!)

2 ¼ cups prunes or dates, pitted
1 cup water
1 cup sugar
1 cup walnuts, crushed
1 cup butter
2 cups brown sugar
3 eggs, well beaten
4 cups flour
½ teaspoon salt

Blend the pitted fruit in a blender until smooth. Place in a saucepan, add water and sugar, cook slowly until fairly thick. Add nuts and cool. In a larger bowl, cream butter and brown sugar, add beaten eggs, flour and salt, mix well. Chill the dough, divide into 4 parts. On a floured surface, roll out a portion at a time into a rectangle, not too thin. Spread ¼ of the fruit mixture on each rolled out portion. With floured fingers roll up from the wide side. Chill the rolls. Slice rolls into ¼ inch wide slices. Place slices on lightly greased cookie sheet. Slices can be placed fairly close together, they do not rise much. Bake in a 350° F. oven for 12 -15 minutes

"The secret of staying young is to live honestly,
eat slowly, and lie about your age." ...Lucille Ball

SESAME WAFERS

(Called benne wafers in the south- benne means sesame
and the seeds were first introduced by African slaves.)

1 cup sesame seeds
½ cup butter, softened
1 ½ cups brown sugar, packed
1 egg
¾ cup flour
¼ teaspoon baking powder
1 teaspoon vanilla

In small skillet, toast sesame seeds over medium heat, stirring
occasionally, until lightly browned. Set aside to cool. In small
bowl, cream butter, sugar, and egg until light and fluffy. Stir
flour and baking powder together; add to creamed mixture and
beat until well mixed. Add vanilla and sesame seeds; continue
beating until well combined. Drop batter by ½ teaspoonfuls on
greased cookie sheets about 1 ½ inches apart. Bake at 350° F.
for 8-10 minutes until slightly brown around the edges. Remove
and cool completely on wire racks. Makes 10-12 dozen.

If pro is the opposite of con - does that mean that
Progress is the opposite of Congress?

THE BEST OF THE BREAST
CHOCOLATE CHIP COOKIES
(Everyone has a "best" chocolate chip cookie – this is it!)

4 ½ cups all-purpose flour
2 teaspoons baking soda
½ teaspoon salt
2 cups butter, softened
1 ½ cups packed brown sugar
½ cup white sugar
2 -3.4 ounce packages instant vanilla pudding mix
4 eggs
2 tablespoons vanilla extract
4 cups semi-sweet chocolate chips
2 cups chopped walnuts (optional)

Preheat oven to 350° F. Sift together the flour, baking soda and salt, set aside. In a large bowl, cream together the butter, brown sugar, and white sugar. Beat in the instant pudding mix until blended. Stir in the eggs and vanilla. Blend in the flour mixture. Finally, stir in the chocolate chips and nuts. Drop cookies by rounded spoonfuls onto ungreased cookie sheets. Bake for 10-12 minutes in the preheated oven. Don't over bake - edges should be golden brown.
* A great variation is chocolate pudding and mint chips or chocolate pudding and a mix of peanut butter and chocolate chips or French vanilla pudding and white chocolate chips – we could go on and on – just use your imagination!!

YO - YO COOKIES

¾ cup shortening

1 ¾ cups brown sugar

1 teaspoon baking soda

2 tablespoons warm water

2 eggs, beaten

2 cups flour

1 teaspoon vanilla

¼ teaspoon salt

raspberry jam

Cream shortening and sugar. Dissolve soda in warm water and add to beaten eggs. Add to creamed mixture. Mix in flour, salt and vanilla. Drop by teaspoons onto greased cookie sheet, spaced well apart. Bake at 375° F. for 8-10 minutes. Cool slightly and put together with raspberry jam.

You might not know this, but some non living things are
actually male or female.
Freezer bags are male - they hold everything in,
but you can see right through them.
Tires are male - they go bald easily and are often over inflated.
Hammers are male- in the last 5000 years, they have hardly
changed at all, and are occasionally handy to have around.
Remote control - female - ha! - you probably thought it would
be male, but consider this: It easily gives a man pleasure, he'd
be lost without it, and while he doesn't always know which
buttons to push, he just keeps trying.

BUTTERCRUNCH ALMOND CUPS

3 ½ cups sliced almonds
1 cup butter
1 cup sugar
1/3 cup honey
1/3 cup whipping cream

Spray 40 tin foil baking cups well, with no-stick cooking spray. Heat butter, sugar, honey, and cream over medium heat and boil gently 1 ½ minutes stirring constantly. Stir in almonds. Pour into prepared foil cups and bake 375° F. for 12-13 minutes. Tarts should be golden brown before you remove them from oven. Wait until cooled before you take them out of foil cups. They should pop out. * make sure tinfoil cups are not paper lined — small tart tinfoil liners work great.

A girl is looking up at the sky. "Look," she says "Angels!" Passersby laugh, "You fool, that is only a cloud."

How wonderful it would be to see angels where there are only clouds! How awful to see only clouds, where there are angels.

Happiness comes in through doors you didn't even know you left open

CHOCOLATE ORANGE TRUFFLES

(For anyone that loves the chocolate orange flavour combination — this is for you! (And me!)

1 pound icing sugar
1 -12 ounce package vanilla wafers, crushed
1 cup walnuts, chopped
½ cup butter
1 -6 ounce can frozen orange juice concentrate, thawed
1 ½ pounds milk chocolate, melted

In a large bowl, combine the icing sugar, vanilla wafers, walnuts, butter and orange juice. Mix well and shape into 1 inch round balls; allow to dry for 1 hour. Place chocolate in top of double boiler. Stir frequently over medium heat until melted. Dip balls into melted chocolate and place in decorative paper cups

* To decorate — melt ¾ cup of white chocolate chips — tint with orange food coloring and drizzle over the tops.

When the mother returned from the grocery store, her small son pulled out the box of animal crackers he had begged for, then he spread the animal-shaped crackers all over the kitchen counter. "What are you doing?" his Mom asked...
"The box says you can't eat them if the seal is broken," the boy explained. "I'm looking for the seal."

GOLDEN GRAHAM CANDY

1 pound white chocolate wafers
4 cups golden graham cereal
1 cup pecans, chopped (you may substitute peanuts or other nuts)

Melt the wafers in a bowl in the microwave on defrost. Stir until melted. Add cereal and nuts. Put on cookie sheet and cool. Break into pieces.

EATMORE BARS

2 cups corn syrup
1 ½ cups peanut butter
1 ½ cups chocolate chips
3 cups blanched peanuts
1 teaspoon vanilla

Boil syrup, peanut butter and chocolate chips for 2 minutes. Add peanuts and vanilla. Spread on a greased cookie sheet. Cool and cut into bars.

"Integrity is doing the right thing, knowing that nobody's going to know whether you did it or not".... Oprah Winfrey

TAFFY Q'S
(Little people love these!)

3 bars taffy
½ cup sweetened condensed milk
¼ cup butter or margarine
3 cups cornflakes

In medium saucepan over low heat melt taffy, milk and butter stirring constantly. Bring to a boil, remove from heat and add cornflakes. Mix and drop by spoonfuls on waxed paper. Cool and enjoy!

TOBLERONE FUDGE

½ cup margarine
½ cup sugar
¾ cup evaporated milk
1 -400 gram Toblerone chocolate bar

Bring margarine, sugar and milk to a boil; cook for 5 minutes over medium heat, stirring constantly. Remove from heat and add chocolate bar. Mix until melted. Line 9 x 9 inch pan with wax paper. Pour fudge into pan, cool and cut into squares.

*Sometimes moving forward means
leaving something behind.*

CARAMEL APPLES
(Makes 15 treats for children, young or old.)

1 cup sugar
¾ cup corn syrup
1 can sweetened condensed milk
¼ cup butter
1 teaspoon vanilla
15 apples, washed
1 ½ cups pecans, crushed

Heat sugar, syrup, milk, butter and vanilla in saucepan. Mix continually on low heat until mixture comes to a boil. Dip apples into caramel sauce, turning to cover, then dip into pecans to coat. Cool on waxed paper.

EASY PRETZEL TURTLES

30 small mini pretzels, curved not sticks
3 packages Rolo candies or 30 chocolate covered caramel candies — (Dove work well too)
30 pecan halves

Preheat oven to 300° F. Arrange the pretzels in a single layer on a parchment lined cookie sheet. Place one chocolate covered caramel candy on each pretzel. Bake for 4 minutes. While the candy is warm, press a pecan half onto each candy covered pretzel. Cool completely before storing in an airtight container.

ENGLISH TOFFEE

1 can sweetened condensed milk
½ pound butter (not margarine)
½ cup corn syrup
2 cups brown sugar

Mix all ingredients in a large saucepan. Cook over medium heat, stirring frequently until mixture comes to a gentle boil. Continue to cook and stir for 30 minutes or until hard crack on thermometer. Remove from heat and pour onto a greased cookie sheet. When toffee cools it will become hard. Break toffee and store in an airtight container. Delicious!!!

MICROWAVE PEANUT BRITTLE

1 cup sugar
½ cup corn syrup
1 teaspoon vanilla
1 teaspoon butter
1 teaspoon baking soda
1 cup peanuts.

Mix sugar and syrup in a 1 quart casserole. Microwave on high for 4 minutes. Add vanilla and butter; stir and microwave on high for 1 ½ minutes. Stir in baking soda until foamy. Add peanuts. Quickly spread on well buttered cookie sheet. Cool and break into pieces.

I have gradually started to believe that I will survive this. For at least two years after my treatment, I still had doubts about cancer and read almost obsessively about recurrent cancer. I read about women who die from breast cancer, but I have changed my attitude about a lot of things; about death and about health in general. I live a more healthy lifestyle. I give myself a break and don't worry so much anymore about things that used to seem so important. I have a more positive outlook on life, and I don't visualize a black, insidious cancer inside me anymore. I still pay attention to my regular check-ups, but I don't obsess about them anymore.

I think I was lucky, but I was also assertive about my treatment. I didn't just let doctors tell me what to do and suffer the consequences. I was proactive and I got involved. It was the most difficult thing I've had to do, but I had a lot of support, from my husband, my daughter, my extended family and friends, even my co-workers and my boss helped to make my treatment a positive force for getting healthy again.

Realistically, I'm probably healthier today than I was ten years ago! I would encourage anyone facing the difficulty of breast cancer to reach out for the support that is available. There are a number of women's cancer resource centers and there are support groups that are right for any individual, no matter what your situation. There are women who survive breast cancer and go on with their lives…listen to them…..they have much to share.

If someone has been diagnosed with breast cancer, the one thing I would say is: Never, never give in to it. Always be positive. If for some reason you are not happy with the course of treatment laid out for you, seek other opinions until you are happy, and ask as many questions as you can. If you are armed with knowledge, you can go forward and give yourself the best treatment and the best survival rate. When I was first diagnosed, I was quite depressed, and it takes a lot of courage to get yourself out of that. I just looked at myself one day and thought, 'I can't live like this - depressed and worried about my cancer - Get on top of it, try and fight it, and get through it being happy and positive'. It is really hard to do that, but one day I just decided to fight it and get through it and get to my five years. I'm there next March.

CLINICAL BREAST EXAMINATION

Clinical breast examination (CBE) is a physical examination of the breasts by a trained health professional. Regular clinical breast examinations can help find cancer early.

If you are over the age of 40, you should have a CBE every two years.

If you have a higher than average risk of developing breast cancer, you will most likely be screened more often or earlier (before age 40). Talk to your doctor about a screening plan that will be right for you.

SCREENING MAMMOGRAPHY

Screening mammograms are done in a clinic or screening centre.

A mammography exam is a low-dose x-ray. Mammography pictures (*mammograms*) show detailed images and views of the breast taken from different angles. The breast is placed between two plastic plates. The plates are then pressed together to flatten the breast. This may be uncomfortable, but it lasts only a few seconds. Compressing the breast tissue helps make the images clearer while using as little radiation as possible. Discuss the risks and benefits of mammography with your doctor.

Reprinted with permission from –
The Canadian Cancer Society - 2007

RECIPE INDEX

APPETIZERS

Apple Dip 1
Artichoke and Leek Dip 2
Baked Atlantic Scallops 3
Bread Fondue 4
California Rolls 5
Cheddar Roasted Red
   Pepper Dip 10
Cheesy Bits 6
Cinnamon 'N Sugar Tortillas.. 18
Cornmeal Tortillas 7
Crab Phyllo Tarts 8
Cream Cheese and Pepper
   Jelly 21
Devilled Eggs 9
Feta Cheese Dip 4
Four Cheese Crab Dip 10
Fresh Mexican Salsa 11
Guacamole 12
Ham and Cheese Puff.......... 13
Homemade Salami 14
Hot Mushroom Dip.............. 15
Lemon Pepper Chicken
   Wings 16
Maritime Shrimp Dip 17
Mexican Cherry Cheese Dip... 18
Monkey Bread......................2
Parmesan Biscuit Sticks........ 19
Pizza Spread...................... 20
Pumpkin Dip 21
Salmon Ball 22
Sassy Saucy Meatballs 23
Savory Party Bread.............. 24
Shrimp Wheels................... 25
Spinach Bacon Dip.............. 30
Spinach Cheese Bake.......... 26
Stuffed Mushrooms.............. 27
Taco Dip 12
Tortilla Beef Tidbits.............. 28
Tortilla Crisps 6
Traverse Bay Dip................. 29
Tzaziki Dip 30
Welsh Cakes...................... 31
Yummy Potato Skins........... 32

BEVERAGES

Banana Yogurt Shake...........38
Chocolate Malt 37
Cocomoka Cold 45
Cranberry Punch.................42
Floats, Shakes, Sodas and
   Malts...........................35
Harvest Coffee Cider 40
Hot Spicy Punch 43
Mock Champagne 40
Morning Mocha..................42
No Time for Breakfast
   Smoothie......................39
Old Fashioned Soda 37
Puerto Rican Coquito...........44
Root Beer Float 36
Sangria Blanca 47
Slushie Punch.....................46
Sun Tea 39
Tropical Fruit Punch 41
Wake Up Shake..................38
Yummy Strawberry
   Milkshake 36

BRUNCHES

Apple and Cinnamon Baked
   French Toast 49
Apple Flax Pancakes............50
Baked Breakfast Frittatas......51
Breakfast Couscous.............52
Breakfast Lasagna 53
Caramel Cream Banana
   Stuffed Crepes................54
Classic Cheese Soufflé..........55
Eggs On Bagels with
   Hollandaise Sauce...........60
Favorite Egg Casserole 56
Favorite Neighbours'
   Waffles........................57
Flax Porridge.....................58
Ham and Swiss Quiche 59

Kick Start Breakfast 60
Make Ahead Breakfast
    Casserole 61
Orange Almond Brunch
    Biscuits 62
Orange Cottage Crepes 63
Overnight Breakfast 64
Peach Puff Pancake 65
Pink Ribbon Breakfast
    Casserole 66
Unique Egg Casserole 67

BREADS AND MUFFINS

Biscuits
Bran and Oat Scones 69
Lemon-Filled Ginger
    Scones 70
Orange Raisin Scones 71
Potato Best Biscuits 72
Scottish Oat Crisps 73
Spinach Feta Biscuits 74

Breads & Buns
Bannock 75
The Best Pizza Crust 87
Chapattis Bread 77
Cinnamon Buns 78
Corn Bread 81
Easter Babka 80
English Muffins 82
Fantastic Focacia Bread 83
Great Brown Bread 76
Molasses Cornmeal 84
Naan Bread 85
Orange Crescents 86

Loaves
Chocolate Zucchini Bread 88
Cranberry Orange Loaf 89
Double Lemon Zucchini
    Poppy Loaf 90
Glazed Lemon Nut Bread 91
Lemon Poppy Seed Bread 92
Sour Cream Banana Bread 93
Sweet Potato Bread 94

Muffins
6 Week Yogurt Bran Muffins .. 95
Applesauce Walnut Low
    Fat Muffins 96
Banana Bran Applesauce
    Muffins 97
Berry Lemon Muffins 98
Cherry Muffins 99
Chocolate Squash Muffins ... 100
Corn Muffins 102
Doughnut Muffins 101
Flax Seed Muffins 102
Irish Coffee Muffins 103
Orange Bran Flax Muffins 104
Orange Tea Muffins 105
Rhubarb Orange Muffins 106
Ricotta Pineapple Muffins 107
Spiced Carrot Bran Muffins .. 108
Spicy Low Fat Squash
    Muffins 109

SOUPS

Beef Noodle Soup 111
Borscht 112
Cabbage and Kielbasa
    Soup 113
Canadian Ham-Bone Soup ... 114
Carollers' Potato Soup 115
Cheese Soup 116
Cheesy Brocolli Soup 117
Cheesy Ham and Rice
    Soup 118
Chicken Chowder Supreme .. 119
Chicken Mushroom Soup 120
Chickpea Chowder 121
Corn and Chicken Chowder . 122
Creamed Potato and
    Cabbage Soup 123
Creamy Potato and Ham
    Soup 124
Curried Tomato Soup 125
Garden Creamy Tomato
    Vegetable Soup 126
Grandma's Tomato Milk
    Soup 127
Green Split Pea Soup 128

Harvest Pumpkin Soup 129
Lemon Chicken Rice Soup ... 130
Lettuce Cream Soup 131
Minestrone Soup 132
Quick and Easy Mushroom
    Soup 133
Quick Cream Corn Soup 133
Roasted Carrot, Onion
    and Garlic Soup 134
Spicy Curried Carrot Soup .. 135
Tomato Pasta Soup 114
Vegetable Chowder 136
Vegetable Soup 137

Summer Salad 143
Sweet and Sour Dressing 145
Swiss Cashew Salad 160
Tomato and Chick Pea
    Salad 143
Tomato Shrimp Aspic
    Salad 147
Tuna Pasta Salad 156
Vegetable Greek Salad 153

SALADS

Balsamic Grape and Walnut
    Salad 140
Beet Salad 144
Caesar Salad Dressing 162
Chicken Spinach Salad 149
Classic Waldorf Salad 141
Cobb Salad 148
Cranberry Spinach Salad 163
Creamed Coleslaw 156
Creamy Fruit Salad 142
Dill Potato Salad 155
Foo Yung Salad 164
Fresh Beet Salad 139
Hickory Tuna Salad 151
Holiday Cranberry Salad 142
Honey Mustard Dressing 161
Hot Chicken Salad 157
Make Ahead Cabbage
    Slaw 158
Mandarin Orange Cranberry
    Salad with Caramelized
    Almonds 166
Mango Salad 165
Marinated Carrot Salad 159
Parsnip Salad 151
Potato Salad 154
Pretzel Salad 146
Ranch Pasta Salad 150
Sesame Broccoli Salad 152
Sour Cream Fruit Salad 145

ENTREES

Beef

Beef Burgundy 169
Beef Pepper Quesadillas 170
Grandma's Cabbage Rolls 171
Leftover Roast Beef
    Favourite 172
Liver, Bacon and Onions 173
Mozzarella Spaghetti
    Skillet 174
No Fuss Stroganoff 175
Polynesian Satay 176
Porcupine Meatballs 177
Rullapylsa 178
Sloppy Joe's 179
Spaghetti and Meatballs 180
Steak In Foil 181
Stuffed Steak 182
Sweet and Sour Beef Stew .. 183
Thirty Minute Casserole 181

Chicken

and Red Pepper Sauce 187
Apricot Chicken 201
Basil & Pimento Cream
    Chicken Breasts 184
Chicken Cacciatora 185
Chicken Stir Fry 186
Chicken With Feta 187
Classy Chicken 188
Easy Chicken Dinner 189
Grilled Chicken Breast in
    Mango-Curry Marinade .. 190
Jamaican Chicken 191
Lemon Chicken Breasts 192

Lemon Chicken Pasta Toss.. 193
Lettuce Cashew Chicken
    Wraps.......................... 194
Mandarin Orange Chicken ... 195
Moist Poultry Stuffing......... 200
Pad Thai........................... 196
Pineapple Chicken Curry..... 198
Roast Turkey, Gravy and
    Stuffing...................... 199
Salsa Chicken 201
Slow Cooker Orange
    Chicken...................... 197
Soy Ginger Chicken 202
Spicy Peanut Chicken......... 203

Pork
Baked Pork Tenderloin 204
Barbequed Pork Ribs.......... 205
Ginger Spiced Pork 206
Greek Ribs on the BBQ....... 207
Ham Bean Bake 208
Homemade Sausage 209
Honey Mustard Glazed Pork
    Tenderloin 211
Barbequed Pork Chops 212
Pork Chops in Spicy Orange
    Sauce 213
Pork Cutlets with Apple Raisin
    Sauce or Mushroom Cream
    Sauce 214
Sage Stuffed Pork
    Tenderloin 215
Sweet and Sour Country
    Ribs........................... 216

Seafood
Baked Salmon Steaks 217
Baked Trout...................... 218
Salmon or Tuna Casserole .. 218
Caesar Salmon.................. 219
Fisherman's Pie................. 220
Glazed Salmon................. 221
Grecian Baked Fish 222
Manicotti Overboard 223
Maple Glazed Salmon......... 224
Pasta With Shrimp in Tomato
    Cream 225
Salmon Loaf 226

Salmon Skewers with Spicy
    Thai Coconut Sauce....... 227
Sea Loaf........................... 228
Shrimp and Sausage
    Penne 229
Spicy Shrimp with
    Asparagus................... 230

Meat Marinades
Chili Garlic....................... 232
Herb 232
Lemon Dill Sauce.............. 231
Red Wine......................... 232

**VEGETABLES AND
SIDE DISHES**

A Side Of Stuffing 265
Awesome Applesauce 235
Baked Rice........................ 239
Bean Wraps 237
Beans, Sumptuous and Slow
    Cooked....................... 236
Beet Leaf Rolls 238
Brown Rice Almondine........ 239
Carrots and Sprouts
    Almondine 240
Cauliflower and Broccoli with
    Lemon Cheese Sauce..... 241
Celebration Cranberry
    Sauce.......................... 235
Cheesy Green Bean Bake.... 242
Classic Italian Risotto 243
Coconut Rice..................... 264
Copper Pennies 244
Corn Casserole 245
Corn Pudding 267
Creamed Corn 249
Creamed Peas or Carrots 249
Creamy Potatoes 246
Creamy Scalloped
    Potatoes 247
Easy Potatoes 246
Fried Green Tomatoes 248
Homemade Creamed
    Vegetables................... 249
Lemon Cheese Sauce 241

384

Lemon Risotto.................. 250
New Potatoes in Cream...... 251
Oriental Rice.................... 252
Orzo Rice Pilaf 253
Oven-Baked Fries............. 247
Pasta Vegetable Scramble... 254
Perfect Steamed Rice......... 255
Potato Puffs..................... 256
Red Cabbage 257
Rice Cabbage Rolls in Tomato
    Sauce 258
Roasted Butternut Squash &
    Sage Risotto with
    Pine Nuts 260
Roasted Cauliflower and
    Garlic......................... 262
Roasted Yams and
    Potatoes..................... 263
Romano Rice 264
Spaghetti Squash
    Casserole 266
Stuffed Green Peppers 268
Stuffed Tomatoes.............. 269
Turnip Bake..................... 242
Veggie Bake 270

Half Hour Pudding.............288
Heaven in a Pan 292
Lemon Angel Delight 293
Lemon Fluff Dessert...........280
Lemon Lime Cheesecake.....294
Lemon Semifreddo with
    Raspberry Coulis...........296
Lemon Snowball 298
Merry Berry Cheese Bars 299
Peach Melba.....................275
Raspberry Dessert 300
Rhubarb Crunch Dessert.....301
Saskatoon Cream
    Cheesecake..................302
Strawberry Shortcake
    Trifle..........................303
Tapioca Custard................304
Traditional German
    Cheesecake..................305

DESSERTS

Apricot Creams 277
Baked Alaska.................... 273
Baked Chocolate Pudding ... 278
Black Forest Cake.............. 279
Brandied Peaches.............. 297
Caramel Grapes 281
Cheese Cake with Orange
    Glaze......................... 282
Cherries Jubilee 276
Cherry Crunch 283
Cherry Trifle 284
Chocolate Caramel Pecan
    Cheesecake 285
Chocolate Jelly Roll............ 286
Chocolate Pavlova 287
Crown Jewel Dessert.......... 289
Fruit Flax Crisp................. 291
Great Grandma's Famous
    Apple Strudel............... 290

CAKES AND PASTRIES

Cakes & Squares

Applesauce Spice Cake 307
Butter Tart Square.............308
Choco Caramel Bars...........312
Chocolate Banana Cake 309
Chocolate Banana Frosting ..309
Chocolate Cake 310
Chocolate Fleck Cake 311
Chocolate Toffee Square 313
Cinnamon Bars..................314
Coconut Pecan Cake with
    Coconut Pecan Frosting..315
Cranberry Almond Coffee
    Cake 317
Dad's Chocolate Slice 318
English Tea Cakes..............319
German Cheesecake
    Squares......................320
"Hip Padder" Bars 321
Krispy Peanut Butter
    Square 322
Lemon Chiffon Cake 323
Peanut Butter Brownies 324
Pineapple Slice 325

Pralines 'N Cream Pecan
 Cake............................ 326
Pumpkin Dump Cake.......... 316
Rhubarb Cake 328
Scrumptious Almond
 Squares 329
Sour Cream Cake 330

Pies & Pastries
Butternut Squash Pie with
 Gingersnap Crust.......... 331
Cape Cod Cranberry
 Velvet Pie 333
Creamy Cherry Pie............. 334
Cupar Raisin Cream Tarts ... 335
Impossible Carrot Pie 336
Perfect Pumpkin Pie 337
Raisin Buttermilk Pie.......... 338
Rum Tarts 339
Pecan Tarts 339

COOKIES AND TREATS

Anise Cookies 351
Banana Cookies 352
Buttercrunch Almond Cups.. 373
Caramel Apples................. 377
Carrot Cake Cookies 353
Cheerio Slice 347
Chewy Coconut Nut Bars 346
Chocolate Chip Peanut
 Butter Cookies 354
Chocolate Chip Toffee
 Almond Cookies............ 355
Chocolate Orange Truffles... 374
Chocolate Peanut Butter
 Cookies....................... 356

Coconut Almond Slice......... 349
Coconut Mango Macaroons .. 357
Coffee Time Biscotti 344
Cookies for Breakfast 358
Date Filled Oatmeal
 Cookies 359
Easy Pretzel Turtles........... 377
Eatmore Bars 375
English Toffee 378
Famous Department Store
 Cookies 360
Flax Pecan Chocolate Chip
 Cookies 361
Fudge Brownies................. 350
Ginger Drop Cookies 362
Gingerbread Men 363
Golden Graham Candy........ 375
Halloween Granola Cookies . 364
Hazelnut Biscotti............... 342
Lemon Crisps 365
Microwave Peanut Brittle..... 378
Mommy's Break Time
 Biscotti........................ 343
Monster Cookies 366
O'Henry Bars 345
One Hundred Best Cookies .. 367
Peanut Crackles................. 368
Prune or Date Pinwheels 369
Self-Icing Cupcakes 348
Sesame Wafers 370
Shortbread Meltaways 368
Taffy Q's 376
The Best of the Breast
 Chocolate Chip Cookies.. 371
Toblerone Fudge................ 376
Turtle Tarts...................... 341
Yo - Yo Cookies 372

CANOLA OIL

The Breast Friends have chosen to use canola oil in many recipes in *Breast Wishes*, because of its nutritional value. Not all fats are created equal. Some fats are good for you, some are not. Your body needs fat to provide energy and help you absorb fat-soluble vitamins. Certain fats, such as omega-3 and omega-6 are essential for good nutrition and must be consumed as part of a healthy diet. It is important to choose fats wisely. Canola oil provides more of the healthier fats than any other vegetable oil.

Everybody needs good fat to stay healthy!

Canola oil is:

- <u>low in saturated fat</u> (that is good) Saturated fat raises the bad LDL cholesterol in your blood and has been linked to increase risk of coronary heart disease.

- <u>a source of omega-6 fat</u> (that is good) Omega-6 is important for the brain and essential for the growth and development of infants.

- <u>high in omega-3 fat</u> (that is really good) Omega-3 helps protect against heart attacks and strokes.

- <u>high in monounsaturated fat</u> (very good) Monounsaturated fat may reduce the risk of coronary heart disease by lowering bad LDL cholesterol in the blood and helping control blood glucose.

- <u>cholesterol and trans fat free</u> (fantastic) Trans fat raises bad LDL cholesterol and lowers good HDL cholesterol.

Health Canada advises, "for good heath, include a small amount (2-3 tablespoons) of unsaturated fat and limit the amount of saturated and trans fat in your day."

Saskatchewan Canola Development Commission

canola*info*.org

"The Saskatchewan Canola Development Commission is proud to promote the health benefits of canola oil through partnering with the Breast Friends cookbooks. We applaud their fundraising efforts and thank them for creating this unique set of cookbooks in support of cancer causes."

Metric Conversion Chart

Because we are old-fashioned cooks you will notice that the recipes in this book are given in Imperial measurements. For anyone that has converted to metric, we are sorry. Hope this helps you out!

Oven Temperatures

250°F = 120°C
275°F = 140°C
300°F = 150°C
325°F = 160°C
350°F = 180°C   Slow oven ...250°F - 325°F
375°F = 190°C   Moderate .....325°F - 375°F
400°F = 200°C   Hot .... 425°F - 450°F
425°F = 220°C
450°F = 230°C
500°F = 260°C

Volume

¼ teaspoon = 1 ml
½ teaspoon = 2 ml
1 teaspoon = 5 ml
1 tablespoon = 15 ml
¼ cup = 50 ml
⅓ cup = 75 ml
½ cup = 125 ml
⅔ cup = 150 ml
¾ cup = 175 ml
1 cup = 250 ml

Weight

1 ounce = 30 g
2 ounce = 55 g
3 ounces = 85 g
4 ounces = 115 g
5 ounces = 140 g
6 ounces = 170 g
7 ounces = 200 g
8 ounces = 250 g
16 ounces = 500 g
32 ounces = 1000 g

A Gift of Hope
Order Form - Breast Friends Cookbooks

All three books are **$19.95 each**, plus 5% GST = **$20.95 each**.

Please send me:

____Book one "**For the Breasts of Friends**" @ 20.95 _____

___Book two "**For the Breasts and the Rest of Friends**" @ 20.95_____

____Book three "**Breast Wishes**" @ 20.95 _____

Shipping and handling in Canada (includes GST): Please enclose: $6.00 for one book, $10.00 for two to 5 books, $15.00 for 5 to 10 books. Over 10 books- call or email to make shipping arrangements. For out of country orders, please contact us by email or phone to order.

Total for books$_____ plus shipping $_____= total enclosed _____

Net profits from the sale of the books go to cancer agencies, patient needs, equipment and research.
See our website for examples of agencies that have received donations or sold our book for their cause.

Name _____

Street or Box_____

City, Province_____

Country, Postal Code (Zip code)_____

Make cheques payable to **Breast Friends**. Send order to Breast Friends, Box 436, Foam Lake, SK S0A 1A0. Email **breastfriends@sasktel.net** for information, bookings or to order cook books. Visa and MasterCard orders are accepted at 1-877-723-6828. The website **www.breastfriends.ca** features information about the group and the cookbooks, sample recipes, donation information and an ordering link.